D0611764

ECLIPSE

Living in the Shadow
of China's Economic Dominance

Arvind Subramanian

PETERSON INSTITUTE FOR INTERNATIONAL ECONOMICS
Washington, DC
September 2011

Arvind Subramanian is senior fellow jointly at the Peterson Institute for International Economics and the Center for Global Development. He was assistant director in the Research Department of the International Monetary Fund. He served at the GATT (1988–92) during the Uruguay Round of trade negotiations and taught at Harvard University's Kennedy School of Government (1999–2000) and at Johns Hopkins University's School for Advanced International Studies (2008–10). He advises the Indian government in different capacities, including as a member of the Finance Minister's Expert Group on the G-20. His previous books include *India's Turn: Understanding the Economic Transformation* (2008) and *Efficiency, Equity, and Legitimacy: The Multilateral Trading System at the Millennium* (2002).

**PETER G. PETERSON INSTITUTE
FOR INTERNATIONAL ECONOMICS**
1750 Massachusetts Avenue, NW
Washington, DC 20036-1903
(202) 328-9000   FAX: (202) 659-3225
www.piie.com

C. Fred Bergsten, *Director*
Edward A. Tureen, *Director of Publications,
  Marketing, and Web Development*

Typesetting by BMWW
Printing by United Book Press, Inc.
Cover design by Sese-Paul Design
Cover photo: © Ron Sachs/Pool/CNP/Corbis
Author photo by Jeremey Tripp

Printed in the United States of America
13 12 11   5 4 3 2

**Library of Congress Cataloging-in-
Publication Data**
Subramanian, Arvind.
  Eclipse : living in the shadow of China's economic dominance / Arvind Subramanian.
     p. cm.
  Includes bibliographical references.
  1. Economic development—China.
2. Economic development—United States. 3. Economic forecasting—China.
4. Economic forecasting—United States.
5. International economic relations.
I. Title.
  HC427.95.S862 2011
  330.951—dc23
                              2011030066

To
Parul,
Tia, Kartikeya, and Rohan, and
My parents

Contents

Tables

Figures

Boxes

Preface

The Peterson Institute's research and publications over the years have focused to a considerable extent on China and its economic rise. One of the early books in this regard was Nicholas Lardy's *China in the World Economy* (1994) followed most notably by *China: The Balance Sheet—What the World Needs to Know Now about the Emerging Superpower* (Bergsten et al. 2006) and *China's Rise: Challenges and Opportunities* (Bergsten et al. 2008).

Most of these analyses focus on the opportunities for, and challenges facing, China itself rather than its impact on the rest of the world (though chapter 1 of *China's Rise* addresses that issue and elaborates my earlier proposal for a G-2 between China and the United States). There are, however, two major exceptions. Morris Goldstein and Lardy's *Debating China's Exchange Rate Policy* (2009) analyzes the effects of China's exchange rate policy on its trading partners and Gary Hufbauer et al.'s *US-China Trade Disputes: Rising Tide, Rising Stakes* (2006) examines trade disputes between China and the United States.

In this book, Senior Fellow Arvind Subramanian extends this line of inquiry by examining the rise of China from the perspective of its impact on the world economic system. He explores this through the key concept of economic dominance, focusing on whether and how China might attain future dominance.

Subramanian anchors the analysis by adopting a historical perspective in comparing China's future rise with the past hegemonies of Great Britain and the United States. He attempts to quantify and project both economic dominance and currency dominance, arguing that China's future dominance could be more imminent, broader in scope, and much larger in magnitude than is currently imagined. The profound effect that this might have on the United States and the world financial, and especially trading, system is explored at some length. The book concludes with a series of proposals for reconciling China's rise with continued openness in the global economic order.

The Peter G. Peterson Institute for International Economics is a private, nonprofit institution for the study and discussion of international economic policy. Its purpose is to analyze important issues in that area and to develop and communicate practical new approaches for dealing with them. The Institute is completely nonpartisan.

The Institute is funded by a highly diversified group of philanthropic foundations, private corporations, and interested individuals. About 35 percent of the Institute's resources in our latest fiscal year were provided by contributors outside the United States. The Smith-Richardson Foundation and the Eranda Foundation provided generous support for this study.

The Institute's Board of Directors bears overall responsibilities for the Institute and gives general guidance and approval to its research program, including the identification of topics that are likely to become important over the medium run (one to three years) and that should be addressed by the Institute. The director, working closely with the staff and outside Advisory Committee, is responsible for the development of particular projects and makes the final decision to publish an individual study.

The Institute hopes that its studies and other activities will contribute to building a stronger foundation for international economic policy around the world. We invite readers of these publications to let us know how they think we can best accomplish this objective.

C. FRED BERGSTEN
Director
September 2011

Acknowledgments

When Keynes famously noted that practical men believe themselves to be exempt from any intellectual influences, he probably had in mind some iron law of vanity that says that the debts we really owe (even if to defunct economists) considerably exceed those we recognize and acknowledge. The obligatory filling of an acknowledgments page is a discipline, however weak, to guard against this law. So here goes.

My foremost general debt is to C. Fred Bergsten, who persuaded me to forgo being a "lifer" at the International Monetary Fund, with all its variable charms, yo-yo excitements, but unquestionable security, and join the Peter G. Peterson Institute for International Economics. The intellectually fertile and stimulating environment of the team at the Institute, under his superb direction, has allowed me to work with delight and inspiration every day that I have been here since April 2007. I owe a similar debt to Nancy Birdsall and the Center for Global Development, with which I have been associated for as long as the Institute.

I owe specific debts, connected directly to the book, to several people. All my colleagues at the Peterson Institute have directly or indirectly contributed to this book. They include Fred Bergsten, Anders Åslund, William Cline, Mac Destler, Joe Gagnon, Morris Goldstein, Gary Hufbauer, Randy Hemming, Olivier Jeanne, Brad Jensen, Simon Johnson, Mohsin Khan, Jacob Kirkegaard, Barbara Kotschwar, Nicholas Lardy, Michael Mussa, Marcus Noland, Adam Posen, Carmen Reinhart, Jeffrey Schott, Ted Truman, Nicolas Veron, Steve Weisman, and John Williamson. Presenting my ideas on a number of occasions at the Institute and to be at the receiving end of many a scathing reaction from my colleagues has made the book a better—or at least less bad—product.

I am also grateful to Barry Eichengreen, Richard Cooper, Josh Felman, Dani Rodrik, and Yu Yongding for reviewing the first draft of the book and providing excellent comments. Discussions (including e-mail exchanges) over the course of the last few years with Liaquat Ahamed, Montek Ahluwalia, Alan Beattie, Nancy Birdsall, S. Jaishankar, Rahul Khullar, K. P. Krishnan, V. S. Krishnan, Ed Luce, C. Raja Mohan, Shivshankar Menon, Zanny Minton-Beddoes, David Roodman, and Martin Wolf have helped directly and indirectly.

Some friends and colleagues deserve special mention for special contributions. Bill Cline helped clarify my thinking on the gravity model and GDP projections. Angus Deaton and Alan Heston have been my gurus, helping me understand the purchasing power parity concept and its applications. Alan Deardorff has done the same for sections in the book that draw upon the gravity model. Randy Henning guided me through the international political economy literature. Simon Johnson, Adam Posen, and Dani Rodrik were indispensable founts of encouragement and morale-sustenance. Simon was also an invaluable sounding board for a number of the ideas and arguments in the book. Deena Khatkhate read the entire manuscript with care and insight, offering constructive ways of reshaping the arguments. Carmen Reinhart generously provided data that I have used in chapter 5. Ted Truman read and re-read, with great care, patience, and insight, several versions of the sections on reserve currencies and the international monetary system. Steve Weisman was a constant source of support and provided guidance on various aspects relating to substance and presentation. John Williamson was always available to share his wisdom and depth of knowledge on all issues related to international monetary economics and the monetary system.

Devesh Kapur and Pratap Mehta, in addition to helping shape key arguments in the book, have been long-standing friends and confidantes, and their presence during the dark moments of soaring self-doubt and plummeting self-esteem is worthy of special mention. The same applies to my close friend and long-standing collaborator, Aaditya Mattoo, who also helped in innumerable other ways: Chapters 8 and 9, in particular, benefited from his ideas and criticisms and draw upon ongoing work with him.

Finally, Fred Bergsten and Josh Felman (whose quiet brilliance remains underappreciated) were especially generous with their time, reading drafts of the book several times and providing excellent and detailed comments. Their responses forced me to rethink and revise many parts of the book and sharpen and clarify ideas and arguments. To them, I am deeply indebted and grateful.

Jolly La Rosa provided excellent research assistance over the course of a year and a half. Janak Mayer provided superb help with the empirical work in chapters 4 and 7. David Einhorn did a wonderful job of editing the manuscript and suggested a key change in the sequencing of an idea in the book. Madona Devasahayam, Ed Tureen, and Susann Luetjen, who skillfully shepherded the book through the publication process, have been a joy to deal with.

Sir Evelyn Rothschild and Lynn Forester de Rothschild generously supported this project through the Eranda Foundation, in addition to suffering cheerfully through an early version of the book. Generous support from the Smith-Richardson Foundation is also gratefully acknowledged.

My parents, grandmother, mother-in-law, and siblings have been unfailing supporters. Most of all, I dedicate this book to my wife, Parul, and our children, Mrigaya (Tia), Kartikeya, and Rohan. They have kept me grounded and put up with me through this book but also through the course of their whole lives.

ARVIND SUBRAMANIAN
Washington, DC
September 2011

Introduction

The British action [at Suez] was the last gasp of a declining power ... perhaps in two hundred years the United States would know how we felt.

—Harold Macmillan to John Foster Dulles on December 13, 1956, after economic pressure from the United States persuaded the United Kingdom to withdraw its forces from the Suez Canal zone

February 2021. It is a cold, blustery morning in Washington. The newly inaugurated Republican president of the United States is on his way to the office of the Chinese managing director of the International Monetary Fund (IMF) to sign the agreement under which the IMF will provide $3 trillion in emergency financing (about 12 percent of GDP) to the United States and the conditionality to which the United States will have to adhere.

Over the preceding decade, the US economy has had to contend with three interconnected problems: slow growth, a fragile fiscal situation, and a beleaguered middle class. Under the weight of public and private debt accumulated after the crisis of 2008–10, high and persistent unemployment, and diminished participation in the labor force, the US economy has grown at just below 2 percent in the 2010s. As a consequence, and despite intermittent attempts to come to grips with the rising costs of entitlements, especially related to health care, public finances are not on fundamentally secure footing. Public-sector liabilities have built up to 50 percent of GDP, as Peter Boone and Simon Johnson warned a decade ago, because the US financial system has remained as cavalier in its risk-taking and as toxic-asset-laden in its balance sheets as before the financial crisis of 2008–10. And inequality has increased even further, with income gains at the very top (.01 percent of the population) becoming even larger. Economic and social mobility have declined, giving rise to a middle class that understandably does not want to move down the skill spectrum but whose prospects of moving up, through education and skill acquisition, are increasingly limited by competition from India and China.

At the same time, China, despite the slump of 2012–13, has recovered its growth momentum and is economically dominant: Its trade and GDP are nearly 50 percent larger than those of the United States, and it remains the largest bankroller to the world with the United States still its largest bankrollee. The renminbi is increasingly in demand as a reserve currency, and the sheen has come off the dollar.

In the months preceding the 2020 US election, inflation became the primary global problem because commodity and oil prices soared due to rapid growth in the emerging markets. Growth in the United States has slowed, threatening to further expose the fiscal and financial sector vulnerabilities. Rumors are swirling in global financial markets that China is planning to wield its financial power because it can no longer countenance substantial US naval presence on the Indian and Pacific Oceans. The dollar is under intense pressure and China has reinforced that pressure by selling some of its $4 trillion worth of reserves. The dreaded dollar collapse is imminent. Bond markets have turned on US government paper, the country has been stripped of its AAA rating, and investors are suddenly absent from US Treasury auctions.

To maintain confidence, the US Federal Reserve has raised interest rates sharply—much more than it might have had to when it enjoyed the "exorbitant privilege" of the dollar as the world's near-exclusive reserve currency. The United States has started to face the dilemma that many developing countries faced during the Asian financial crisis of the late 1990s: While necessary to keep inflation in check and maintain confidence in the currency, higher interest rates are threatening growth and hurting the viability of the financial sector. US debt dynamics look ominous because interest rates substantially exceed growth rates. Significant economic and social costs loom. America, in short, appears like any emerging-market country.

Cheap financing is the need of the hour—especially since the loss of confidence is related to fiscal sustainability, as many advanced economies discovered years earlier (Iceland, Greece, and Ireland in 2010 and 2011 and Spain and Portugal in 2012). The oil-rich countries have refused to extend emergency financing to the United States, because the friendly autocrats of yore have all been replaced by "illiberal democrats" (to use Fareed Zakaria's phrase) of various Islamic persuasions, moderate to extreme, with long memories of US intervention in the Middle East. The IMF seems the only option left.

The presidential motorcade reaches the plush IMF headquarters, but the leader of the free world has not arrived alone. Because the elections of 2020 resulted in divided government, the managing director has insisted that, to reassure the financial markets of the credibility of the IMF loan-cum-conditionality package, US congressional leaders of both parties be present to signal that bipartisan legislative approval for the package will be forthcoming. (The United States, however, is able to resist pressure that the chief justice of the Supreme Court, representing the remaining branch of government, also be present.)

China—which is now the largest contributor to IMF resources and, pursuant to the reform of the IMF's voting structure in 2018, now has veto power at the Fund—makes the removal of US naval bases from the Western Pacific a precondition for the United States to receive the financing necessary to make its debt dynamics sufficiently stable to satisfy bond markets. This precondition has bite because China can easily get a majority of IMF members—beneficiaries of Chinese trade and financial largesse—to block a US financing program. The terms of the IMF program are clear, onerous, and delicately balanced between tax increases and expenditure reductions and are therefore equally distasteful to Republicans and Democrats. The US government must introduce a national value-added tax, restore the highest marginal tax rate to 40 percent, institute means testing for Medicare and Social Security benefits, and substantially reduce defense expenditures. The president grimly accepts. Under the calm gaze of the managing director and flanked by leaders of both houses of Congress, he signs the letter of intent that elaborates the terms and conditions of IMF financing.

This scene of stark symbolism is relayed instantaneously around the globe. It is eerily reminiscent of 1998, when with arms crossed and a smug expression, West-embodying IMF Managing Director Michel Camdessus watched as Indonesian President Suharto signed off on an IMF program and, in the eyes of Asia, signed away sovereignty and self-respect. Except that the roles have been reversed. The handover of world dominance is complete.

****

Is this scenario merely fantasy, or could it actually play out in the not-too-distant future? Mainstream opinion in the United States clearly rules out the latter possibility: A central tenet of America's self-perception is that its economic preeminence cannot be seriously threatened because it is America's to lose, and sooner or later the country will rise to the challenge of protecting it. China may be rising as an economic superpower, and the United States may have to cooperate more with China and others to share the global stage. But the Chinese threat is neither imminent nor sufficiently large in magnitude or broad in scope to dislodge the United States from the driver's seat. Moreover, if the United States can get its economic house in order, the Chinese threat can be headed off.

Tinges of hubris (or complacency) that have long lurked behind that tenet could be detected in Larry Summers's speech just before his departure as President Barack Obama's national economic advisor in December 2010:

> America's history, in a certain sense, has been one of self-denying prophecy—a history of alarm and concern, but alarm and concern averted by decisive actions to assure our prosperity. As one former CIA director warned of our largest competitor, that industrial growth rates of eight or nine percent per year for a decade would dangerously narrow the gap between our two countries. That was Allen Dulles in 1959 referring to the Soviet Union. And when the Soviet Union collapsed instead, the *Harvard Business Review* in 1990 proclaimed in every issue—every issue—in one way or another that the Cold War was over, and that Germany and Japan had won. Now we hear the same thing with re-

spect to China. Predictions of America's decline are as old as the republic. But they perform a crucial function in driving the kind of renewal that is required of each generation of Americans. I submit to you that as long as we're worried about the future, the future will be better. We have our challenges. But we also have the most flexible, dynamic, entrepreneurial society the world has ever seen. If we can make the right choices, our best days as competitors and prosperous citizens still lie ahead (Summers 2010).

In concluding his book on reserve currency status or "dollar power," another manifestation of economic dominance, economist Barry Eichengreen (2010, 177) sounds a similar theme: "The good news, such as it is, is that the fate of the dollar is in our hands, not those of the Chinese."

These beliefs are not confined to economists such as Summers and Eichengreen. They are quite widely shared. Political scientist Michael Mandelbaum (2010, 182) asserts: "When Britain could no longer provide global governance, the United States stepped in to replace it. No country now stands ready to replace the United States. . . ."

In a similar vein, Joseph Nye (2010, 11–12), an eminent international relations expert and former senior official, offers this assessment: "The United States is not in absolute decline, and in relative terms, there is a reasonable probability that it will remain more powerful than any single state in the coming decades. . . . The problem of American power in the twenty-first century, then, is not one of decline but what to do in light of the realization that even the largest country cannot achieve the outcomes it wants without the help of others."

These perspectives flow from a deep and noble fount: the wells of belief in American exceptionalism, that something special about the nation's past and present will carry into the future. That sentiment was, of course, also widely shared in the United Kingdom. When the anti-imperialist Irishman Stephen Dedalus in James Joyce's *Ulysses* is asked about the Englishman's proudest boast, his irony-laced response is, "That on his empire, . . . the sun never sets."[1]

This book, then, is an attempt to question this central tenet of US economic preeminence trumpeted by the experts from the different fields cited above. Its aim is to quantify relative economic dominance and its manifestations, including currency dominance; to track the history of dominance; and to project it over the next 20 years.

This quantification yields some surprising conclusions. First, the economic dominance of China relative to the United States is more imminent (it may already have begun), will be more broad-based (covering wealth, trade, external finance, and currency), and could be as large in magnitude in the next 20 years as that of the United Kingdom in the halcyon days of empire or the United States in the aftermath of World War II.

---

1. Nearly every empire in history has shared and expressed a similar belief in its enduring dominance; the "sun never setting" metaphor can be traced to a speech in Herodotus's *Histories* made by Xerxes I of Persia before invading Greece.

Second, since size—of an economy, its trade, and its creditor position—is a key determinant of reserve currency status, China's growing size and economic dominance are likely to translate into currency dominance. The calculations, as well as a new reading of the history of the transition from sterling to the dollar, suggest that the renminbi could surpass the dollar as the premier reserve currency well before the middle of the next decade. The probability and speed of this transition will greatly increase if China undertakes some key reforms of its financial and external sector, even more so if China makes the political transition to democracy. And if the renminbi ascends to become the premier international reserve currency, China might be reluctant to lose the strength and prestige that comes with that status by disrupting financial and trade relations in any serious way.

Third, these overwhelming numbers contain two policy messages, one for all of China's main trading partners and the other for the United States in particular. China's future dominance need not pose a threat to the current open and rules-based economic and trading system. Indeed, China is so unusually open in terms of actual trade outcomes that a large and growing private constituency is being created with an awareness of mutual dependence, the benefits from it, and hence a stake in maintaining it. Moreover, China is so dependent on trade as an engine of growth and continual improvements in living standards—which are key to the legitimacy of the Chinese leadership— that the private stakes for maintaining openness are matched and reinforced by public interests.

But the world cannot be entirely sure of what actions China will take in the future, especially if fundamental political transformations continue to lag behind economic changes, and if uncertainty remains about China's territorial ambitions. The world needs insurance against the possibility of a future with an economically dominant but less than benign China. And that insurance must take the form of reviving multilateralism and tethering China to it. China, in short, offers the new case for reviving multilateralism.

The message for the United States is that rising economic and currency dominance of China might well be determined to a greater extent by Chinese policy and performance than by US actions. Dominance might be more China's to lose than America's to retain. America cannot escape the inexorable logic of demography and the phenomenon of "economic convergence," the process by which hitherto poor countries, and especially China, catch up with their richer counterparts. A country that is four times as populous as the United States will be bigger in overall economic size, once its standard of living exceeds a quarter of that of the United States.

In principle, the baseline scenario of a dominant China can be altered materially by a resurgent America. In some ways, the United States did just that in the early 1990s to head off the challenge to its dominant status from Japan. But that analogy might be less applicable in the future. Japan's dynamism collapsed in a way that is less likely for China, whose room for growth remains considerable not least because it is still so far away from the frontier.

Moreover, the conditions in the United States now are more difficult than before: The fiscal and external situation are more fragile, the outlook for growth less promising, and above all, the structural malaise of economic and social stagnation of its middle class has worsened.

Moreover, even if the United States found new founts of technological dynamism, that will still not necessarily give it an edge over China and others because in the new "flattened" world, technological progress in one country can be more easily replicated elsewhere (Friedman 2005). If rich countries stagnate, countries such as China will catch up as they have been doing. But if rich countries become technologically dynamic, they may not be able to pull ahead. The asymmetry might be that rich countries can fall behind, but their ability to stay ahead in growth terms is inherently limited by convergence and by the nature of new technologies and the ability of countries such as China to more quickly use them.

One lesson from the last great transition of dominance from the United Kingdom to the United States is that it is a combination of broad internal economic weakness, external vulnerability, and the presence of a dominant power that makes the status quo power vulnerable. In the present case, this vulnerability would be to a dominant power that is not only not an ally—unlike the United States and the United Kingdom before and after World War II—but also a country that has yet to sufficiently reassure the world about its internal politics and its extraterritorial ambitions. The prospect, however remote, of being at the receiving end of a less-than-benign exercise of power by a dominant China should serve as a loud wake-up call for the United States.

What can this book possibly add to an overgrazed field? The related themes of the changing world order, American decline, and China's rise have not suffered from lack of insightful attention. Besides the scholars mentioned above, thoughtful contributions have recently come from C. Fred Bergsten (2008), Niall Ferguson (2010), Thomas Friedman and Michael Mandelbaum (2011), Robert Kagan (2008), Parag Khanna (2011), Henry Kissinger (2011), Gideon Rachman (2011), Adam Segal (2011), Anne-Marie Slaughter (2009), Martin Wolf (2010, 2011), and Fareed Zakaria (2008a, 2008b), to name just a few.

In questioning the wisdom going forward of clinging to the notion of America's invulnerability, this book will not introduce any new theories. It does not attempt to break any new ground in terms of economic or geopolitical insights, and its projections do not go beyond 2030, when a lot can and will change, not least the rise of countries such as India, Brazil, and Indonesia, which by that time will have the demographic weight and levels of affluence to knock on the doors of the economic dominance club. Rather, the book will look at some numbers from the past and for the future, which form the core of the case presented here, leavened by historical narrative. The innovation, such as there is, will be to present new and relevant numbers, produce them in a reasonably consistent and defensible manner, combine them in new ways, and look at them through a new lens.

For example, I attempt to look at GDP numbers for the future that correct for differences in future purchasing power across countries. Similarly, there are very few numbers on how trade will evolve in the future. Nor have there been successful attempts to understand and quantify the determinants of reserve currency status. In this book, these numbers are assembled and combined to create a new "index of economic dominance" to quantify the strength of countries and compare them across countries and time. The index goes back to 1870 and projects forward to 2030.

These numbers draw on well-established methodologies, whose plausibility is tested against historical experience. Since the period of greatest interest for this study is the next 20 years, the focus here is on the past century or so, because that window provides two historical parallels to the possible future dominance of China: the United States after World War II and the United Kingdom before World War I.

What is the justification for the 20-year time horizon? Twenty years may not be the optimal time frame for analyzing all questions about the future, but it seems an acceptable compromise. On the one hand, if the horizon of analysis is too long, the uncertainties increase and the confidence bands surrounding projections can become uncomfortably large. On the other hand, a shorter horizon seems less meaningful for discussing issues such as dominance and drawing out their implications for individual countries and the system. The 20-year horizon is thus an attempt to navigate between the clamorous cycle and the tenuous trend.

I begin this book with the story of how the acquisition and loss of the Suez Canal by the United Kingdom coincided with the peak and end of empire and end it by comparing the Suez Redux scenario—as described in the "handover" fantasy at the beginning of this introduction—with the original Suez episode in 1956 to assess how plausible the former might be.

Chapter 2 quantifies economic dominance by constructing an index for different countries across time. Quantification is preceded by a discussion of the universe of possible determinants, the rationale for narrowing this universe to a few key determinants (wealth, trade, and external finance), and the complicated issues of measurement and weighting. The quantification is validated in a number of ways: by comparison with real-world examples of power allocations such as those of the IMF and by testing whether the index can track the history of economic dominance since 1870.

Chapter 3 turns to currency dominance. After reviewing the history, the chapter undertakes a new analysis of the determinants of reserve currency status going back to 1900. The key finding is that size—in terms of GDP, trade, and external finance—is the fundamental determinant of reserve currency status. These variables explain about 70 percent of the variation in reserve currency status of the major currencies over the last 110 years. This finding also serves to validate the index of economic dominance because the determinants of currency dominance seem to be similar to those of economic dominance.

Chapters 2 and 3 provide the basis for projecting, respectively, future economic and currency dominance. GDP and trade are the underlying determinants of that dominance, so they need to be projected out. Chapter 4 takes on these long-term projections, which are driven by "economic convergence," whereby poor countries catch up with the rich ones, and by "gravity," whereby trade between countries is determined by their GDPs. Convergence and gravity help quantify future GDP and trade. The chapter shows that convergence, which was selective until recently, has become much broader in scope and faster in pace. Many more countries are catching up, and doing so more quickly, with the rich countries. This is true in spades for some of the larger emerging-market countries such as China, India, and Brazil, which will be key to determining future dominance.

Equipped with the framework and the numbers, chapter 5 projects economic and currency dominance until 2030. The main conclusions relate to the timing, magnitude, and breadth of future Chinese dominance. Like the two previous economically dominant powers, China's dominance will be broad-based. By 2030, China will account for close to a quarter of the world's GDP measured in purchasing power parity terms (compared with 12 percent for the United States), which is roughly similar to that of the United States in 1950 and greater than that of the United Kingdom in 1870. China will account for between 15 and 20 percent of world trade, while the United States will account for 7 percent. The projected figure for China is greater than what the United States posted in its heyday but somewhat below what the United Kingdom achieved (24 percent) in 1870.

Chinese dominance would also extend to the currency, with the renminbi starting to compete with the dollar for reserve currency status. The econometric results combined with a slightly different reading of the historical experience of the sterling-dollar transition yields a more dramatic fate for the dollar and renminbi. The conventional view on the sterling-dollar transition is one of persistence and inertia. This is based on comparing the period when the United States became the largest economy (around 1870) and the period when it became the premier reserve currency (around World War II). The rise of the dollar then is supposed to have lagged the rise of the US economy by more than 65 years.

But this view needs to be qualified on two grounds. First, the analysis here suggests that reserve currencies are determined not just by income but, crucially, by trade and external finance. On this broad-based index, the United States surpassed the United Kingdom and became the world's economically dominant power closer to World War I rather than in 1870.

Second, as Barry Eichengreen and Marc Flandreau (2008) have argued, the dollar first eclipsed sterling in the mid-1920s, and although sterling and the dollar shared near-equal status during the interwar years, the persistence of sterling during this period was driven to a considerable extent by the politics of the sterling area. Correcting for these two factors, the lag between the rise to economic dominance of the United States (around World War I) and the establishment of the dollar as the premier reserve currency was considerably shorter—closer to 10 years rather than the 60-plus years conventionally believed. Applying this timing to the current situation suggests that the renminbi could overtake the dollar within the next 10 years because China's index of overall economic dominance overtook that of the United States around 2010.

The currency dominance transition is far from inexorable. It will be conditional on China undertaking far-reaching reforms of its financial sector and exchange rate policies. China will need to eliminate restrictions on foreigners' access to the renminbi for the entire range of financial and trade transactions and deepen its financial markets so that investors gain confidence in their liquidity and depth. However, if these policy initiatives are indeed undertaken—and many have already been initiated—the fundamentals will be in place to facilitate the rise of the renminbi and its eclipsing of the status quo reserve currencies, the dollar and the euro.

Skeptics of these projections will concede that size and policies are important determinants of reserve currency status but would argue that the deepest determinant of this status is confidence and trust, especially in hard times. Their telling question will be: In a crisis, when the chips are down, will investors feel that their money is safer in China than in the United States or at least safe enough against expropriation or nationalization by Chinese authorities?

Of course, broader political developments—especially Chinese political stability accompanied by transition toward greater democracy and freedoms—will be important in reassuring investors. But there are grounds for believing that China, regardless of the political transition, is unlikely to act in a manner that should worry investors. China, through its policy actions, is signaling its desire to elevate the status of the renminbi, not least because internationalization of the renminbi offers China's policymakers a possible political exit from the current mercantilist strategy. Having worked hard to secure reserve currency status for the renminbi, China is unlikely to jeopardize it. It goes without saying that if the United States suffers a failure of policy and performance (even without it being as bad as the fantasy scenario outlined at the outset of this chapter), the transition to the renminbi would occur with greater certainty and speed.

Chapter 6 elaborates on three distinct aspects of China's dominance. First, China will be a precocious power, in that dominance will occur at living standards associated with middle-income countries. In contrast, the United States and the United Kingdom were among the richest countries in the world during their periods of dominance. Second, China's mercantilism has also been somewhat unusual. Like the United States and the United Kingdom during comparable periods, China has run current account surpluses. But unlike the United States, China has consciously targeted mercantilist outcomes through exchange rate or trade policy. And unlike the United Kingdom, which relied primarily on trade policy, China's mercantilist instrument has been exchange rate policy. China has been unique in that its rise to dominance and its mercantilism are associated with being closed to capital, whereas the United Kingdom and United States were highly open to capital.

Finally, China, although mercantilist now, is a highly open economy, measured in terms of trade outcomes. This is the paradox of a China that is both mercantilist and highly open. And China's openness is unusual for such a large country, especially when compared with the United States during the heyday of its dominance.

All projections are problematic, not least because they extrapolate the recent past. So chapter 7 asks what can go wrong with the analysis, especially regarding the numbers for China. The chapter suggests that the China projections are appropriately cautious. The projections of dominance do not require China to replicate its performance of the last three decades—they assume China's growth slowing to 6 percent a year in PPP terms (less than 7 percent in dollar terms) over the next two decades, which would be about 40 percent slower than in recent years. A historical comparison, based on looking at how countries fared when they had reached China's situation today—namely one-quarter of the standard of living of the United States during its postwar economic heyday—suggests that there are enough countries that have done in the past what China is projected here to do in the future. It should be noted that some countries have also slipped and encountered long periods of decline. But a lot will have to go wrong for China to find itself in the latter rather than the former category.

Chapters 8 and 9 draw out the possible implications for economic cooperation with a rising China. The big question here is whether the open, rules-based trade and financial system bequeathed by the United States after World War II will survive China's economic dominance?

It will almost be true by definition that as a dominant power, China—as for the United States during Pax Americana—will increasingly be beyond the influence of outsiders, especially on key issues such as exchange rates, climate change, and technology protectionism. Self-interest will, largely, rule.

The pursuit of self-interest per se need not undermine the current system. For one, China's unique features—especially the fact that it is one of history's most open superpowers—will invest it with a stake in broadly maintaining the current trade and financial system. The commitment of the United States to an open system after World War II was less economic because it was not a very open economy and was more the product of a broader strategic vision: An open economic system would promote prosperity elsewhere, especially for its allies in Europe and Japan, reduce the prospects of another global conflagration while consolidating the dominance of the United States. China's stake in market openness will be existential and substantial because delivering development to its people—the basis for the regime's legitimacy—is crucially predicated on markets remaining open.

The importance of trade for China going forward, the likelihood that China will exit from its mercantilism by internationalizing the renminbi, and the relative ineffectiveness of the IMF as a forum for cooperation between systemically important countries, makes it likely that engagement—and the scope for friction—between China and the other large economies will relate more to trade than macroeconomic issues. In turn, this will make the World Trade Organization (WTO) not the IMF the key forum for and locus of cooperation between China and these economies.

The high probability scenario must still be one of China having a vested interest in an open trading system and hence acting, even leading, to preserve it. Moreover, modern trading relationships, notably the slicing up of the value-added chain, and the globalization of foreign direct investment, have resulted in much larger two-way flows of goods, capital, people, and ideas. This criss-crossing globalization has created enmeshing private interests with a stake in preserving this globalization to a greater degree than ever before. And if the renminbi ascends to becoming an international reserve currency, China might be reluctant to lose the strength and prestige that comes with that status by disrupting financial and trade relations in any serious way.

But there is a small but finite probability that China's perception of its self-interest conflicts with the requirements of an open system and that it exercises its dominance in a less-than-benign manner. A dominant China could pursue industrial and quasi-protectionist policies domestically, capture resources abroad, enter into bilateral and discriminatory arrangements with selected partners, all of which, given China's size, could affect the fundamental character of the current open economic system. How can the world today secure some protection against, or diminish the chances of, a damagingly assertive China in the future?

The world—more specifically, China's large trading partners, including the United States, Europe, Japan, India, and Brazil—needs to take out an insurance policy today or sometime during the period of transition to greater Chinese dominance to provide some protection against or diminish the chances of a not-so-benign exercise of China's economic hegemony in the future. The need for insurance would stem not from alarmism but would simply follow as a matter of prudent risk management. Insurance does not foreclose or preclude the possibility of a positive dynamic of engagement with China based on deepening or strengthening economic and trade cooperation.

History suggests that multilateralism offers the best hope for placing checks on dominant economic powers. The aim of China's trading partners should be to keep China tethered to the multilateral system, but achieving this will not be easy. First and foremost, China's trading partners will need to exercise strategic foresight and restraint in terms of refraining from deepening bilateral ties with China, especially in areas covered by the WTO. If many of these countries do negotiate bilateral trade agreements, then all of them will have less multilateral dealings with China. The problem is not just that bilateral agreements with China might be imbalanced but also that enforcement of rules and agreements is likely to be more difficult bilaterally than multilaterally. In other words, China's economic dominance might play out more under imbalanced bilateral rules and the asymmetry inherent in adhering to them.

A more difficult question is whether a second act of self-restraint by China's major trading partners might be necessary. If the United States, European Union, Japan, India, and Brazil resist deepening bilateral ties with China but go ahead and negotiate free trade or economic partnership agreements with each other, China might legitimately view this situation as "hostile regionalism," as an attempt at the economic and trade encirclement of China. A more positive and less hostile way of keeping China anchored would be for its trading partners to practice a policy of multilateralism not only in their dealings with China but also among themselves. This would signal a belief in the intrinsic value of multilateralism rather than just as an instrument to contain China.

This book is primarily about the rise of China with some implications for the United States and the multilateral system and is somewhat inattentive to Europe and its role in the dominance stakes. In quantitative terms, Europe or the EU-27 is as big today as the United States and hence is a key player in the economic system. The neglect of Europe is in part because Europe today is still a half-way house, with divided responsibilities on decision-making between member countries and Europe. Moreover, as of this writing, it remains unclear which of the two competing forces—sovereignty-preserving and sovereignty-reclaiming versus centralizing and sovereignty-pooling—will gain the upper hand in the wake of the ongoing crisis in the European periphery. The projections suggest that even if the future throws up a more unified Europe that is capable of projecting economic power, China will still remain the biggest individual player by far. But a resurgent America and a unified Europe will play, and need to play, a key role in shaping the multilateralism that represents the best insurance against any unbenign exercise of dominance by China.

It is possible, of course, that China's rise is exaggerated and that American economic preeminence will persist, even if diluted to some extent. On the other hand, the possibility of the United States being dictated to in the near future by an economically dominant and an assertive China is a low but not a zero probability outcome. Regardless of exactly how and how quickly China's rise plays out, the numbers and their implications spelled out in this book stand in stark contrast to the immutable belief among some of America's enduring economic dominance in the years ahead. Can history—or rather China—abbreviate the duration of dominance of the United States to much less than the 200 years anticipated by Harold Macmillan in the opening quote to this introduction?

1

A Brief History
of Economic Dominance

The United States has the sticks and carrots.

—John Foster Dulles in a memorandum to
President Dwight Eisenhower in the aftermath of the Suez crisis[1]

The Suez Canal is as good a metaphor as any for economic dominance. It is well known that the Suez crisis of 1956 irretrievably buried any hopes (or illusions, some would say) that the United Kingdom might retain its status as a great power. But the history of the canal actually bookends both the apogee and collapse of the British empire. And at both points in time, the economically dominant creditor country gained at the expense of the enfeebled and indebted power.

Opposed originally to the canal's construction, which began in 1859, the United Kingdom subsequently rued its lack of a direct stake once the waterway's strategic possibilities as its "highway to India" and "backdoor to the East" became evident. The original Suez Canal company was majority-owned by the French, with the Egyptian ruler, Ismail Pasha—the *khedive* or viceroy nominally representing the Ottoman ruler in Istanbul—enjoying a 44 percent stake.

By 1875, however, Egypt teetered on the edge of insolvency, overstretched by military adventurism in the Sudan and Ethiopia, seduced into profligacy stemming from the *khedive's* grandiose ambition to make Cairo the Paris-on-the-Nile, and debilitated by dwindling export revenues once stability returned to international cotton markets after the US Civil War. A debt-to-GDP ratio of close to 200 percent, mostly owed to restive European bondholders, forced the *khedive* to sell his stake for a paltry sum of 4 million pounds, which amounted to 4 percent of his debt and 7 percent of Egypt's GDP at the time.

Spotting the opportunity, the British government, with the assistance of the Rothschilds, acquired the viceroy's stake—amounting to 0.3 percent of UK GDP compared with the 3 percent of GDP that the United States paid for

---

1. As reported by Kunz (1991).

13

the Louisiana Purchase—with lightning speed. "You have it, Madam," Prime Minister Benjamin Disraeli wrote to Queen Victoria upon completion of the transaction. So rapid was the transaction that Disraeli's arch enemy, William Gladstone, fumed that parliamentary procedure was being circumvented (Ferguson 2000). The Suez Company became an Anglo-French concern, but the United Kingdom exerted effective control over the Suez zone and its sea traffic until the early 1950s.

But just as the United Kingdom acquired the canal by virtue of its economic dominance, and in particular as a net creditor to the rest of the world, it lost it when it faded as a power and became a net debtor. Following a long sequence of events, including the withdrawal of US and British support for the World Bank to finance construction of the Aswan dam, Egyptian President Gamal Abdel Nasser nationalized the Suez Canal in July 1956. The United Kingdom, France, and Israel mounted an attack in late October and November of that year and Egypt responded by sinking all the ships and vessels in the canal, thereby blockading the vital oil tanker traffic.

Investor anxiety about this campaign and its consequences for the United Kingdom led to sterling coming under attack, and the Bank of England was forced to draw down its reserves to defend sterling. By December, the threat of a devaluation was very real, especially since there was a fear that the United Kingdom's reserves might fall below the target level set by the UK authorities, which would signal the need for a devaluation of sterling.

Heading off a sterling devaluation was thought imperative for two reasons. Oil prices (denominated in dollars) spiked because of the Suez blockade, which reduced tanker traffic and global oil supplies, and a devaluation would make oil even more expensive in the United Kingdom, fueling inflation. Second, United Kingdom was still clinging to the vestiges of empire and the sterling area, which yoked together the United Kingdom and the Commonwealth countries through preferential trade and a loose monetary arrangement. A de-based sterling would threaten these arrangements and hence the remnants of empire. The then-governor of the Bank of England, Cameron F. Cobbold, emphasized that a sterling devaluation "only" seven years after the previous one in 1949 "would probably lead to the break-up of the sterling or (possibly even the dissolution of the Commonwealth) . . . a reduction in the volume of trade and currency instability at home leading to severe inflation." Consequently, "we should regard a further devaluation of sterling as a disaster to be fought with every weapon at our disposal" (Boughton 2001a, 435, parentheses in original).

The United Kingdom turned to the United States for financial help, relying on their "special relationship" for assistance either in the form of interest waivers on the United Kingdom's lend-lease credits (the system of financial assistance extended by the United States to its World War II allies) or new loans through the US Export-Import Bank. But President Dwight Eisenhower—furious about the attack because it occurred during the presidential campaign in which he was campaigning as a man of peace after having ended the fighting in Korea—refused to help. In addition, the United States made it clear that, unless the United Kingdom complied with a US-sponsored United Nations resolution involving quick and unconditional withdrawal of British forces from the canal area, it would not allow the British to access resources from the International Monetary Fund (IMF).[2] UK compliance would enable it to access Export-Import Bank loans as well as substantial IMF resources.

"This was blackmail. . . . But we were in no position to argue," recalled a senior adviser to Prime Minister Anthony Eden (who resigned in the wake of the Suez crisis) (Andrews 2006, 7). Once the United Kingdom agreed to a deadline for withdrawal, the United States in fact supported a massive financial package that included unprecedented borrowing from the IMF worth $1.3 billion and a $500 million loan from the Export-Import Bank. The United States also allowed the United Kingdom to postpone about $175 million of its payments under lend-lease.[3]

Four aspects of this episode are worth highlighting from the perspective of dominance and power. First, economic means were used by the dominant power to secure noneconomic objectives. Second, power was exercised by the rising superpower not against some small country but against the power that it was displacing, which was a political, economic, and military ally rather than an adversary. Third, the exercise of economic power was directed against a country to secure national objectives, not to change the rules of the system. National rather than systemic objectives were the motives for exercising dominance.

Finally, a key and less recognized aspect of the Suez episode was that the dominant power used not just sticks but carrots to change outcomes. The hardball played by the United States, and its ability and willingness to use tough financial sanctions before the crisis was resolved, were matched or even surpassed by its generosity after the United Kingdom agreed to the conditions imposed. Indeed, US willingness to go to bat for the United Kingdom was reflected not just in the unprecedented magnitude of the IMF loan[4] but also in the fact that the loan violated IMF rules at the time that prohibited lending to support large capital outflows, which the United Kingdom experienced during the Suez crisis.[5] Economic dominance is thus not just about penalties but also about incentives, and indeed one might argue that carrot-based dominance might have greater legitimacy than stick-based dominance.

---

2. The IMF functions like a credit union, with contributions from each member country. These contributions have a hierarchy. The first 25 percent is called the gold tranche, which the country can withdraw at any time without permission from the IMF membership. Withdrawals beyond this gold tranche require approval of 50 percent of the IMF's membership. The United States made clear that it would block any UK request to access resources beyond the first 25 percent.

3. In fact, the lend-lease arrangement was renegotiated seven times to allow the United Kingdom the unconditional right to postpone payments of principal and interest (Kunz 1991, 181).

4. Indeed, the package was designed to be so big as to immediately deter speculation against sterling, which had the desirable effect that the United Kingdom ended up borrowing only $560 million of the total of $1.3 billion that was approved by the IMF.

5. IMF rules only allowed lending when a country's current account (consisting of trade in goods and services), not its capital account, was jeopardized.

Whether irony or symmetry, the upshot of it all was that as an economically dominant net creditor, the United Kingdom, acquired the Suez Canal, and as an economically enfeebled net debtor, she lost it. The enfeeblement, of course, was a gradual process that had begun long before 1956. The Suez episode simply marked, dramatically and definitively, the relegation of the United Kingdom from the top league.

Systemic Manifestations of US Economic Dominance

The Suez episode illustrates one facet of economic dominance, namely dominance directed at one or a set of countries to attain direct national objectives. In this respect, the United States has used economic power in countless ways on innumerable occasions. For example, since World War II, the United States, acting alone or in concert with other countries, has accounted for nearly 70 percent of economic sanctions used or threatened to achieve foreign policy goals (Hufbauer et al. 2007).

As important as its exercise of economic power against individual countries has been the imprimatur of the United States in creating and shaping the overall economic, trade, and financial system. The measure of its economic preeminence has been the fact that in the postwar period the United States has been able to define the rules and exceptions of this system and change them when its perceived interests have so dictated. It is not that the United States has always achieved its economic objectives by successfully changing the actions of other countries or insulating its own actions from external influence. Nor is it the case that economic dominance has always been achieved by unilateral US actions, or that the changes sought by the United States have necessarily occurred speedily or by the use of threats alone. But the fact remains that, by and large, for much of the 20th century, the United States had the ability to influence outcomes. The sections that follow consider some major ways in which the United States has shaped the financial and trade system over time.

International Financial System

Designing the rules for the IMF was a contest between Harry Dexter White, a senior US Treasury official, and Lord John Maynard Keynes, bravely seeking to hold the fort on behalf of a diminished and indebted the United Kingdom (Harrod 1951). Collectively, they designed a relatively open system and one that would keep in check the worst beggar-thy-neighbor instincts that prevailed during the interwar years. But it was a system that was partial to creditors over debtors, and in several important respects, White, representing the interests of the world's then-largest creditor, prevailed over Keynes. Of the technical discussions that eventually formed the core of the IMF, Robert Skidelsky (2003, 736) writes: "The seminars tended to follow a pattern: the

British proposed, the Americans disposed. This was the inevitable consequence of the asymmetry of power."[6]

Keynes wanted more symmetric adjustment between surplus and deficit countries. He wanted to impose financial penalties on countries that ran excessively large current account surpluses, ease the burden of adjustment on deficit countries by providing more resources to the IMF, and have the IMF run more like an international central bank with less political control exerted by the United States.[7] White mostly rejected or significantly attenuated these ideas. It is either irony or historic justice that the refusal of the United States to institute more stringent rules on surplus countries to adjust has come back to haunt it today, when it has been asking China (and Germany) to do—reduce their surpluses—what it would not contemplate back in 1945.

Less well known is that Keynes wanted IMF quotas to be decided on the basis of the importance of a country in world trade, which would have reduced the disparity between the United Kingdom and the United States. White would have nothing of that. The United States decided on quota shares on explicitly political grounds and a (convoluted) technical formula was conjured up to give expression to, and provide cover for, clearly political decisions (Mikesell 1994, Boughton 2006). President Franklin Roosevelt wanted to give the largest quotas to his military allies in World War II—the United Kingdom, Russia (which did not become an original IMF member), and China. When the French protested at their demotion behind China, Treasury Secretary Henry Morgenthau explained that President Roosevelt had already promised the fourth largest quota to China, although cool relations between Roosevelt and Charles de Gaulle were thought to have played a role (Mikesell 1994).

What is as telling about US economic dominance, however, has been its ability to change the rules of the system. Between 1971 and 1973, the United States was essentially and unilaterally able to blow up the Bretton Woods

---

6. Louis Rasminsky, the Canadian representative who played an important role in drafting the Bretton Woods agreement and became Canada's first Executive Director to the IMF, put it much more starkly: "We have all been treated to a spectacle of American domination and domineeringness through their financial power which has to be seen to be believed. . . . US foreign economic policy seems to be in the hands of the Treasury who are insensitive to other people's actions and prepared to ram everything they want down everyone's throat" (as quoted in Pauly 2006, 191).

7. In his speech at the first meeting of the IMF Board of Governors in Savannah, Georgia, Keynes warned about US political control over the IMF and the World Bank with typical eloquence. Expressing the hope that the two Bretton Woods twins would not be cursed by the malicious fairy, Carabosse, he nevertheless feared that they would: "You two brats shall grow up politicians; your every thought and act shall have an arrière-penseé; everything you determine shall not be for its own sake or on its own merits but because of something else" (Skidelsky 2003, 829). Fred Vinson, the US Treasury Secretary, sensing that these words were targeted at him, responded, "I don't mind being called malicious but I do being mind called a fairy" (Skidelsky 2003, 829). To help minimize the political pressures from the United States, Keynes urged—unsuccessfully—that the IMF and World Bank be located in New York rather than Washington, DC.

international monetary system of fixed exchange rates because fixed rates became an unacceptable straitjacket on US domestic policies.

In 1971, the United States, in violation of the spirit and also the letter of the IMF Articles of Agreement, suspended the convertibility of dollars into gold and refused to keep its currency within the bands required by IMF rules. Then, in violation of the letter and spirit of the rules of the General Agreement on Tariffs and Trade (GATT) in place at the time, the United States imposed an across-the-board import surcharge of 10 percent as a means of persuading partner countries to revalue their currencies (and hence indirectly devalue the dollar).[8] This action worked, reflected in the Smithsonian Agreement of December 1971, to change the values of the currency pegs. But when even this currency realignment proved insufficient to meet the needs of its domestic policies, the United States in March 1973 abandoned the fixed exchange rate system in favor of floating exchange rates, driving the final nail into the coffin of the original Bretton Woods agreement.

This process was neither smooth (domestically or with trading partners) nor speedy enough to allow any inference of unconstrained US economic power.[9] Nor, importantly, was it the case that other countries had not changed the value of their currencies prior to the US action—France, the United Kingdom, and Germany all did that. Nor indeed was it the case that the outcome—the move to flexible exchange rates—was undesirable from a global perspective. But at the end of the day, the US government "was exercising the unconstrained right to print money that others could not (save at unacceptable cost) refuse to accept" (Strange 1987). The hegemonic power was unwilling to accept the domestic costs of supplying the public good—which the fixed exchange rate system was considered to be then—and was able to change the terms of international cooperation. The abrasive US Treasury Secretary John Connally—author of the "dollar-is-our-currency-but-your-problem" quip—is reported to have told a group of experts at this time, "Gentlemen, the foreigners are trying to screw us, but I intend to screw them first."[10]

---

8. That this action was extreme is suggested by the fact that to implement it, President Richard Nixon had to invoke very unusual domestic legal authority—emergency banking legislation from 1933, also known as the Trading with the Enemy Act of 1918—because normal authority to apply tariffs under the US Constitution rests with Congress.

9. The fact that the United States tolerated the yoke of fixed exchange rates throughout much of the 1960s, when it was running expansionary domestic policies, is invoked as evidence that even the economic superpower had to accept the rules of and constraints imposed by the system (that it had created). Put differently, even the power of the United States was not uncircumscribed (Gilpin 2001, 131–42).

10. Then-US Treasury Secretary John Connally also exercised American power in more personal ways. The IMF Managing Director at the time, Pierre-Paul Schweitzer, brother of Nobel Prize-winning doctor and philanthropist Albert Schweitzer, attempted to convince the United States that any change in the value of the pegs of the different currencies should involve both devaluation by the United States (to which Connally was adamantly opposed) and revaluation by the other currencies. An irate Connally subsequently ensured that Schweitzer would not secure reappointment as Managing Director.

Now, fast forward 20 years. The counterpart of the current Chinese export juggernaut in the 1980s was Japan. Then, like today, Japan was the target of accusations of unfair trade (Lawrence 1987, Noland 1995, Bhagwati 1999). The recession of the early 1980s, and the sharp rise in the dollar, led to record US current account deficits (and counterpart surpluses in Japan). Protectionist rhetoric surged in the United States. But in this episode, with greater cooperation from European trading partners, the United States was able to get its way both on the currency and on actual protectionist action.

Under the Plaza Accord negotiated in September 1985, the United States, Japan, and European partners agreed to coordinated foreign exchange market intervention to appreciate the yen and Deutsche mark against the dollar. The United States also engaged in "talking down" the dollar. These official actions combined to reinforce market-determined appreciations of the yen and deutschemark, the consummation desired by the US authorities. In addition, the United States had been able to secure Japan's agreement earlier in the 1980s to "voluntarily" reduce its exports of cars, steel and machine tools, and other products. And the United States also was able to use antidumping actions and voluntary import expansions to secure changes in the semiconductor industry.

Multilateral Trading System

In the multilateral trade system as well, the United States was able to determine rules, exceptions, and outcomes. Just after World War II, the United States sought to eliminate the system of imperial preferences whereby the United Kingdom and its colonies discriminated in their trade relations against the rest of the world and strenuously worked to enshrine a system based on nondiscrimination,[11] usually referred to as the most favored nation (MFN) principle.[12] Having done this, the United States indulged Europe's efforts to integrate in a discriminatory fashion because of the broader political objec-

---

11. The United States did not immediately achieve this objective. Imperial preferences declined gradually over time not because the preferences themselves were eliminated but because the tariffs applicable to other countries were reduced under successive rounds of tariff negotiations under the GATT. Schenk (2010a) notes that the average preference margin on trade between the United Kingdom and the Commonwealth remained at about 5 to 6 percent as late as 1953, which was about half the level in 1937.

12. There is some semantic irony in the term "most favored nation," which connotes discrimination rather than its opposite. But the point was to suggest that a member of the GATT should treat another GATT member no worse than any other country (including nonmembers of the GATT). The MFN principle made its first appearance in the 17th century (WTO 2007, 132) but was seriously tested during the opium wars between the United Kingdom and China. It was incorporated in the 1842 treaty between the United Kingdom and China signaling the end of the first opium war. In that context, China was required to extend to the United Kingdom any (not just trade) favor it extended to any other country. China's refusal to extend benefits it had granted the United States led to another war between the United Kingdom and China in 1854.

tives related to European reconstruction in the aftermath of World War II.[13] This discrimination could be intellectually rationalized as an overall gain for the world on the grounds that the trade-creating effects of preferential tariff cuts would outweigh the negative trade-diverting effects. But discrimination it was, and it was institutionalized for political reasons.

Then, when the United States started to feel the discriminatory effects of European integration, it pushed strongly for reductions in MFN tariffs under various "rounds" of multilateral trade negotiations, especially the Dillon (1960–62) and Kennedy (1962–67) Rounds. President John F. Kennedy, in his special message to Congress seeking support for the eponymous round, cited European integration at the top of the list of reasons for undertaking multilateral trade negotiations. Between 1956 and 1967, tariffs on nonagricultural goods in the United States and Europe were reduced from 20 percent to below 9 percent (WTO 2007).

The major motivation of the US administration to start the Tokyo Round of trade negotiations in 1973 was to respond to its difficult economic times, including high and rising unemployment, chronic trade deficits, and rising inflation (WTO 2007, 185).[14] The Bretton Woods system of fixed exchange rates had collapsed, the first oil price shock reverberated through the world, and, above all, a rising Japan embodied the larger competitive threat facing the United States. As a result, the Tokyo Round focused more on making trade fair rather than free, stemming from the widespread perception in Washington that other countries were taking advantage of the United States and reflected in the emphasis on disciplining subsidies and permitting contingent protection actions (safeguard, antidumping, and countervailing duties) against surges in imports. Congress made clear to the US administration that disciplining subsidies should be a priority in the Tokyo Round. As Mac Destler (1992, 148) writes: "The codes on subsidies and countervailing measures and on antidumping, however, were the MTN's (Tokyo Round of multilateral trade negotiations) centerpieces." In other words, the Tokyo Round was as much about disciplining and sanctioning the departures from free trade—to reflect the US economic situation—as it was about promoting free trade.

Furthermore, for most of the postwar period, the United States ensured that agriculture and textiles would remain beyond the scope of serious liberalization because of the political strength of its domestic farm and textile interests. The textile sector was regulated by a series of periodically deter-

---

13. Jean Monnet, one of the moving spirits behind early European integration, had close connections with prominent US officials and financiers, including John Foster Dulles. The United States financed the first integration initiative—the Economic Coal and Steel Community—to the extent of $100 million. And even before that, the United States financed the creation of the European Payments Union—the precursor of European monetary and currency integration—to the tune of $50 million.

14. Another motivation was the fear that enlargement of the European Economic Community (EEC) would have a negative impact on US trade and investment, and in particular that UK membership in the EEC would adversely affect US exports of agricultural goods to Europe.

mined bilateral quotas agreed to among the major importing and exporting countries. This arrangement began in 1961 under the so-called Short Term Agreement on Cotton Textiles (STA), which gave way to the Long Term Agreement Regarding International Trade in Cotton Textiles (LTA), which became the Multi-Fiber Arrangement (MFA) in 1974. In other sectors, especially steel and autos, whenever the domestic industry came under pressure from foreign competition, the United States was able to minimize this competition, notably by securing "voluntary export restraints" from its trading partners or by seeking recourse to antidumping and countervailing import restrictions.

In the 1980s, when its near-abroad foreign policy considerations became important, the United States itself departed from the cherished MFN principle for which it had long crusaded by negotiating a free trade agreement with Israel in 1985 and Canada in 1987. The latter was later extended to Mexico as part of the North American Free Trade Agreement (NAFTA). These agreements presaged and indeed galvanized the negotiation of other free trade agreements around the world. In some ways, the embrace of discriminatory free trade agreements by the United States—rather than its enthusiastic support of European integration—might have been the great betrayal of the nondiscriminatory trading system that it had worked hard to create after the Great Depression.

Also in the 1980s, the United States began to perceive that its comparative advantage lay in the intellectual property and service sectors, so it pushed for new international rules to open international markets for intellectual-property-intensive products (e.g., pharmaceuticals, software, and movies) and especially financial and telecommunications services. This push led to the Uruguay Round of multilateral trade negotiations completed in 1994. The move to incorporate intellectual property in the multilateral system was especially controversial both in terms of the means deployed and the objectives targeted by the United States. Several analysts wrote that intellectual property was unlike trade liberalization in that the global benefits were questionable because up to the first order, the economic impact was a rent transfer from poor to rich countries. Achieving these objectives was sought by threatening countries with trade retaliation unless they agreed to increase the standards of intellectual property protection in their markets. Special domestic legislation—the infamous Section 301 of US law—was enacted in the United States to authorize such retaliation.

Finally, the United States was able to secure significant opening of China's goods and services markets as part of China's accession to the World Trade Organization (WTO) in 2001. Again, it is true that the United States was pushing on a door already slightly opened because the Chinese leadership under Zhu Rhongji was attempting to use external pressure to further reform domestically. But it is a measure of how radical the opening was that a senior Chinese negotiator—10 years later—cast the Doha impasse as payback by China for the concessions it had to make under its WTO accession.

After WTO Director General Pascal Lamy proposed his compromise in the Doha Round, and after it was tentatively accepted by most of the G-7 (not including India), some US negotiators went to the Chinese embassy in

Geneva to try to pry loose some additional concessions. Paul Blustein (2009, 271) writes that "the U.S. negotiators knew they would have a tough sell, because the Chinese have nursed grudges ever since the 1999 talks concerning their entry into the WTO; [they] feel that the United States bullied them into accepting excessively stringent terms. . . ."

Perhaps an even more telling illustration of the radical nature of China's opening is the fact that China embarked on a mercantilist exchange rate strategy (to push exports and reduce imports) in part to offset the trade opening brought about by its WTO accession.[15]

In many of these proliberalization and occasionally antiliberalization efforts of the United States, it is not that the United States did not have the complicity of trading partners in achieving some outcomes. Most notably, many developing countries were quite happy to have textiles and clothing beyond the scope of international rules as a quid pro quo for not having to undertake liberalization obligations in the manufacturing sector (Wolf 1987), since they were ideologically committed to import-substitution and protectionist polices at home. And many if not most of the inefficient textile exporters were glad to have guaranteed quotas rather than face open competition from other, more competitive exporters. This was the dirty secret of the MFA and the main reason why it persisted for so long.

Nor was it true that the United States always got its way; for example, in the Tokyo Round, the United States was unable to significantly discipline agricultural practices of the then European Economic Community (EEC). Neither did the United States get its way expeditiously: It took same 12 years of protracted and tortuous negotiations from the initial effort to secure global intellectual property and services liberalization in 1982 until the final agreement in the Uruguay Round of trade negotiations in 1994. And the United States indeed had to "pay" to achieve its objectives: For example, in return for opening up intellectual property and service sectors globally, the United States had to offer to open up its own apparel sector.

But broadly speaking, the trading system and the rest of the world proved malleable to the efforts of the United States: The system may not have been putty in the hands of the United States to shape entirely to its liking, but it did shape it, and much moreso than any other country.

Contrast this history of US dominance with that today, in particular vis-à-vis China. For the last five years, the United States has been attempting to change China's exchange rate policies. China has maintained a consistently undervalued exchange rate (Cline and Williamson 2010) and as a result has run consistently large current account surpluses (Goldstein and Lardy 2008), leading to a historically unprecedented level of foreign exchange reserves totaling $3 trillion. Since the global economic crisis of 2008, China's exchange rate policies have acquired greater political salience in the United States, where high levels of unemployment and underutilization of economic resources

---

15. See chapter 6 for further discussion of this point.

make China's undervalued exchange rate seem more demonstrably a beggar-thy-neighbor policy. And yet, the United States has been largely ineffective acting unilaterally in its efforts to change China's policies.

The United States has threatened unilateral trade actions but has been unable to translate these threats into any meaningful legislative action. The initiative by Senators Charles Schumer (D-NY) and Bob Graham (D-FL) in 2005 to impose across-the-board tariffs on imports from China never saw the light of day. And the bill passed by the House of Representatives in October 2010 looks decidedly weak in that it would affect a small fraction of China's imports in contrast to the Nixon surcharge of 1971.[16]

This inability to act reflects in part growing Chinese dominance. Action against China does not command broad support in the United States: Labor may be in favor of tough actions against China's undervalued exchange rate, but capital—that is, US firms—are at best ambiguous. US firms located in China and exporting abroad might actually benefit from the undervalued exchange rate, and other US firms that are invested in or do business with China are vulnerable to Chinese retaliatory action, such as by being denied access to Chinese government procurement contracts. Thus, the United States barks but cannot bite. The balance of power in the US-China relationship is especially striking given that it was only about a decade ago that the United States was able to muscle China into radically opening its agriculture, goods, and services market as part of China's accession to the WTO (Bhattasali, Shantong, and Martin 2004).

China has, of course, facilitated this strengthening of its own economic power by encouraging US foreign direct investment (FDI) and influencing American politics and political economy by building a stake for these firms in China. In the 1980s, Japan was the target of US trade action, but Japan was less successful in fending off trade measures taken against it. Japan did not have the economic heft that China currently enjoys, and by limiting US FDI in Japan, it had forgone the opportunity to create a constituency in the United States to speak up for Japanese interests.[17]

If China has been able to resist the exercise of US power through its size and strategic use of FDI, it has also been able to do so indirectly. For example, China has used its surpluses to provide aid to and finance investments in Africa, extracting in return the closure of Taiwanese embassies. It has used its size to strengthen trade and financial relationships in Asia and Latin America. (China's offer to build an alternative to the Panama Canal to boost Colombia's prospects is one dramatic illustration of this phenomenon.) More recently, it has offered to buy Greek, Irish, Portuguese, and Spanish debt as a way of forestalling or mitigating financial-market chaos in Europe. ("China is

---

16. At the time of this writing it is unclear if this measure will also be passed in the Senate.

17. Interestingly, Japan's response was to build factories, especially in the contentious automotive sector, in the United States. By doing so, it has now built a stake for US labor and suppliers, and hence made US politics a little more sympathetic to Japan and Japanese investments.

Spain's best friend," effused Spanish Prime Minister José Luis Rodríguez Zapatero in April 2011 on the occasion of the Chinese president's visit.)

Chinese exchange rate policy has adversely affected emerging-market and developing countries as much as the United States. But Europe and emerging-market countries have stood on the sidelines while the United States has had to carry the burden of the crusade and, for that reason, not very successfully. China has had more allies and fewer critics in part because of the support it has been able to buy and the potential opposition it has been able to ward off through financial generosity and trade links. Many countries—including Brazil and India—chafe at their competitiveness being undermined by the undervalued renminbi, yet they maintain a studious public silence, refraining from criticizing Chinese policy. If dominance is as much about being able to not do what others want you to do, China's dollar stockpile and large market have already conferred dominance.

Another illustration of declining US influence relates to trade. Today, the politics of the Doha Round is very complicated because of US ambivalence under the Barack Obama administration about completing it. But it must be remembered that a Republican president and Republican Congress between 2000 and 2006—generally considered to be a combination that is more conducive to trade opening—were unable to wear down opposition from major emerging-market countries, including China and India, and successfully complete the Doha Round of trade negotiations.

Caveats to US Dominance and Decline

The foregoing should not be interpreted as portraying some golden hegemonic era of US dominance during which the country got all that it wanted, as soon as it wanted it, and from whomsoever it wanted it. Nor does the recent change in fortunes by any means suggest that the United States has suddenly gone from omnipotent to impotent. First of all, in several respects the United States did *not* get its way.[18] It did not eliminate imperial preferences, even though it wanted to; it failed to persuade the United Kingdom to become a charter member of the EEC; it did not stop the creation of the European free trade area; and it was unable to change European agricultural policies. Moreover, the United States often had to pay or incur some domestic political costs to secure outcomes of interest, often securing them only after considerable delay, and possibly more easily when there was a weaker or more compliant trading partner (than Europe, for example). In the trade arena, it also helped that the European Union partnered with the United States in pushing the broad agenda of market opening.

And of course, the lack of complete hegemony in the noneconomic sphere was also clear, as described by Joseph Nye (2010, 4): "After World War II, the

---

18. For example, the Hufbauer et al. (2007) database suggests that in the postwar period, economic sanctions by the United States were partially or fully successful in about 45 percent of the cases studied.

United States had nuclear weapons and an overwhelming preponderance of economic power, but nonetheless was unable to prevent the 'loss' of China, to roll back communism in Eastern Europe, to overcome stalemate in the Korean War, to stop the 'loss' of North Vietnam, or to dislodge the Castro regime in Cuba."

On the other hand, it is certainly not accurate to say that the United States has suffered such a loss of dominance as to render it unimportant today. During the recent global financial crisis, the United States—or rather the US Federal Reserve—performed a key role traditionally associated with a hegemony: supplying countercyclical liquidity during a financial crisis. The Federal Reserve was the central banker to the world, providing $600 billion in credit via foreign exchange swaps (not including the foreign institutions that participated in the various US programs). Countries such as Brazil, Singapore, Mexico, and Korea not only participated in these swaps but they actually sought help from the United States rather than turn to the IMF for similar financial assistance.

The fact that, on the one hand, the United States could not secure all the outcomes in the past, or, on the other, that it continues to have influence in the present is undeniable. But these facts cannot be invoked to obscure the possible and possibly clear differences in the breadth and magnitude of influence then and now; simply put, the probabilities associated with the United States being able to successfully shape outcomes were greater in the past than today. The question today is whether US economic dominance in this more nuanced sense of some clear loss of ability to influence outcomes is declining, and if so what are the economic causes.

There is now a cottage industry of writings arguing that the world is on the cusp of a change in economic dominance, with power and influence moving away from the United States toward Asia. Niall Ferguson's dramatic description states that "on closer inspection, we are indeed living through a global shift in the balance of power very similar to that which occurred in the 1870s. This is the story of how an over-extended empire sought to cope with an external debt crisis by selling off revenue streams to foreign investors. The empire that suffered these setbacks in the 1870s was the Ottoman empire. Today it is the US. . . ."[19] The question is whether there might be some economic antecedents to such alarmist prophesying.

Defining Dominance and Power

Power or dominance is not easy to define. Hans Morgenthau (1949, 13) wrote: "The concept of political power poses one of the most difficult and controversial problems of political science." But one can talk more easily about or around power. Power can have intrinsic and instrumental value. Countries might seek power for its own sake or in order to influence the actions of others

---

19. Niall Ferguson, "An Ottoman Warning for Indebted America," *Financial Times,* January 1, 2008.

and insulate their own actions from external influence (Kagan 2008). Robert Dahl's celebrated and widely accepted definition of power was "the ability to induce another party to do something it would not otherwise do" (cited in Scott Cooper 2006, 80).

Another aspect of power, of course, is that it has a zero-sum quality to it. Paul Kennedy cites two early thinkers who saw power up to the first order in these terms. "Whether a nation be today mighty and rich or not depends not on the abundance or security of its power and riches, but principally on whether its neighbors possess more or less of it" (Philipp von Hornigk, the mercantilist German writer, cited in Kennedy 1989, xxii); "Moreover national power has to be considered not only in itself, in its absolute extent, but . . . it has to be considered relative to the power of other states" (Correlli Barnet cited in Kennedy 1989, 202).

Power can broadly derive from military strength. Mao Zedong famously noted that power flows from the barrel of a gun; "How many battalions does the Pope have?" Josef Stalin is supposed to have asked his aides on being informed that the Allied cause had the support of the Vatican. Military might has clearly been seen as a source of power and influence throughout history, and, conversely, overreaching by the military has often been the cause of the decline of great powers.

If hard power occupies one end of the spectrum, Nye's soft power occupies the other. According to Nye (2004, 31), "the primary currencies of soft power are a country's values, culture, policies and institutions"—and the extent to which these "primary currencies," as Nye calls them, are able to attract or repel others to "want what you want."

Between hard and soft power, or perhaps even underpinning both, is economics. Seldom in history have economically small or weak nations dominated others. Kennedy (1989, xv) argues that, "the triumph of any one Great Power . . . has also been the consequences of the more or less efficient utilization of the state's productive economic resources in wartime, *and, further in the background, of the way in which that state's economy had been rising or falling, relative to the other leading nations, in the decades preceding the actual conflict.* For that reason, how a Great Power's position steadily alters in peacetime is as important to this study as how it fights in wartime."

This suggests not only that economics is a key factor in shaping great power status but also that what matters are economic factors not in some absolute sense but in a relative sense. It is this economic dimension and these economic determinants of power that will be the focus of much of this book. But even as I assert the importance of economics, it immediately gives rise to questions about the specific economic attributes that confer economic power and whether economic dominance can be quantified. These issues are taken up in the next chapter.

2

Quantification and Validation of Economic Dominance

Everything should be made as simple as possible, but no simpler.

—Albert Einstein

Mindful of and inspired by Einstein's exhortation, this chapter attempts to quantify economic dominance—a daunting task indeed, as economic dominance, like power more broadly, has many dimensions. It can have intrinsic value (e.g., having one's currency as the world's reserve currency can provide national prestige) or instrumental value. As an instrument, it can be deployed to achieve economic and noneconomic outcomes. In turn, these outcomes can be national or systemic. Also as an instrument, economic dominance can be wielded both as a stick and carrot, as the previous chapter showed. And dominance can encompass many areas of economics, including resources, trade, finance, and currency.

Richard Cooper (2003, 1–2) captures many of these points: "Economic power . . . involves the capability decisively to punish [or to reward] another party, according to whether that party responds in the desired way, combined with a perception that the possessor has the will or political ability to use it if necessary."

While useful and multiple distinctions can be made between various aspects of dominance, the aim of this chapter is simply to project economic dominance more broadly over the next 20 years. This requires quantifying the concept of economic dominance, which is done here by constructing an index. This is an exercise fraught with pitfalls. Indices, and quantification more broadly, can be reductive, obscuring the richness of the underlying phenomenon they try to measure. They can also be political or politically manipulated, aimed at perpetuating or justifying certain inequitable outcomes.[1]

---

1. Morris (2010, 141) cites the example from the field of archaeology, where quantification by evolutionists was criticized by the anthropologists Michael Shanks and Christopher Tilley as justifying "the priorities of the West in relation to other cultures whose primary importance is

Further, because of the complexity and multidimensionality of the underlying concept, an index of economic dominance might be particularly unhelpful or meaningless.

Having said all that, at least the extreme manifestations of economic dominance—the apogee and the loss or disappearance—can be identified and even dated, as the story of the Suez Canal shows. The challenge is whether dominance can be measured outside of these extreme and clear-cut situations.

The chief virtue of quantification is that it can make explicit what is often not, thereby helping to push forward discussions and debates about economic dominance and power. But for any such exercise to be taken seriously, at least five broad principles must be respected.

First, quantification must be simple in the sense of being parsimonious in the number of determinants and/or attributes of dominance that are included while still capturing its main features. There is a balance to be struck here between being indiscriminately inclusive and being objectionably selective, as captured in Einstein's remark. One way of achieving this balance is to see how much additional or independent information an attribute adds to those that are already included.

Second, all the attributes should be amenable to relatively uncontroversial measurement, and the data for these variables should be easily available, especially going back in time. Third, since the aim is to look into the future, there should be something beyond an ad hoc basis for projecting the variables over the 20-year time horizon that is the focus of this exercise. The greater the need to predict future policy behavior, the less confidence the projections will inspire.

Fourth, there should be some reasonable and justifiable basis for weighting the variables and computing an index. And finally, there should be some way (or ways) of validating the whole business of quantification and index building.

This chapter proceeds in four steps. I first present the list of possible determinants of economic dominance based on an admittedly selective reading of the history of the exercise of dominance (identification). Using the criteria described above, I then narrow the list and offer explanations as to why some of the potential candidates are excluded (what one might call "Occam razorization").[2] This is followed by a discussion of some of the issues involved in measuring the variables retained in the index (measurement). Finally, the

---

to act as offsets for our contemporary 'civilization'." A more positive use of indices is the World Bank's Cost of Doing Business indicators, which have on occasion been used to name-and-shame governments that have fallen behind others in creating an investor-friendly regulatory environment.

2. "Occam's razor" is the principle associated with a medieval Franciscan monk, William of Ockham, that extols simplicity over complexity. In Ockham's words, "plurality should not be posited without necessity." This has, over time, become an important principle in distinguishing good from less-good science and useful from less-useful descriptions of reality.

different variables are weighted in order to construct the index and then validate it in different ways (weighting and validation).

Even in discussing the various stages of building the index, several limitations will become evident, leaving room for experimenting with alternatives.[3] So what follows should be seen as a preliminary but transparent, difficult but careful, and controversial but hopefully useful attempt to understand and quantify economic dominance.

Identifying the Potential Attributes of Economic Dominance

What are the possible determinants or correlates of economic dominance? Based on history and intuition, six candidates plausibly suggest themselves for inclusion as determinants of dominance: economic wealth and resources, fiscal strength, military strength, trade, finance, and currency. Intuitively, it would seem that the size and wealth of an economy and the resources at its disposal, as well as its role in trade and finance, are important determinants of dominance. One indicator of trade and finance as determinants of dominance is the extent of their use as tools to secure foreign policy goals. Gary Hufbauer et al. (2007) find that in 204 episodes they studied, financial sanctions alone were used in 54 instances; trade sanctions in 40 instances; and the combination in 100 instances. Human capital and technological strength are two other plausible candidates for inclusion, but these tend to be highly correlated with wealth and resources and can thus be excluded on the Occam's razor principle.

Resources and Wealth—and Which Resources?

That a nation's wealth is one of the key determinants of economic dominance is uncontroversial. "Wealth is power, and power is wealth" wrote the English philosopher Thomas Hobbes. Above all, it is wealth that provides the economic resources to project power to deploy against potential rivals and others in influencing outcomes.

But opinion has varied about whether particular types of wealth and resources are more important than others. In principle, one might think of at least four different types of resources that could be relevant for determining power: overall resources, fiscal resources, military resources, and foreign resources.

The overall resources at the disposal of a country or its government, measured by its GDP, can be one simple and broad measure of dominance. Historically, since power was associated with military supremacy, certain kinds of economic activity that were particularly important for military strength were considered crucial, as in the cases of shipbuilding in the 1600s, coal and steel

---

3. Virmani (2004) offers one such alternative.

leading up to World War I, and industrial strength more broadly leading up to World War II.

Is military strength a determinant or correlate of economic strength? Historically, there was a mutually reinforcing relationship between the United Kingdom's ability to control the seas and its ability to further its economic objectives to expand markets and access cheap resources. One of the most famous pieces of governmental intervention to promote trade was the Navigation Act passed under Oliver Cromwell to ensure that all goods imported into England be carried in English ships or in ships of the country of origin of imported goods. The act's clear purpose was to dominate overseas trade by undermining Dutch domination of the seas.

The fact that Japan benefits from the security umbrella provided by the United States was not an irrelevant factor conditioning Japan's vulnerability or susceptibility to US influence, including during the negotiation of the Plaza Accord in the 1980s that led to an appreciation of the yen and depreciation of the dollar. Similarly, US support for Russia after the collapse of communism was influenced by Russian possession of nuclear weapons. Thus, military strength can be argued to be a determinant of economic dominance and power.

Is fiscal strength also a determinant of economic dominance? After all, it is the resources that governments can galvanize that provide the wherewithal for converting and projecting national purpose into international power and influence. Throughout history, the ability of governments to finance wars conferred power. Conversely, in the words of the Niall Ferguson (2009), "This is how empires decline. It begins with a debt explosion."

For the early mercantilists, an increase in the wealth of one country was synonymous with an increase in power. But in the mercantilist doctrine, increases in wealth were not associated with particular domestic resources or activities but rather with acquiring foreign resources, namely specie (gold or silver), at the expense of trading partners (Hirschman 1945). This aspect of resources is discussed below.

Trade

That a country's dominance in trade also affects its power will again not be controversial given the history of imperial conquest. At the zenith of its power, the United Kingdom dominated world trade, accounting for nearly a quarter of world exports (and probably imports). Britannia ruling the waves (often by waiving the rules, some critics contended) enabled it to control its colonies.

Voltaire had no doubts about the source of power and dominance of imperial Britain: "What made the power of England is that all the parties have . . . combined since the time of Elizabeth to promote trade. The same Parliament, which had the head of its King cut off, busied itself with maritime projects, like in the most untroubled times. The blood of Charles I was still warm, when that Parliament, though almost made up entirely of fanatics, passed in 1650 the famous Navigation Act."

Hufbauer et al. (2007) find that trade sanctions were used in about 20 percent of the instances in which countries used sanctions to achieve foreign policy goals. But how exactly does trade confer economic dominance and power? Is it imports, exports, trade, product composition, or the number and identity of trading partners that confer power?

Today, importing and the size of imports confer power because they determine how much leverage a country can get from offering or denying market access to goods and services from other countries. And indeed postwar history is replete with examples of powerful countries using market access as a stick or carrot to secure economic and noneconomic objectives (Hufbauer et al. 2007, Bayard and Elliott 1994).

Recall the examples in chapter 1 of Richard Nixon using import tariffs to secure exchange rate changes by partner countries in the 1970s and then of the threat of protectionist action instigating exchange rate and trade policy changes in Japan in the 1980s.

Other examples abound. The 1974 Jackson-Vanik Amendment denied trade access for countries that violated human rights. The threat of trade sanctions under Section 301 was an important instrument in getting developing countries to tighten their intellectual property laws in the 1980s and 1990s. China was willing to liberalize its trade regime as part of its accession to the World Trade Organization (WTO) in part because the United States agreed in return to guarantee nondiscriminatory access for Chinese exports to its own market. That is, it is not that the United States as a quid pro quo was offering new access to China; rather, it was offering security of access by committing to eliminate the procedure whereby Congress decided annually whether to continue providing nondiscriminatory access to China.

Trade preferences for low-income countries—first under the Generalized System of Preferences and later under the European Union's Everything But Arms initiative[4] and the US African Growth and Opportunity Act—have been a standard instrument of development policy in the United States and European Union. And, of course, offering preferential trade access under free trade agreements has been an important instrument of foreign policy best illustrated by integration in North America under the North American Free Trade Agreement (NAFTA) and enlargement of the European Union to countries in the eastern periphery.

But exports too can confer power.[5] A strong current of opinion in Europe before and after World War I held that Germany had made war with the instruments of peace, namely through silent economic penetration of other countries through trade, and above all by the rapid expansion of its exports and by attempting to dump products in overseas markets with the aim of pre-

---

4. That the Everything But Arms initiative does not cover migration and movement of skilled people earned it the moniker of "everything but arms and legs."

5. Hufbauer et al. (2007) note that the United States used export restrictions far more often than import restrictions as tools for achieving foreign policy goals.

venting industrialization overseas. So strong was this perception that six Allied nations—the United Kingdom, France, Italy, Russia, Belgium, and Japan—adopted resolutions at the Paris Economic Conference in 1916 to not only deny most favored nation (MFN) treatment to German exports but to subject them to prohibitions or to special regimes. This spirit carried over to the Versailles Conference and was one that US President Woodrow Wilson sought to fight against.

Moreover, in a world where consumption determines welfare, exports confer power because they give a country the ability to determine another country's living standard and access to goods and services, especially if these are considered "essential." China has recently used export controls to deny Japan access to important rare earth minerals. Russia uses gas exports as an instrument of foreign policy in its relations with neighbors. The United States has extensive restrictions on exports of high-technology products and military hardware to countries that are deemed to be potential enemies or security threats. And most famously, oil has been used as a weapon by exporting countries, most notably by Saudi Arabia and other Organization of Petroleum Exporting Countries (OPEC) countries in 1973 when they imposed export embargoes directed at the United States in retaliation for US support of Israel in the Yom Kippur War with Egypt (Yergin 2008).

But exports also create vulnerabilities because of their dependence on other countries' actions.[6] The irony in the case of pre–World War I was that the alarm over German exports was matched within Germany by the concern that it was becoming overly dependent on foreign markets and was thus vulnerable to actions abroad that would deprive it of raw materials and food. It was this fear that in part led Germany in 1879 to reverse its policy and turn protectionist, especially in agriculture, to attain self-sufficiency in food. This concern also underlay Germany reversing Bismarckian policy and joining other European countries in the "scramble for Africa" and African markets.[7]

Similarly, in the financial crisis of 2008–10, China found that its export-led growth strategy was rendered vulnerable to downturns in its markets abroad, creating severe dislocations for its own workers as exports contracted sharply. Trade is thus a double-edged sword, creating power and dependence, strength and vulnerability, at the same time.

Finally, trade vulnerability can arise from having excessively concentrated sources of supply, especially of essential goods such as oil, and from having one's exports too concentrated in terms of markets.

---

6. A variant of this argument comes originally from John Stuart Mill, whose eulogy of free trade was based on the view that trade created mutual dependence and would thereby constitute a force for peace (Hirschman 1945).

7. As Hirschman (1945, 148) notes, "The alarm cry, 'export or die,' is one of the many slogans Hitler did not invent."

External Financial Relations: Debtors and Creditors

How much economic dominance derives from or is related to a country's external financial relations? Historically, the mercantilist school of thought maintained that economic dominance and power derived from running current account surpluses. Power derived from wealth, wealth meant the accumulation of specie, and the accumulation of specie resulted from exporting more than importing (current account surplus). The added advantage of running current account surpluses was that the accumulation of specie was at the expense of trading partners, which meant a corresponding reduction in their wealth and power (Hirschman 1945). Today, of course, instead of specie we get creditor and debtor relationships: Countries that run current account surpluses acquire claims on foreign goods and services and are net creditors to the world (and vice versa for countries running deficits).

In the late 19th century, all the major powers were net foreign creditors. Being a creditor meant that a country controlled the capital in countries where this capital was invested. Creditors called the shots. According to Niall Ferguson, being a creditor was important for British rule: "Britain was also the world's banker, investing immense sums around the world. By 1914 the gross nominal value of Britain's stock of capital invested abroad was £3.8 billion, between two-fifths and a half of all foreign-owned assets. That was more than double French overseas investment and more than three times the German figure. No other major economy has ever held such a large proportion of its assets overseas. More British capital was invested in the Americas than in Britain itself between 1865 and 1914. Small wonder the British began to assume that they had the God-given right to rule the world."[8]

In the aftermath of World War II, the United Kingdom's indebtedness was widely considered to have contributed to its decline as a world power (Harrod 1951, Skidelsky 2000). The more famous example of vulnerability as a result of dependence on foreign capital—and, conversely, power as a result of being a supplier of capital—was the Suez Canal crisis, with the United States (the creditor) dictating terms to the debtor (the United Kingdom). This dependence was also evident—well before the 1956 crisis—in the agreement signed between the United States and the United Kingdom as part of the negotiations leading up to the creation of the International Monetary Fund (IMF).

As a condition of receiving an overall financial package that included a new loan ($3.75 billion), a write-off of about $20 billion to settle the lend-lease arrangements, and transfer of property to the United Kingdom of $6.5 billion, the United Kingdom was required to ensure that its currency was convertible and did not discriminate against US exports and to eliminate discriminatory quantitative import restrictions. The latter included a broader requirement, which was subsequently implemented through the General Agreement on Tariffs and

---

8. Niall Ferguson, "Why We Ruled the World," June 1, 2003, www.niallferguson.com.

Trade (GATT), for the United Kingdom to phase out its system of imperial preferences that discriminated against countries not part of the British empire.[9] In the Suez episode, dominance was used to secure foreign policy goals; in the Anglo-American agreement of 1945, dominance was used to secure economic objectives.

Less well known but perhaps even more dramatic an illustration of the United Kingdom's long-gone preeminence were the events in 1966, when Prime Minister Harold Wilson's government tried to coerce Malaysia into negotiating a monetary union with Singapore. According to David Andrews (2006), this threat backfired when Malaysia threatened to pull out of the sterling area. Malaysia's sterling reserves amounted to 14 percent of the United Kingdom's net liabilities to sterling area countries. Converting them into dollars would have had serious repercussions for the United Kingdom's external situation, which was already under threat. In 1956, the United Kingdom was blackmailed by its successor to economic power status; in 1966, the blackmailer was not the mighty United States but tiny Malaysia.

Similarly, the fact that Saudi Arabia obtained an exclusive chair with a sizable chunk of voting power on the IMF's Executive Board in the aftermath of the oil price shocks of the 1970s had a lot to do with it acquiring large current accounts surpluses and becoming a large net creditor to the rest of the world.[10]

In the Asian financial crisis, Korea had to open its domestic financial services sector, which US export interests had long been pushing for unsuccessfully. Korea's letter of intent "included specific items that the United States had long demanded of Asian governments, and that the latter had rejected" (Gilpin 2001, 159). Larry Summers has stated that "the IMF has done more to promote America's trade and investment agenda in East Asia than 30 years of bilateral trade negotiations," a sentiment echoed by former US Trade Representative Mickey Kantor, who hailed the IMF as "a battering ram" that was used to open Asian markets to US products in the wake of the Asian financial crisis (Kirshner 2006, 159).

One distinction is between a real creditor and an implicit or institutional creditor. As the statements by Summers and Kantor attest, the United States has continued to wield influence and achieved outcomes through the IMF

---

9. Imperial preferences were not eliminated directly. They were reduced indirectly and gradually as a result of the decline in MFN tariffs that was achieved through various rounds of tariff negotiations in the GATT.

10. When Saudi Arabia became one of the two largest creditors, it was able to appoint its own Executive Director rather than participating in the election of directors like other developing countries. And after the second oil shock, IMF Managing Director Jacques de Larosiere fought off opposition from the industrial countries to raise Saudi Arabia's quota share to the sixth highest, above Canada and Italy. De Larosiere was keen to increase resources for the IMF, and Saudi Arabia's quota increase paved the way for the largest-ever loan (about $9 billion) made by a country to the IMF. Note that this privileged status for Saudi Arabia was entirely due to its net creditor status, because the application of the normal quota formula would not have warranted such favorable treatment (Boughton 2001b, 890).

despite having turned net debtor some three to four decades ago. In economic terms, the United States has been a net debtor to the rest of the world since the 1970s, but institutionally—or more specifically by ensuring early on that it had a decisive say in IMF decision-making—it has de facto remained a net creditor, able to press its views and ply its influence.[11] Of course, this anomaly cannot persist indefinitely, and calls for the reform of the Bretton Woods institutions are aimed precisely at rectifying this anomaly. But institutions have proved remarkably immune to real change, and one consequence is the persistence of power acquired long ago.

Currency Dominance

Having one's currency as the world's reserve currency—which is widely accepted, demanded, traded, and transacted—can confer power and prestige. In the most recent global financial crisis, for example, the United States, or rather the US Federal Reserve, supplied countercyclical liquidity to the extent of $600 billion to Europe and several emerging markets. Partly by virtue of its reserve currency status, the Federal Reserve could essentially use its balance sheet to help the world. This conferred prestige, and had the United States wanted to, it could have exploited this source of power.

History provides at least two other interesting examples of the use of reserve currency status by the United States for achieving noneconomic and economic objectives.

The first relates to the Panamanian experience of the 1980s. Panama was effectively a completely dollarized economy. In 1988, following accusations of corruption and drug dealing against General Manuel Noriega, the United States froze Panamanian assets in US banks and prohibited all payments and dollar transfers to Panama. The economy was afflicted by a severe liquidity shortage and effectively demonetized, and output shrank by nearly 20 percent. In the words of a former US ambassador to Panama, these actions had done the most damage to the economy ". . . since Henry Morgan, the pirate, sacked Panama City in 1671." These sanctions were not enough to overthrow

---

11. At the founding of the IMF, the United States, as the dominant economic power at the time, was given about a third of the voting power. The United Kingdom had the second largest quota (nearly 15 percent), followed closely by the Soviet Union and then by China, France, and India. Boughton (2006, 2), the IMF's historian, notes that, "The significance of the United States having a third of the total was that certain policy decisions required qualified majorities, ranging from two thirds up to 85 percent, for approval. The U.S. share thus made it the only country with a veto over major decisions, although other countries could (and still can—and they do) form coalitions to block proposals that they dislike. The Soviet Union—a key military ally at the time—was assigned a large quota as an inducement to persuade it to join (which, in the end, it declined to do). China—another important wartime ally of the United States—also received favorable treatment. As an additional benefit, the countries with the five largest quotas were entitled to appoint their own Executive Directors and avoid having to join forces with other members to elect directors to look after their interests."

Noriega, but the power to inflict pain on others from possessing a reserve currency was clear (Cohen 1998, 44–46).

Another interesting if less known example illustrating the use of currency dominance to achieve other economic objectives—in this case promoting the interests of a country's financial sector—dates to pre-Castro Cuba. Andrews (2006, 88) is worth citing:

> Like many other Caribbean-basin countries that fell under the direct and indirect influence of the United States during this period, Cuba's domestic monetary system became increasingly dollarized during the first two decades of the twentieth century. When a financial crisis struck in 1920–21, Cuban-owned banks collapsed because they had no access to the lender-of-last-resort facilities of the U.S. central bank. U.S. banks then quickly emerged in a dominant position in the Cuban financial system. In this way, the United States exerted a major influence over the Cuban financial system simply by a 'non-decision'—that is, by not providing lender-of-last resort support to Cuban banks. Interestingly, after this crisis, the U.S. Federal Reserve Bank of Atlanta (as well as that of Boston, between 1923 and 1926) established an agency in Cuba to carry out lender-of-last-resort functions.

In other words, through nonaction, the power from reserve currency led to a competitive advantage for US banks, and through subsequent deliberate action the interests of these banks were consolidated.

Occam Razorization: Narrowing the List

In the interests of simplicity and transparency, of the six potential determinants of economic dominance—overall resources, military resources, fiscal resources, trade, external finance, and currency—this study retains only three: overall resources or GDP, trade, and finance. The reasons for discarding the others follow.

Fiscal strength, which is the ability of a government to mobilize resources to achieve dominance, and military strength, which is the ability of a government to mobilize resources for one particular objective, ultimately stem from overall wealth or resource availability. Countries may be able to spend more on their militaries than might be warranted by their economic strength (e.g., Russia after 1950), but the discrepancy eventually tends to correct itself, as the Russian experience ultimately showed. In other words, military strength, while important, may not be an independent or additional (additional to aggregate wealth/GDP) determinant of economic dominance.

The data also tend to support such a conclusion. Data on military expenditures of the economically dominant powers for selected years from 1880 to 2010 show that the correlation between aggregate wealth and military strength is high (figure 2.1). Specifically, the correlation between the share of a country in world GDP (a measure of aggregate wealth) and its share in world military expenditure is nearly 0.7 for the major countries over the long run.

Figure 2.1 Military expenditures of economically dominant powers, 1880–2009

share of total military expenditure by dominant powers

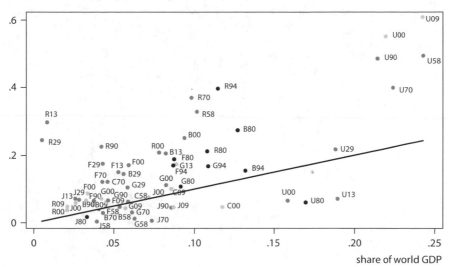

Notes: The numbers denote years (1880 and 1894 are shown in black; 1900–1990 in medium grey; and 2000 and 2009 in light grey). The letters denote countries (B: United Kingdom; C: China; F: France; G: Germany; J: Japan; R: Russia; and U: United States).

Sources: Kennedy (1989), Maddison (2010), and Stockholm International Peace Research Institute (SIPRI) Military Expenditure Database.

The correlation between measures of wealth, trade, and external finance are substantially smaller, suggesting that each of these have independent origins and idiosyncratic factors driving them. In contrast, military strength seems to be derivative to a greater extent of overall wealth. The figure also shows that the real outliers in this relationship, in terms of military spending exceeding that of the typical country, are Russia (shown as points with the prefix R) for much of the period before the collapse of communism and some European countries in the late 1800s and early 1900s. Outliers in terms of military spending below the typical country are Japan and, more recently, Europe.

A more mundane reason for ignoring military strength is that it is more difficult to project. Military expenditures are key policy choices that governments will make. Predicting the future behavior of governments is a difficult and fraught exercise.

What about fiscal strength as an attribute of economic dominance? First, the correlation between government deficits and debt and economic dominance is far from clear. Figure 2.2 plots the government debt (as a share of GDP) for some of the major economic powers in history. Consolidation and exercise of British imperial power after the mid-1600s was associated with rising deficits

Figure 2.2   Public debt in the United Kingdom, United States, and Germany, 1692–2010

percent of GDP

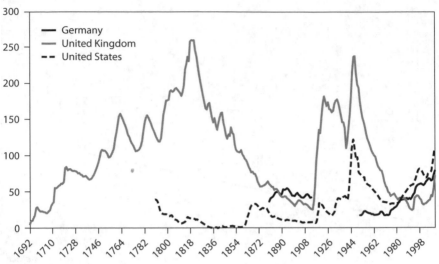

Source: Reinhart and Rogoff (2009).

and debt. British success over the French in the Napoleonic wars did not necessarily occur because the United Kingdom could raise taxes to finance the wars, but because it was able to successfully run deficits through bond financing (Bordo and White 1991). France, in contrast, had higher taxes and lower deficits, and this "did not reflect any superior fiscal virtues but rather the opposite" (Bordo and White 1991, 316). Running large deficits was thus a sign of strength rather than weakness. Similarly, the United States ran up massive fiscal deficits to finance World War II, and that episode reflected, perhaps even caused, economic dominance rather than decline. Conversely, the decline of British power after World War II was associated with fiscal surpluses and declining debt.

Second, and perhaps more fundamentally, government fiscal strength is a function of overall economic strength, and whether the latter can be translated into the former is less a matter of economics and more one of politics and history. The key question is whether the domestic social compact is sufficiently robust and credible (from the perspective of investors) to allow countries to tax and spend in a manner necessitated by domestic objectives and external imperatives.[12] Thus, at least up to the first order, economic strength can proxy for fiscal strength.

---

12. The ability of the United Kingdom to run larger deficits during the Napoleonic wars was at least in part due to its record of fiscal probity and the open budgetary process in Parliament. France, on the other hand, had squandered her reputation during the ancient regime, and then again following the revolution, through expropriation and hyperinflation.

Finally, there is a more practical reason not to include fiscal strength as a determinant of economic dominance. Dominance is relative, so one needs measures that are comparable across countries. But assessing relative fiscal strength across countries is not easy. One could look at government indebtedness (as a share of GDP), but cross-country comparisons are fraught with difficulties. For example, countries have different debt tolerance depending on their history of honoring obligations, whether they borrow in domestic or foreign currencies, and what their respective growth potential is.[13] Figure 2.2 shows that there have been periods when dominant powers have had larger debts than others (e.g., the United Kingdom in the 1800s and the United States after the 1980s), rendering cross-country comparisons difficult.

Should a country's reserve currency status be included in measures of overall economic dominance? It is not included here for two reasons. Having a reserve currency can be a source and instrument of strength, but as explained in chapter 3, it can also create vulnerabilities. A reserve currency, at best, is a double-edged sword and hence fails to satisfy the criterion of being an unambiguous source of dominance. More important perhaps is the fact that having a reserve currency is more a proximate than a fundamental determinant. Reserve currency status is itself an outcome and in turn determined, as shown in chapter 3, by GDP, trade, and external financial strength—the three variables retained here for construction of a parsimonious index of economic dominance.

Measuring the Three Determinants

Having identified the list of potential determinants of economic dominance, and then narrowed it to include just three, I turn now to measuring the three determinants selected: resources, trade, and external finance. A first point worth noting is that all measures for a country with regard to these three determinants are expressed as a country's share of the world total: By construction, the larger a country's share, the smaller that of others, including rivals. This captures the essential zero-sum nature of power and dominance.

Resources

The simplest measure of a nation's wealth or resources is, of course, its GDP. But the question is whether GDP should be valued using market exchange rates or in terms of the true purchasing power of a nation's currency. Using purchasing power parity (PPP) to compare standards of living is well accepted. But using PPP to assess economic dominance is less so, the contrary view being that what matters for power and dominance is "dollars," which would argue in favor of conventional market exchange-rate-based measures of GDP.

---

13. See Reinhart, Rogoff, and Savastano (2003) for an analysis of debt tolerance.

But dominance is about the real resources (or the real services provided by them) that a country can muster relative to other countries in the exercise or projection of power. So the question is: What resources are potentially used for power and how should they be valued? Note that this question does not arise in measuring other determinants of dominance—trade and external finance—which must be valued in conventional or market-exchange-rate-based dollars. It is only when evaluating broad resource availability that the question of PPP or market exchange rates becomes relevant.

As an exercise, imagine a future military confrontation (the extreme example of exercising dominance) between China and the United States. Then ask: What are the relative resources (real resources) that each country can muster in this confrontation?

If the real resources required for this war were all tradable goods (e.g., military equipment that was not available in China), then it is true that GDP measured in PPP terms would be overstating the real resources available to China. "Real" dollars would be all that matter. But if waging this war were to require domestic, nontradable, resources (e.g., soldiers or equipment that could be made at least in part in China), then GDP measured in PPP terms would in fact be a good, or even better, proxy for dominance. So as long as power and its use require economic resources that are part domestic (which will always be the case given people are involved) and part tradable, a combination of market-based and PPP-based exchange rate measures is the right way to value these resources.

In fact, Alan Heston and Betina Aten (1993) calculate internationally comparable military expenditures using PPP exchange rates, arguing that market exchange rates inaccurately reflect differences in salaries and procurement across countries, and hence the real military resources available to different countries. And what is true in the military context (that real resources are not just about dollars) is true more broadly. Thus, the index will measure GDP only half in PPP terms and the remaining in dollar terms.[14]

Trade

One issue in measuring trade is whether imports, exports, their product composition, their geographic concentration, or some combination of these is the right measure of dominance.[15] To avoid complexity, and dictated by data availability, I simply use a country's trade—measured as the sum of exports and

---

14. It could be argued that GDP should be measured entirely in PPP terms because the power that comes from command over foreign resources—and captured in the trade and external finance variables in the index—are measured in dollar terms. But to be conservative, the index measures GDP only half in PPP terms.

15. Hirschman (1945) attempts a more complex measure of trade dominance that takes account of these various considerations.

imports of goods—expressed as a share of world trade as the relevant measure for the economic dominance index.

A problem with measuring trade over time, as is done in this index, is that the measure might be distorted because of the increasing fragmentation of the value-added chain through supply chains and outsourcing. This could lead to overstatement of trade over time and hence overstating dominance from trade. This potential distortion is limited, however, by the fact that all the measures are in relative terms. If world trade is generally increasing because of fragmentation, no one country's measure will be prone to bias, unless it is uniquely or disproportionately a beneficiary of trade fragmentation, as China's might possibly be.

External Financial Strength

The preceding discussion suggested broadly that net creditors or suppliers of finance have power and net debtors are vulnerable. So some measure of net creditor status is necessary to compute the index of economic dominance. In principle, this measure could be a stock or flow. Stock measures could include a country's or government's net foreign assets or foreign exchange reserves. The problem with a stock measure such as net claims is that these claims may not be worth much unless a country has the power and other means to compel foreigners to honor those claims. As John Maynard Keynes (1981, 277-78) put it: "To lend vast sums abroad for long periods of time without any possibility of legal redress if things go wrong is crazy construction; especially in return for a trifling extra interest." The problem with reserves as a measure of economic power is two-fold. Economically dominant countries tend to have reserve currencies and hence have less need and incentive to hold reserves. Moreover, a country holding foreign reserves (for example, China today) is vulnerable to seeing their value erode through policy actions of the reserve currency issuing country.

For these reasons, it seems preferable to measure power stemming from net creditor status in flow terms. Having a current account surplus is indeed a source of power because adjustment is so painful to the deficit countries if the flow is cut off, as the numerous instances in history have illustrated. Taking this into account, I define external financial strength in the following manner. For any given time period, the cumulative current account balance of a country (over the preceding 10 years) is measured. The cumulative net flow of capital for the world as a whole is calculated by adding up the surpluses for all countries running such surpluses.[16] The measure of economic power

---

16. For the world as a whole, the sum of current accounts of countries must add up to zero. Here, the denominator is the sum of all the positive current account balances (which should equal the sum of all the negative balances) and is a measure of cumulative net global capital flows (outflows for the surplus countries and inflows for the deficit countries). This way of measuring the dominance deriving from creditor/debtor status is possible because of data compiled by Taylor (2002) on current accounts for the major countries going back to 1870.

stemming from creditor/debtor status is computed as the country's cumulative balance as a share of the world's cumulative balance. The reason I do the calculations over a slightly longer period is to avoid anomalies arising from cyclical factors (current account balances are typically sensitive to the cycle) and to ensure that countries are indeed structural creditors or debtors as the case may be. If a country is a large net creditor relative to world flows of capital, I posit that it will have more economic power. If a country is a net debtor, it will suffer from a loss of power by being dictated to by creditor countries.[17]

This is by no means the only way of measuring dominance arising from external financial strength. Capital flows could have been measured in gross rather than in net terms as done here. Claims could have been measured as a share of global GDP rather than as a fraction of total capital flows. And, arguably, even the size of the creditor claims relative to global GDP is less important than who is holding the claims, or who is indebted.[18] As the Suez example makes clear, if a government is indebted, especially to a foreign government, it has far more serious implications for dominance than claims within the private sector.

Validating Economic Dominance

Given all the problems associated with the concept of dominance and the difficulties of measurement, is the attempt at quantification too theoretical and otherwise misguided? One important real-world example suggests otherwise: the IMF, which exemplifies dominance and its exercise.

At the IMF—for so long a much-derided institution—there is an explicit attempt to allocate power (and determine dominance) in the form of voting rights based explicitly on economic factors. IMF governance procedures certainly constitute a refutation to the possible critique that dominance is a vague concept. The formula that determines a country's share in total voting rights includes its share in (1) the world's economy measured at market exchange rates; (2) the world's economy measured at PPP exchange rates; (3) world cross-border current account transactions;[19] (4) the variability of cur-

---

17. Thus, the range of this variable is between plus 1 (when there is one country exporting all the world's capital to all the other countries) and minus 1 (when one country is receiving all the world's net capital from all other countries).

18. When capital becomes less publicly controlled and more dispersed, both on the lender's side and the borrower's side, the power associated with being a creditor and the vulnerability associated with being a debtor are arguably diluted. For example, the fact that China's large current account surpluses have resulted in readily available cash in the hands of the government—as opposed to the private sector—gives China clout in a number of its dealings with countries. The government can provide financial assistance to poor countries and can shore up interest rates in the United States or, more recently, Greece, by buying assets of foreign governments. These are currencies of power.

19. Specifically, the underlying data are a member's sum, and the corresponding world aggregates, of current account payments and receipts (goods, services, income, and transfers).

rent account receipts and net capital flows; and (5) the world total of official reserve assets (foreign exchange, special drawing right holdings, reserve position in the IMF, and monetary gold) (Bryant 2010).

So, to the possible critique that dominance is a vague and not meaningful concept, one can respond that IMF governance procedures constitute a real-world refutation of that critique.

Validation of the construction of the economic dominance index in this book comes first and foremost from the broad overlap between the previously discussed determinants selected to build the index and the variables listed in this IMF formula. The first two IMF variables capture wealth or economic size; the third variable relating to current account transactions is simply an expanded definition of trade; and the fifth variable—holdings of reserve assets— really corresponds to the mercantilist view that power derives from holdings of assets that have international purchasing power. The IMF's determination of dominance (voting rights), echoing the earlier discussion in this chapter, has no role for fiscal, military, or reserve currency variables.

The second point worth noting is that the IMF too views power in explicitly relative terms because all the variables (with one exception, dropped here for reasons explained below) are expressed as a country's share in the world total: by construction, the larger a country's share, the smaller that of others, including rivals.[20]

Third, while there are two sources of discrepancy between the variables in the IMF voting formula and in the index presented here—the first relating to the list of determinants and the second to measurement—they can be easily explained. The IMF's formula includes a variable for the variability of foreign exchange receipts, which the index here does not. Why so? It is well known that the quota formula tries to meet three different objectives: in addition to being the basis for determining dominance (via voting power) it also serves to determine the maximum borrowing limits for countries and their financial contributions. The variable relating to fluctuations in foreign exchange earnings aims to capture the potential borrowing need of a country from the IMF, and is therefore less relevant in broader measures of economic power. This variable is thus not a celebration of dominance but a concession to weakness.

Further, the IMF's quota formula attempts to capture the command over foreign resources by including holdings of official foreign exchange reserves as a determinant of power. While this may have been relevant for the pre–World War II period, it is irrelevant and indeed perverse in the environment since the

---

20. The importance of economic size, trade, and creditor/debtor status as three key determinants of power reflected in the IMF formula was foreshadowed in the original US proposal for what would eventually become the IMF. This was the Harry Dexter White proposal for an International Stabilization Fund (ISF) that envisaged quota allocations according to four variables: national income, foreign trade, population, and holdings of gold. Keynes's alternative for the ISF, namely the International Clearing Union, envisaged allocations based on foreign trade, which would have favored the United Kingdom relative to the ISF proposal. The holdings of gold in the White proposal correspond to the net creditor variable in the index of economic dominance presented here.

1970s. Perverse because, as explained earlier, the rich and powerful countries, whose currencies serve as reserve assets for others, tend not to hold any significant quantities of reserves (put starkly, by virtue of being reserve currencies, they can just print them). Reserve holdings are thus not a very good proxy for power that stems from enjoying net creditor status and the associated command over foreign resources that being a creditor confers. For this reason, net creditor status is measured differently here.

Finally, by including two measures of GDP, the IMF recognizes that domestic resources can be valued in different and complementary ways for the purpose of measuring dominance.

If the IMF is the first source of validation cited here, the second comes from the analysis of reserve currency status in chapter 3, which shows that the three determinants of economic dominance are also associated strongly with a market-based or, rather, outcome-based measure of economic dominance, namely reserve currency status. Not only is the association strong for each of the determinants; collectively they also explain a large share of the variation in reserve currency status. This provides some additional, if indirect, validation of the choice of the three variables as determinants of economic dominance.

Weighting and Constructing the Index of Economic Dominance

Finally, the three underlying determinants need to be aggregated into a summary measure of dominance. The main reason for aggregation is for presentational simplicity and tractability (the results are not materially altered by the manner in which these variables are aggregated). It would be cumbersome to track all the determinants of dominance for all the relevant countries for several time periods. But aggregation raises a big problem: How should one weight all the determinants to arrive at a single summary measure? To do this, I construct an index of economic dominance, which can be represented as shown in the footnote.[21]

Can the weights be determined in a manner that is not completely arbitrary so that one can get a number from the three different determinants of dominance? Clearly, no weighting scheme can be defended on some a priori theoretical grounds. Any choice of weights will be indefensibly arbitrary. I show below that the projections are unaffected by the weighting scheme, so

---

21. I define an index of economic dominance (IED) as follows:

$$\phi_i^{\text{IED}} = \alpha_1 \phi_i^{\text{GDP}} + \alpha_2 \phi_i^{\text{TR}} + \alpha_3 \phi_i^{\text{CR}} \tag{1}$$

where the index ϕ_i^{IED} is expressed as a share, say, of world economic power, and as such is inherently a measure of relative power. ϕ_i^{GDP} is the share of a country in world GDP (average of dollar and PPP GDP); ϕ_i^{TR} is the share of a country in world trade; and ϕ_i^{CR} is, as described earlier, a country's share in world net flows of capital. Note that the equation has a simple interpretation because the left- and right–hand-side variables are expressed as a share. The alphas are weights to be accorded to each of the determinants of power, and these weights add up to one.

that scheme should be seen as a means to simplify tracking dominance across countries and over time rather than expressing some definitive judgment about the determinants of dominance. In what follows, two different weighting schemes are adopted for illustrative purposes, both of which have some external underpinnings.

These weighting schemes draw respectively on the IMF precedent and the work in the next chapter on reserve currency status. If one looks at the current IMF formula, and ignores the variable that captures the fluctuations in foreign exchange flows (which is less relevant for a broader index of power), one sees that the weights are 0.3 for aggregate GDP at market exchange rates, 0.2 for aggregate GDP at PPP exchange rates, 0.3 for foreign exchange flows, and 0.05 for holdings of gold (which was a historic proxy for creditor status). Disregarding for the moment the distinction between the two different ways of measuring GDP, and recalibrating the weights to reflect excluding the variable for fluctuations and to ensure that they add up to one, one sees that the IMF formula accords a weight (after suitable rounding) of 0.6 for GDP, 0.35 for trade, and .05 for creditor/debtor status.[22] This is the first set of weights (with the slight difference that within economic size, GDP at market and PPP exchange rates are weighted equally), which might be called "IMF weights."[23]

The second set of weights is derived from the next chapter on reserve currencies. Trade, GDP, and net creditor/debtor status are all important determinants of reserve currency status. Interestingly, the numbers yield a weighting scheme for the variables that is very similar to that practiced by the IMF, with the difference being that trade and GDP are switched in importance. Thus, an alternative weighting scheme—"reserve currency weights"—derived from the next chapter yields weights of 0.6 for trade, 0.35 for GDP (divided equally between market-based and PPP exchange rate measures), and .05 for net creditor status.[24] Surprisingly, and reassuringly, the weights for net creditor status are nearly identical between the reserve currency analysis and the IMF's weighting procedure.[25]

---

22. Although the weights add to one, the IMF quota formula is algebraically calculated and implemented in a way that provides discretion to reduce the shares of richer countries relative to what is given by the formula and reallocate these shares to poorer countries (Bryant 2010).

23. The IMF as inspiration and justification for the variables to be included in an economic dominance index and how they might be weighted can be criticized on the grounds that the IMF decisions are entirely political, not economic. But if power is about politics as practiced in the real world, the outcome of this political process may not be so inferior to measuring dominance than any theoretical reasoning might yield. That it is a political decision might even be a virtue. At the very least, it can be thought of as a kind of revealed preference measure of the practitioners of power.

24. The quantitative analysis of reserve currency yielded a weight of .37 for GDP, .59 for trade, and .04 for net creditor status. This was close enough to the IMF weights that it was decided to retain the symmetry with them.

25. I thank Simon Johnson for suggesting that the IMF as inspiration for quantifying economic dominance and Aaditya Mattoo for suggesting that the reserve currency analysis could be a basis for assigning weights in computing the index of dominance.

Figure 2.3 Economic dominance index from 1870 to 2010 for the top three countries using IMF weights

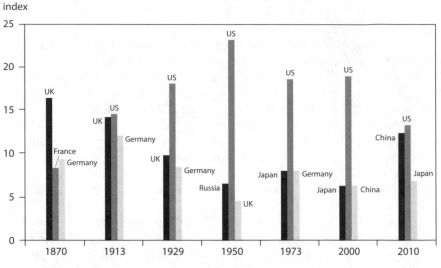

IMF = International Monetary Fund

Notes: This index is a weighted average of the share of a country in world GDP, trade, and world net exports of capital. The index ranges from 0 to 100 percent (for creditors) but could assume negative values for net debtors. The weights for this figure are 0.6 for GDP (split equally between GDP measured at market and purchasing power parity exchange rates, respectively); 0.35 for trade; and 0.05 for net exports of capital.

Source: Author's calculations.

Having constructed the index, does the resulting translation into economic dominance for the past accord with what one broadly knows about history? To determine this, the next section looks at a third—and historical—validation for the quantification of economic dominance.

Results: Economic Dominance in the Past

The index of economic dominance is computed for the following years: 1870, the heyday of UK imperialism; 1913, just before the onset of World War I; 1929, just before the onset of economic instability and political turmoil; 1950, in the immediate aftermath of World War II; and 1973, 2000, and 2010.[26] The index is computed for eight countries that either wielded power in the past or were contenders for doing so: the United Kingdom, United States, France, Germany, Japan, Russia, China, and India.

The index for the top three powers at any given point in time is plotted in figures 2.3 and 2.4. The difference between the two relates to the weights—figure 2.3 uses the modified IMF weights and figure 2.4 uses the weights that

---

26. The choice of dates for the past is to a large extent also dictated by data availability.

Figure 2.4 Economic dominance index from 1870 to 2010 for the top three countries using reserve currency weights

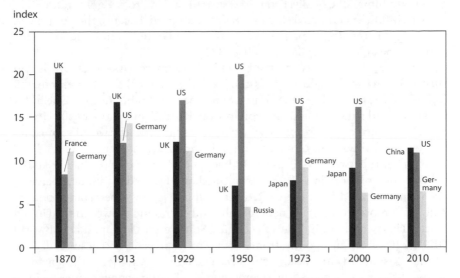

Notes: This index is a weighted average of the share of a country in world GDP, trade, and world net exports of capital. The index ranges from 0 to 100 percent (for creditors) but could assume negative values for net debtors. The weights for this figure are 0.6 for trade; 0.35 for GDP (split equally between GDP measured at market and purchasing power parity exchange rates, respectively); and 0.05 for net exports of capital.

Source: Author's calculations.

come from the reserve currency analysis in chapter 3. The index appears to broadly track the history of dominance since 1870.

In 1870, the United Kingdom was the most dominant power (index value between 15 and 20 percent) and substantially greater than that of its closest rivals, Germany and France (the United States at this stage was not among the world's top three on the index). In the case of the United Kingdom, empire was dominance: At the turn of the 20th century, an island with less than 5 percent of the world's population controlled close to 25 percent of the world's land area and population. Empire meant, of course, that government and administration controlled by the United Kingdom extended to trade, finance, and currency. It turns out that the high value of the index for the United Kingdom for 1870 stems from it having been a dominant exporter, accounting for nearly 25 percent of world exports, compared with 13 percent for Germany, its closest competitor; a very rich country (25 percent richer than the United States and 50 percent richer than Germany and France); and a substantial net creditor, accounting for 50 percent of the world export of capital. In short, the United Kingdom was dominant on all economic attributes.[27] This

27. The United Kingdom was not the most populous country, but at that time, population was nearly equally distributed across the four major powers.

period also coincided with the United Kingdom setting the standard for the international monetary system. An increasing number of countries that were either on a bimetallic or silver standard started moving to the gold standard in the late 1800s, which was de facto a sterling standard, because the pound had been pegged to gold formally since 1821.[28] The United States and Germany adopted the gold standard de facto in 1873.

By 1913, the gap between the United Kingdom and its closest rivals had shrunk dramatically, and vis-à-vis the United States it had been eliminated (on one of the two indexes the United States has the higher rating). The index for the United Kingdom remains roughly unchanged, but those of the United States and Germany increase substantially. By that time, the world seemed no longer to be unipolar in terms of economic fundamentals.

This shift between 1870 and 1913 happened in part due to changes in the volume and composition of trade (the UK share declined by about 6 percentage points, while that of the United States increased by 4 percentage points) and much more to changing demography and economic growth in the United States. This combination led to the United States increasing its share of world GDP by 10 percentage points, from about 9 to 19 percent, with a small decline in the UK share in world economic size. The United Kingdom still remained the world's largest net creditor, its position not having changed since 1870.

By 1929, even bigger changes were evident. The position of the United Kingdom and United States had reversed dramatically and the United States had become the world's dominant power with an index of 18 compared with 13 just before World War I. The United Kingdom's index had declined to 11 from 18 in 1913. While this change happened in part as a steady and inexorable rise in the United States as a generator of wealth and trade, a big change also occurred in net capital flows. The United States became a large net creditor while the United Kingdom's role as a creditor diminished. Barbara Tuchman captures this transition to the ascendancy of the United States, which from the time of World War I became, in her words, Europe's "larder, arsenal, and bank."

By 1950, the picture changed even more dramatically. The United States had become the unrivalled world economic hegemonic power. The index for the United States rises to between 20 and 25 (depending on the weights), while that of its closest competitor, Russia stands at 7. The United States accounted for 27 percent of global GDP; it had become the world's largest trader, accounting for 15 percent of world trade; and it was the world's largest exporter of capital, and a substantial one at that. The dramatic decline in the fortunes of the United Kingdom stemmed in large part from it becoming a large net debtor because of World War II, in contrast to its net creditor status in the late

---

28. Britain had been on a bimetallic standard for some time. In 1717, Sir Isaac Newton established a new conversion rate that overvalued gold relative to silver in Great Britain compared with other countries. Exports of silver from, and imports of gold to, Great Britain increased, thereby driving silver out of circulation and putting the country on a de facto gold standard.

1800s and early 1900s. The sun had set on the British empire and the 1956 Suez Canal fiasco lay ahead. US economic hegemony continued through the 1970s and 1980s.

By 1990, Japan was mounting a challenge to US dominance (Russia had faded) on the strength of its trading situation (accounting for 7.5 percent of world trade) and its growing net creditor status. The United States continued to be the largest economy and largest trader, but the big change was that it had started becoming a consistent net debtor. The index of economic dominance for the United States declines to 16, while that of competitors, Japan and increasingly China, start rising. It is still a unipolar world but less so than in the previous four decades.

By 2010, the Japanese challenge faded, and China now seems on the rise. Consistent with the historical experience, economic dominance for China is based on its rapid growth in GDP and trade, as well as financial dominance, related to its large current account surpluses. Depending on the weight to be assigned to the latter, China's index is close to or even greater than that for the United States. And, of course, the big difference between China and some of the historical pretenders to economic superpower status is that demography works overwhelmingly in China's favor. China is as big as the United States in terms of economic size and trade, but the United States is a large net debtor while China is a large net creditor.

Having quantified and validated economic dominance, I turn to currency dominance in the next chapter.

Quantifying Currency Dominance

> *[T]he currency of a country which is important in world markets will be a better candidate for an international money than that of a smaller country.*
>
> —Paul Krugman (1994)

An iconic expression of a country's economic dominance is its currency. Even if the economic benefits of currency dominance are questionable, countries and their governments do seem to prize that status. Some of the benefits could be psychic captured for example, in the Archbishop of Canterbury's insistence that, "I want the Queen's head on the banknotes. . . ." (Goodhart 1995). Others could be political, for example, when the United Kingdom tried to salvage some prestige for its postempire status via its currency. Prime Minister Harold Wilson said in 1964 that "To turn our backs on the sterling area would mean a body-blow to the Commonwealth and all it stands for."[1]

Even if currency status is not prized for one's own currency, at the very least countries seem to resent the currency dominance of others. This resentment could be based on a perception of economic gain for the other. Charles de Gaulle, for example, complained bitterly of America's privileged use of "dollars, which it alone can issue, instead of paying entirely with gold, which has a real value, which must be earned to be possessed, and which cannot be transferred to others without risks and sacrifices" (quoted in Frieden, 2006, 345).

Today's version of the ongoing currency debate centers on the fate of the dollar, which has once again become ragingly topical. Questions relating to reserve currencies have periodically obsessed the economics profession, typically under two circumstances. First, when the policies of the principal reserve currency (the dollar) threaten to erode confidence in it (e.g., in the 1960s and

---

1. Quoted in Scott Cooper (2006, 172). There was another strand of opinion in the United Kingdom during the 1950s and 1960s that saw sterling's reserve currency status as a burden and wanted to see its gradual demise, but in a manner that would not disrupt the UK economy or the international monetary system (Schenk 2010a).

1970s), as captured in French President Georges Pompidou's famous metaphor: "We cannot keep forever as our basic monetary yardstick a national currency that constantly loses value. . . .The rest of the world cannot be expected to regulate its life by a clock which is always slow" (quoted in Frieden, 2006, 345). Second, reserve currency issues become topical when potential rivals to the dollar emerge, as with the euro in the 2000s.

With equal periodicity, though, the issue has been quietly consigned to forgetfulness. Today the issue has resurfaced in the aftermath of the global financial crisis with somewhat greater intensity because of a combination of the two factors mentioned above. First, there is the view that the crisis was occasioned in part by reckless US policies, in turn aided and abetted by the dollar's reserve currency role, which allowed the recklessness to be financed by outsiders. Joseph Stiglitz (2009) made this case in his speech to the United Nations in 2009: "The system in which the dollar is the reserve currency is a system that has long been recognized to be unsustainable in the long run." The second reason relates to the rise of China and the possible ascendancy of the renminbi to reserve currency status and the competition that it poses to the dollar.

Similar doubts about the dollar arose in the 1960s, which led to the creation of special drawing rights (SDRs) through the International Monetary Fund (IMF). But back then there was no challenge to the dollar (in fact the SDR was created in anticipation of the fear—that never materialized—there would be too few dollars relative to the growing demand for them). In the early 2000s, the euro represented a challenge to the dollar but there was no systemic crisis that created theoretical angst about the status quo. Today, there is both the concern about the economic strength and policies of the United States and the fact of the emergence of a potential rival, which makes discussions about reserve currency and the fate of the dollar much more salient.

The recent economic crisis has led some—including most famously the governor of the People's Bank of China—to question the legitimacy and effectiveness of having the dollar as the international reserve currency. There are calls to strengthen the role of the real currencies such as the euro, artificial ones such as SDRs, or both as an alternative to the dominant status of the dollar.

The question addressed here is not the normative one of the desirable composition and configuration of reserve currencies, but a positive one: Will changes in the world economy lead to or be accompanied by any changes in the status of different currencies as international reserve currencies? In particular, is it possible that the dollar will be eclipsed as the unrivaled international reserve currency or at least be relegated to one among two or three other currencies that vie with each other for reserve currency status? Further, is it possible that the renminbi will be one of these two or three or perhaps even *primus inter pares* among them? This chapter presents some new results on the determinants of reserve currency status. These results inform the conclusion in chapter 5, which projects the course of future economic and currency dominance.

Table 3.1   Roles of an international currency

Function	Use by governments	Use by private agents	Desirable prerequisites of/in country issuing reserve currency
Store of value (allows transactions to be conducted over long periods and geographical distances)	International reserves	Foreign currencies become substitutes for a domestic currency because the latter is prone to inflation and volatility. In the extreme, foreign currencies can even become legal tender	Low and stable inflation; relatively strong and stable currency; financial markets that are deep, liquid, and open to foreigners
Medium of exchange (avoids inefficiencies of barter)	Vehicle for foreign exchange intervention	Means of payment. Invoicing trade and financial transactions	Large global share of output, trade and finance; financial markets that are deep, liquid, and open to foreigners
Unit of account (facilitates valuation and calculation)	Anchor for pegging local currency	Denominating trade and financial transactions	Large global share of output, trade, and finance

Sources: Adapted from Kenen (1983) and Ferguson (2008).

Definition

Before answering the questions posed above, one needs to define reserve currency and assess the benefits (and costs) of being an international reserve currency. Paul Krugman (1984) and Menzie Chinn and Jeffrey Frankel (2008) provide a useful summary. An international currency is simply one that is used outside one's own country. The greater the use, the more it merits the description of a reserve currency. Foreign governments and/or foreign private agents seek to use the currency of another country because of the three functions that a foreign currency can perform, as summarized in table 3.1.

Although much of the research on international reserve currencies has focused on reserve holdings by foreign governments, it must be emphasized that reserve currency status reflects use not just by governments but also the private sector for trade and financial transactions.

The quantitative dimensions of the official holdings of reserve currencies are discussed below, but it is worth recalling some of the basic numbers relating to the international or private-sector dimensions of reserve currencies.

Between 1860 and 1914, nearly 60 percent of world trade was denominated in sterling even though the United Kingdom accounted for about 30 percent of world trade (Schenk 2010a). More recently, when the dollar has ruled, 45 percent of international debt securities were denominated in dollars (as of end-2008), the dollar was used in 86 percent of all foreign exchange transactions (as of 2007), and 66 countries used the dollar as their exchange rate anchor (as of 2008). For many countries, 70 to 80 percent of their trade is denominated in dollars, oil and most commodities are priced in dollars, and in the shadowy world of crime and illicit transactions, "the dollar still rules" (Eichengreen 2010). In some ways, one could argue that private-sector actions are indeed the deep determinants of reserve currency status.[2]

Benefits and Costs to the Country Issuing the Reserve Currency

Countries exhibit a certain ambivalence about their reserve currencies because both benefits and costs are associated with reserve currency status.

Benefits

Convenience for the Country's Residents. A country's exporters, importers, borrowers, and lenders are able to deal in their own currency rather than foreign currencies. Thus, the transaction costs of obtaining another currency and the psychological costs of having to move or convert from domestic to foreign currencies are lowered or eliminated. When an American tourist goes abroad, he or she can, often and in many places, buy goods and services for dollars because the latter are widely accepted or easily exchanged for local currency. A Thai tourist, on the other hand, will have had to go to the bank to get the relevant local currency for his expenditures. For banks and other financial institutions, there may also be some cost advantage of dealing in one's own currency: When transactions are denominated in dollars, foreign economic agents have to convert it back to their local currency to understand the transaction; in contrast, US agents avoid the nuisance of having to do this conversion. This is all rather like the convenience of dealing in one's own language.

Seigniorage or Exorbitant Privilege in Good Times. The advantage that comes from having other governments their citizens hold—or willing to hold—one's currency is a narrow definition of seigniorage captured in this quote from columnist Thomas Friedman:

---

2. As Eichengreen (2010, 125) notes: "Central banks will want to hold reserves in the same currency in which the country denominated its debt and invoices its foreign trade, since they use those reserves to smooth debt and trade flows . . . and to intervene in foreign exchange markets."

The United States has an advantage few other countries enjoy: It prints green paper with George Washington's and Ben Franklin's and Thomas Jefferson's pictures on it. These pieces of green paper are called 'dollars.' Americans give this green paper to people around the world, and they give Americans in return automobiles, pasta, stereos, taxi rides, hotel rooms and all sorts of other goods and services. As long as these foreigners can be induced to hold those dollars, either in their mattresses, their banks or in their own circulation, Americans have exchanged green paper for hard goods.[3]

But a broader definition of seigniorage—and indeed the heart of reserve currency status, also called "exorbitant privilege" (coined by Charles de Gaulle and his adviser Jacques Rueff)—is the ability to borrow abroad large amounts cheaply in one's own currency, especially while simultaneously earning much higher returns on investments (including FDI) in other countries.[4]

Although, the empirical evidence is unclear, exorbitant privilege can be interpreted as the ability to run large current account deficits—and hence run up large debts denominated in one's own currency at low interest rates—safe in the knowledge that others will be willing to finance it on account of the special status for the currency.

Seigniorage or Exorbitant Privilege in Bad Times. Perhaps as important a benefit or even more so might be the attenuation of costs in times of financial crises. Having a reserve currency might imply lower interest costs and more enhanced capital-market access than would otherwise prevail during a crisis. This helps avoid currency meltdowns and the associated dislocations that usually accompany severe financial crises. In the recent crisis, the United States benefited from such a flight to quality, which meant that markets did not start pricing in default probabilities.

Political Power and Prestige. Having one's currency as the reserve currency tends to confer power and prestige. The example of being able to supply countercyclical liquidity, especially in a crisis, and the potential power and influence that can derive from it has already been noted. The United Kingdom's gradual loss of key currency status coincided with its gradual loss of political and military preeminence. The two examples described in chapter 2 relating to Panama and pre-Castro Cuba also attest to the power stemming from having a reserve currency.

---

3. Thomas Friedman, "The World; Never Mind Yen. Greenbacks Are the New Gold Standard," *New York Times,* July 3, 1994.

4. The United States has consistently earned more on it investments overseas than it has had to pay on its debts, a differential of about 1.2 percent per annum (Cline 2005, 49). A few recent studies speak to the seigniorage gain. One study finds 10-year bond yields were 70 basis points lower as a result of foreign capital inflows (Bandholz, Clostermann, and Seitz 2009). Still another suggests that the increase in US treasuries held by foreigners depressed yields by 90 basis points (Warnock and Warnock 2009).

Costs

Exorbitant Curse, not Exorbitant Privilege. Seigniorage has a flip side. The fact that a currency is considered special makes it attractive to hold, increasing the demand for it, and causing the currency to appreciate and render exporters less competitive on world markets. C. Fred Bergsten (1975, 2009) has a stronger version of this curse. In his view, the ability to finance current account deficits more easily can lead to irresponsible government and private-sector behavior, thereby contributing to financial instability. The US experience in the recent global financial crisis is a case in point, the argument being that the large current account deficits—stemming in part from reserve currency status—led to large capital inflows and cheap and easy money, which combined with lax regulations led to reckless behavior and sowed the seeds for the crisis. Thus, reserve currency status may have been the rope that allowed the United States to hang itself because of the cheaper financing that it afforded.

Vulnerability from Exorbitant Privilege. Exorbitant privilege also creates a vulnerability to external actions among those who have bought US assets. China arguably has some leverage over the United States because of its ability to sell its large stockpile of US treasuries. Many of the sterling bloc countries after World War II were in a position to sell their sterling holdings, creating instability and complicating UK macroeconomic management. As discussed in chapter 2, in 1966, Malaysia, which held 14 percent of the United Kingdom's net liabilities to sterling area countries, was able to threaten to sell these holdings and destabilize sterling as a way of successfully staving off UK political pressure to force it to integrate monetarily with Singapore.

Burden of Responsibility. This is the flip side of the power that can come from reserve currency status. The monetary authorities in the country of the leading international currency may have to take into account the effects of their actions on world markets, rather than being free to devote monetary policy solely to domestic objectives. Edwin Truman (2007) argues that the Federal Reserve probably cut interest rates more than it otherwise would have in the second half of 1982, and again in late 1998, in response to international debt problems in Latin America and elsewhere. The United States has also been reluctant to see other countries officially dollarizing (Argentina) for fear of having to accept any burden of responsibility, even if only implicit.

The best example of the costs of preserving reserve currency status comes from the experience of sterling. Susan Strange (1987) argues that preserving sterling's international role required higher defense spending and higher interest rates to keep sterling strong, which also undermined export competitiveness. After World War II, the United Kingdom at several times between 1949 and 1967 chose not to devalue sterling stemming in part from the fear that such a move would destroy the sterling bloc and jeopardize the Commonwealth. In the Suez crisis, part of the United Kingdom's vulnerability stemmed from wanting to avoid the effects of devaluation on the sterling bloc and hence on the remains of empire.

"Costly" Prerequisites. One point that is not sufficiently emphasized and which lies at the heart of China's dilemma in elevating its currency to reserve currency status—or rather allowing its currency to be elevated—relates to the demanding prerequisites. Reserve currency status requires as a sine qua non an openness to capital flows and elimination of domestic financial repression. Put simply, for a currency to become a reserve currency it must be available for use by outsiders, especially for outsiders to buy assets in the country issuing the currency. But a domestic growth strategy that is predicated on maintaining an undervalued exchange rate and generating rapid export growth is difficult to sustain the more open a country is to capital flows: When foreigners buy a country's assets, that increases capital inflows, making the currency stronger and exports less competitive. For China, therefore, there is a tension between the export-led growth strategy, which requires denying foreigners the ability to buy Chinese assets, and promoting reserve currency status, which requires allowing unrestricted access to foreigners to buy Chinese assets.

Short History

One way to answer the question about changes in reserve currency status—especially in relation to the dollar and renminbi going forward—is to turn to history. Which countries have enjoyed reserve currency status historically, and when and why have there been significant transitions?

Figure 3.1 plots the reserve holdings of the top three reserve currencies at selected points in time between 1899 and 2009. Until the post-World War II period, there was never just one reserve currency. Peter Lindert's (1969) analysis showed that in the period before the war, sterling was the dominant reserve currency but by no means the currency hegemon. According to Lindert's calculations, in 1913, sterling accounted for 38 percent of all official currency holdings, while the comparable share of the French franc and German mark were 24 and 13 percent, respectively. In 1899, the figures for the three countries were respectively, 43, 11, and 10 percent. Holdings of nonsterling reserves were especially pronounced in regions commercially and financially linked to France (e.g., Russia) and Germany.

The dollar made its first appearance as a reserve currency in the interwar years. In this period, the pound and the dollar accounted for a roughly equal share of reserve holdings. Although the dollar surpassed sterling around the mid-1920s, according to Barry Eichengreen and Marc Flandreau (2008), they traded places for the top spot afterward. In 1931, when sterling went off the gold standard in the wake of serious economic problems, sterling reserves fell. But when the dollar went off the gold standard some switching occurred back to sterling.

Figure 3.1   Holdings of reserve currencies, 1899–2009

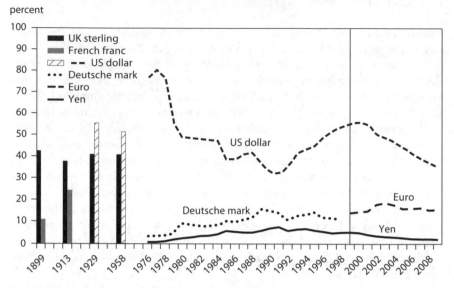

percent

Notes: Holdings are expressed as share of a currency in global holdings of foreign exchange reserves. Part of the foreign exchange reserves cannot be assigned to particular currencies, so the share is expressed in terms of total holdings that can be so assigned.

Sources: Eichengreen and Flandreau (2008); Lindert (1969); Kennedy (1989); Triffin (1961); and International Monetary Fund, Currency Composition of Official Foreign Exchange Reserves (IMF COFER) database.

After the establishment of the Bretton Woods system in 1945, the dollar was the de facto reserve asset (even though all currencies were still denominated in terms of gold) and enjoyed a near-monopoly status. The European currencies, including sterling, were not convertible into gold until 1958. But this dominance of the dollar is not quite reflected in the data because of the persistence of sterling as a reserve currency. According to estimates in Robert Triffin (1961), the share of sterling in world foreign exchange reserves was higher than that of the dollar until 1954 (27 and 26 percent, respectively); thereafter the dollar's share rose steadily, reaching 65 percent in 1973. On other measures of reserves (e.g., liquid foreign assets), the dollar had overtaken the pound by 1945.[5]

The high share of sterling after World War II is misleading because many if not most of these reserves were held by countries (mainly UK colonies) in the

---

5. Schenk (2010b, 2) has a slightly different interpretation: "In the 1950s the sterling area (35 countries and colonies pegged to sterling and holding primarily sterling reserves) accounted for half of world trade, and sterling accounted for over half of world foreign exchange reserves. In the early post-war years, this share was even higher: the IMF estimated that official sterling reserves, excluding those held by colonies, were four times the value of official dollar reserves and that by 1947 sterling accounted for about 87 percent of global foreign exchange reserves. It took ten years after the end of the war (and a 30 percent devaluation of the pound) before the share of dollar reserves exceeded that of sterling."

sterling area. When World War II broke out, the sterling bloc countries within the British empire agreed to protect the external value of sterling by essentially extending credit to Britain and accepting sterling-denominated IOUs. Legislation was therefore passed throughout the empire formalizing the British sterling bloc countries into a single exchange control area.

Thus sterling balances were blocked and could only be used to buy British goods. That sterling was in fact a diminished currency, with its elevated status propped up by the sterling area measures, is revealed by the events of 1947. When, as part of the Anglo-American Agreement negotiated by John Maynard Keynes after World War II, restrictions on the use of sterling had to be removed in 1946, residents in sterling area countries rushed to convert sterling into dollars to purchase US goods. The consequential loss of nearly 40 percent of UK reserves ($1 billion out of $2.5 billion) led quickly to the restoration of restrictions on sterling convertibility (Eichengreen 2010).

Holding European currencies as reserves started to become attractive in the 1960s as the European countries began to gradually relax exchange controls for capital account transactions, as the United States started generating inflation, and as the United States started imposing ad hoc restrictions on capital outflows as a way of protecting the balance of payments.[6] This led to the development of the euro-dollar market. The German mark and Japanese yen started featuring more prominently in official reserve holdings from the mid-1970s onward, according to IMF data, with a corresponding decline in the dollar.

Since the early 1990s, the dollar has made a comeback and the euro—since its introduction in 1999—has increased its share of global reserve holdings (figure 3.1). For much of the post-1973 period, though, the dollar has accounted for a vast bulk of the share of official foreign exchange reserves held by the world.

In 1970, a new reserve currency was issued by the IMF called the special drawing right. This action was in response to the belief, spawned by the analysis of Triffin (1961), that there would be an inherent shortage of international liquidity. The shortage would result because there were limits on the amount that the United States—or any reserve currency center—could supply in its currency to the rest of the world in response to the demand for it. If there is too much supply, as occurred in the United States during the late 1960s and 1970s, leading to current account deficits, foreigners start losing confidence in the currency and its ability to be stable and hold value. And if the United States responded by reducing its deficits, there would not be enough dollars in the rest of the world to grease trade and finance. The solution therefore was to create a synthetic reserve asset, the SDR, to supplement the supply of the reserve currency (and gold).[7]

---

6. The interest equalization tax first imposed by the United States in 1963 is seen as a key trigger for the development of the euro-dollar market.

7. See Williamson (2009) for a lucid history of SDRs.

What Determines Reserve Currency Status?

Table 3.1 relates the desirable prerequisites of the country issuing the reserve currency to its three key functions. To be an attractive store of value, the issuing country should have low and stable inflation as well as a stable and relatively strong exchange rate. To be a good medium of exchange and to serve as a unit of account, a reserve currency must be widely transacted and accepted. A country that is large in output, trade, and finance will naturally find its currency widely transacted and hence more likely to be widely accepted.

There is a certain circularity or self-reinforcing quality here: The more transacted a currency is, the more there will be an incentive to use this currency as a medium of exchange and as a unit of account, and hence the more it will be transacted, and so on.[8] Also, the more deep and liquid a country's financial markets, the easier it will be to raise money in that currency and hence easier to make payments and store value.

Putting all these factors together suggests that any quantitative analysis of the determinants of a reserve currency must include the size of a country's economy, trade and external financing, the development of its financial markets, the confidence that investors have in the currency as a store of value, and how extensive its use already is. This is the approach adopted in Chinn and Frankel (2007).[9]

The analysis used here—described in detail in appendix 3A—departs from the existing literature in two different ways, based on a historical perspective on the issue. First, it spans a much longer time period, between 1900 and 2010, compared with existing contributions that focus on the period after 1973. Second, Occam's razor is wielded to narrow the list of determinants to (1) relative size, albeit measured along three economic dimensions—income, trade, and external finance, which are also the determinants of economic dominance more broadly as discussed in chapter 2; and (2) persistence or the self-reinforcing characteristic of a reserve currency.

Krugman (1984, 274) provides justification for such a simplification. In his view, the two key determinants of a reserve currency are as follows: "First, the currency of a country which is important in world markets will be a better candidate for an international money than that of a smaller country. Second,

---

8. Chinn and Frankel (2008, 9) draw an analogy with language: "If one sat down to design an ideal language, it would not be English. (Presumably it would be Esperanto.) Nobody would claim that the English language is particularly well-suited to be the world's lingua franca by virtue of its intrinsic beauty, simplicity, or utility. It is neither as elegant and euphonious as French, for example, nor as simple and logical in spelling and grammar as Spanish or Italian. Yet it is certainly the language in which citizens of different countries most often converse and do business, and increasingly so. One chooses to use a lingua franca, as one chooses a currency, in the belief that it is the one that others are most likely to use."

9. The contrast between the results here and those of Chinn and Frankel (2007) is discussed in greater detail in appendix 3A.

the use of a currency as an international money itself reinforces that currency's usefulness, so that there is an element of circular causation." Frankel (1995) makes the same case in favor of size while also elaborating that the relevant dimensions of world markets are the share of a country international output, trade, and finance.

The key findings of the analysis based on using a simple and historical approach are discussed below.

First, there is a large and statistically strong relationship between a country's reserve currency status, on the one hand, and its share in global GDP and global trade, on the other.

Second, there is a positive but slightly less strong relationship between the country's net creditor status and reserve holdings.

Third, the surprising finding is that these three variables together—which I argued were also the key determinants of economic dominance more generally—account for reserve currency status. Together, they explain nearly 70 percent of the variation in reserve currency holdings. Thus, seeking parsimony in explaining reserve currency status is vindicated, as Krugman and Frankel have suggested.

Fourth, a surprising finding—and one somewhat different from the results in the literature—is that trade appears to be a much more important determinant of reserve currency holdings. This is consistent with the view that reserve currency status derives in turn from private-sector behavior—that is, the more the private sector desires, uses, or denominates transactions in a particular currency, the more likely it will attain reserve currency status. The results suggest that if a country's share in world trade goes up from, say, 10 to 15 percent, all else being equal, its share in reserve holdings would increase from 20 to 37 percent. In contrast, if a country's share in world GDP increased by the same amount, its share in reserves would increase from 20 to about 30 percent.

Finally, the statistical analysis suggests that the United States is currently punching above its weight, which was not true a decade ago. Given US fundamentals on GDP, trade, and net creditor status, its share in reserve holdings is substantially greater than it ought to be. This finding can give rise to complacency or alarm. Complacency because it suggests or reinforces the fact of persistence and first-mover advantage: Once a currency is entrenched as a reserve asset, dislodging it from its lofty perch is difficult. But the finding could also be a source of alarm because it shows that fundamentals are working against the currency and once some tipping point is reached, the switch away from the dollar could be swift.

Will that happen? The British empire was associated with sterling dominance, Pax Americana with dollar dominance. In the long march from the cowry shell to the greenback (via silver, bimetallism, gold, and sterling), does renminbi dominance await the world? I turn to this question in chapter 5.

Appendix 3A
A Regression Analysis of Reserve Currency Status

There is an extensive literature examining the determinants of reserve currency status.[10] Simple regression analysis is used to relate reserve currencies to the three key determinants to see if there is any strong association between them. Data have been compiled here on the major reserve currencies going back to 1899. The analysis is restricted to the major reserve currencies in each period (sterling, franc, and mark for pre-1913; sterling and dollar for 1929 and 1958; dollar, franc, sterling, yen, and mark between 1975 and 2000; and dollar, sterling, yen, and the euro since then).[11]

Selected years were chosen for the analysis depending on data availability and also because the aim was to estimate long-run rather than high-frequency relationships. Thus, data were selected for every 10 years beginning with the most recent period (1980, 1990, 2000, and 2009) and then for those years for which they were available (1900, 1919, 1929, 1958, and 1976). The longest gap is for the period between 1929 and 1958 because data are most shaky for this period, according to Eichengreen and Flandreau (2008). Chinn and Frankel (2007), in contrast, estimate the relationship for annual data from 1973 onward. They also have a more expanded set of explanatory variables, including inflation differentials, depreciation, and foreign exchange market turnover ratio. As discussed in the chapter, the specification here is more parsimonious, restricted to GDP, trade, and net debtor/creditor status.

One important technical point drawn from Chinn and Frankel (2007) is in specifying the left-hand-side variable. They suggest that the functional form relating reserves to the underlying determinants cannot be linear because the dependent variable (currency shares) is bounded between 0 and 1. They suggest using a logistic transformation to take account of this constraint, which is adopted here. Thus the dependent variable is log (share/(1 − share)), where share refers to the share of a currency in total global holdings of reserves. This functional form also captures persistence in reserve holdings, which Krugman (1984) and others have argued is a key determinant of reserve holdings.[12]

---

10. See Aliber (1966), Alogoskoufis and Portes (1992), Eichengreen and Mathieson (2000), Frankel (1992, 1995), Kenen (1983), Krugman (1984), Kindleberger (1981), McKinnon (1979), Portes and Rey (1998), Rey (2001), and Swoboda (1969).

11. One could add Switzerland to the sample.

12. The basic equation is Log $(\Phi/(1 - \Phi)) = \alpha Y$, where Φ is the reserve share and α is the coefficient on the explanatory variable estimated in table 3A.1. Taking logs yields: dLog Φ + d Log$(1 - \Phi)$ = α d Log Y. Using the fact that dLog Φ = d Φ/Φ and rearranging terms yields an expression for the change in the share, d Φ = $(\alpha$ d Log Y$) \times (\Phi \times (1 - \Phi))$. Now, ceteris paribus, this expression is highest for Φ = 0.5, and declines monotonically for all values of Φ below and above 0.5. That is, the closer the initial share of a reserve currency is to zero or one, the smaller will be its change in response to changes in underlying determinants such as trade and income. This is the sense in which this functional form captures persistence. Thus, for any given change in the right hand side variable (dY), the impact on reserve changes is smaller when the initial share of reserves is very high or very low.

Thus, of the many determinants suggested by Chinn and Frankel (2007), only two are used here—size and persistence. Neglecting the other variables is partly due to limited data availability, because it is not easy to find data on the depth of financial or foreign exchange markets going back in time; and partly due to the fact that over long periods, differences between reserve currency countries in inflation, for example, (which affects the attractiveness of a currency as a store of value) is not that significant. And as the results clearly suggest, ignoring these other factors does not seem to be a major problem, because the limited set of explanatory variables seems to account for a surprisingly large share of the variation in reserve currency holdings.

Table 3A.1 reports results for two ways of calculating reserve holdings. In the first four columns of table 3A.1, the reserves of each currency are expressed as a share of total official reserves; in columns 5 to 8, reserves are expressed as a share of all reserves whose denomination is accounted for. Results do not change significantly across these two definitions, except that in the former specification, the net creditor status variable is statistically more significant. Columns 1 and 5 use all the observations. The specifications in all the other columns drop the observation for the United Kingdom in 1958, which, for reasons discussed in the text, was an outlier because sterling was artificially propped up by special policy measures. In columns 3 and 7, the observation for the United States in 2009 is also dropped.

One caveat about the interpretation of the results. My sample by construction includes only those currencies that already have reserve currency status, so there is selection bias. The results should be interpreted as suggesting something about the relative standing of currencies once they have reached reserve currency status, not necessarily their likelihood of attaining this status. The findings are described below.

First, there is a large and statistically strong relationship between a country's reserve currency status, on the one hand, and its share in GDP and trade, on the other. In columns 2 to 4, and 6 to 8, which are my preferred specifications, the coefficients of these two variables are significant at the 1 percent confidence level.

Second, there is a positive but less strong relationship between the country's net creditor status and reserve holdings. In the specification in column 2, the net creditor variable is significant at the 10 percent confidence level, and at the 5 percent level in the specifications (columns 3 and 7) excluding the dollar in 2009.

Third, the surprising finding is that these three variables together—which I argued were also the key determinants of economic dominance more generally—account for reserve currency status. Together, they explain nearly 70 percent of the variation in reserve currency holdings. In Chinn and Frankel (2007), the proportion of variation that is explained is high but that is because of the presence of the lagged dependent variable on the right-hand side of the regression.

Table 3A.1 Determinants of reserves, 1899–2009

Variable[a]	Reserve shares based on all reserves[b]				Reserve shares based on allocated reserves[c]			
	1	2	3	4	5	6	7	8
Constant	−6.03	−6.18	−6.19	−6.19	−5.75	−5.89	−5.90	−5.90
	−9.14	*−9.46*	*−9.46*	*−9.31*	*−8.36*	*−8.54*	*−8.57*	*−8.43*
Share in world GDP	11.37	12.87	12.67	12.67	13.85	15.24	14.99	14.99
	3.58	*4.52*	*4.42*	*4.35*	*3.61*	*4.24*	*4.09*	*4.02*
Share in world trade	22.13	20.84	20.56	20.56	21.95	20.76	20.39	20.39
	4.32	*4.18*	*4.08*	*4.01*	*4.14*	*3.92*	*3.83*	*3.77*
Share in world's net capital surplus	1.18	1.38	1.74	1.74	1.08	1.26	1.73	1.73
	1.37	*1.77*	*2.10*	*2.07*	*1.09*	*1.31*	*1.77*	*1.74*
Dummy for US in 2009				1.19				1.57
				3.23				*3.79*
R²	0.62	0.67	0.66	0.67	0.63	0.67	0.67	0.68
Number of observations	33	32	31	32	33	32	31	32
Description of sample	All countries	Excludes UK in 1958	Excludes UK in 1958 and US in 2009	Excludes UK in 1958	All countries	Excludes UK in 1958	Excludes UK in 1958 and US in 2009	Excludes UK in 1958

a. The dependent variable is logistic of the share of a currency in world reserves. The dependent variable relates to currencies, while the right-hand-side variables relate to countries issuing the currencies. The *t*-statistics are reported in italics below the coefficients.

b. The denominator in this calculation is the total of reserve holdings even if the currencies are not of accountable denomination.

c. The denominator in this calculation is the total of those reserves whose currency denomination can be identified.

Source: Author's calculations.

Figure 3A.1 Association between reserve currency and GDP, 1899–2009

logistic of share of currency in world reserve holdings

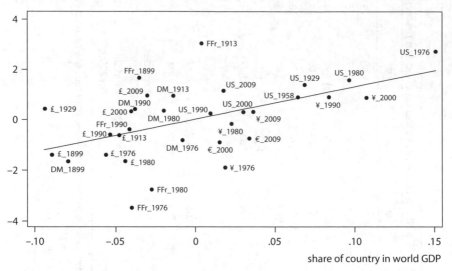

FFr = French franc; DM = Deutsche mark; US = US dollar; ¥ = Japanese yen; £ = UK sterling

Notes: The logistic of a variable is defined as log (share / (1-share)), where share is the share of a currency in world official reserves of foreign exchange. Data points in this figure capture the conditional relationship between the share of reserve holdings and the share of a currency's country in world GDP. Each data point also shows the relevant year. The data correspond to the specification in column 2 of table 3A.1.

Sources: Data are from Eichengreen and Flandreau (2008); Lindert (1969); Triffin (1961); and International Monetary Fund, Currency Composition of Official Foreign Exchange Reserves (IMF COFER) database.

Fourth, again a surprising finding—and one somewhat different from the results in Chinn and Frankel—is that trade appears to be a much more important determinant of reserve currency holdings.[13] The coefficient on trade is substantially larger (between 35 and 60 percent depending on the specification in table 3A.1) than that for GDP. In Chinn and Frankel (2007), the coefficient on GDP is also significant but is about one-fourth the magnitude obtained here and they do not find trade to be a statistically significant determinant.

The regressions also suggest that the dollar is currently punching above its weight. The regression in columns 4 and 8 introduce a dummy for the US dollar in 2010. This dummy is positive and significant at the 1 percent confidence level, which essentially means that given United States fundamentals on GDP, trade and net creditor status, its share in reserve holdings is substantially greater than it ought to be. In contrast, if a dummy for 2000 for the US dollar is added to the regression, that dummy is not significant, suggesting that the

---

13. Chinn and Frankel (2007) report that trade shares do not emerge as significant explanatory variables in their analysis.

Figure 3A.2 Association between reserve currency and trade, 1899–2009

logistic of share of currency in world reserve holdings

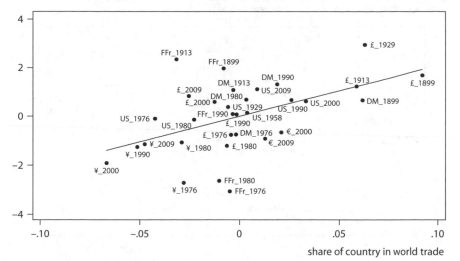

share of country in world trade

FFr = French franc; DM = Deutsche mark; US = US dollar; ¥ = Japanese yen; £ = UK sterling

Notes: Data points in this figure capture the conditional relationship between the share of reserve holdings of a currency and the share of the country issuing the currency in world trade. Each data point also shows the relevant year. The data correspond to the specification in column 2 of table 3A.1.

Sources: Data are from Eichengreen and Flandreau (2008); Lindert (1969); Triffin (1961); and International Monetary Fund, Currency Composition of Official Foreign Exchange Reserves (IMF COFER) database.

reserve holdings in dollars were roughly in line with fundamentals in 2000. It is only in the last decade that the US has been punching above its weight.

Figures 3A.1 to 3A.3 show the relationship between reserve currencies and their three main determinants, respectively. These figures plot the conditional relationship summarized in the regressions (in table 3A.1) between the share of reserve holdings and the share of the country using that particular reserve currency in world GDP (figure 3A.1), the share of the country in world trade (figure 3A.2), and the share of a country in world net exports of capital (figure 3A.3). These figures are not plots of the unconditional relationship. They correspond to the regressions in column 2 of table 3A.1. Each observation denotes a currency and the year, so that it is easy to see where the reserve currencies stand at different points in time relative to the average relationship depicted by the line in these figures.

Alternative Ways of Projecting Currency Dominance

How can this analysis of the determinants of reserve currency status be used to project, in chapter 5, the timing of China's future currency dominance? I do this in two ways, which might be called respectively, "level" and "change" ap-

Figure 3A.3 Association between reserve currency and net creditor status, 1899–2009

logistic of share of currency in world reserve holdings

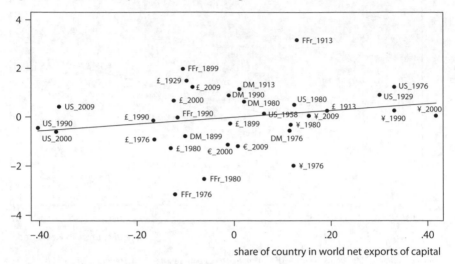

share of country in world net exports of capital

FFr = French franc; DM = Deutsche mark; US = US dollar; ¥ = Japanese yen; £ = UK sterling

Notes: Data points in this figure capture the conditional relationship between the share of reserve holdings and world's net exports of capital. Each data point also shows the relevant year. The data correspond to the specification in column 2 of table 3A.1.

Sources: Data are from Eichengreen and Flandreau (2008); Lindert (1969); Triffin (1961); and International Monetary Fund, Currency Composition of Official Foreign Exchange Reserves (IMF COFER) database.

proaches. In the main text of chapter 5, I focus on the former. This consists of the following steps. First I use the coefficients from the regressions described in table 3A.1 for GDP, trade, and net creditor status to construct the index of economic dominance for different countries, including China. This index is displayed in figure 2.4. I use historical values of this index for the United Kingdom and the United States and go back to history to identify the lag between US economic dominance and dollar dominance. I then project forward economic dominance for China and the United States (using the same weights for GDP, trade and net creditor status) and then apply the historical lag between economic and currency dominance to ascertain the timing of the possible ascent of the renminbi.

An alternative—the change approach—follows these steps. I project changes in GDP, trade, and capital export shares between 2010 and 2030 for the United States and the euro area. These projections combined with coefficients for each of these variables in the regression analysis from table 3A.1 imply changes in the currency holdings of dollars and euros in 2030. The equation that helps this projection analysis is described in footnote 12. I implicitly assume that the decline in shares of dollars in euros in reserve holdings will be reflected in increased renminbi holdings.

4

Forces Driving Dominance: Convergence and Gravity

... the degree of income inequality across societies has reached unprecedented levels. None of this can persist ... [C]ountries that have been kept out of this process of diffusion by socialist planning or simply by corruption and lawlessness will, one after another, join the industrial revolution and become the miracle economies of the future.

—Robert E. Lucas, Jr. (2004)

Shifts in economic dominance seem a real possibility today because the financial crisis that began in 2007 and its aftermath have appeared to economically diminish the United States and Europe. Although US economic growth has recovered somewhat, a long and difficult period of unemployment looms ahead. In Europe, too, the core countries (especially Germany and France) have also put the worst of the crisis behind them, but troubles in the periphery have been so severe that talk of a "two-speed" Europe with a richer northern core and a poorer southern periphery is no longer beyond consideration. In the short run, the world itself seems to be divided into two distinct regions, with the anemic West being pulled up by the dynamic "Rest," to borrow Fareed Zakaria's characterization (Zakaria 2008a).

In fact, though, the post–World War II dichotomy of a rich West economically separated from and situated above the poor Rest has been losing its salience since well before the recent crisis. The twofold developed-developing categorization of the early postwar years was first abandoned to make way for the newly industrialized economies (NIEs) (the original gang of four Asian economies: Korea, Taiwan, Singapore, and Hong Kong), then to a broader set of "emerging-market" countries, and then to these NIEs being elevated to the category of "other advanced economies." Even then, these mutating, proliferating categories seemed unable and inadequate to capture the shifts set in motion by the rise of China and India.

Underlying these taxonomic tweakings is a simple and historic change: catch-up or convergence, the phenomenon of poor countries becoming richer and narrowing the gap with the rich countries. To set the context, it is useful to first document the broader phenomenon of convergence and then focus on those large countries that will be key players in terms of future economic dominance. Consider therefore convergence for the "previously poor" and then for the "populous and previously poor," encompassing Brazil, China, India, and Indonesia (the BIICs).[1]

Convergence of the Previously Poor

Depending on how far back in history one wants to go, the economic history of humankind can be divided into four broad phases. The first and longest is the period of Malthusian stagnation, running from about 13000 BCE to around 1000 CE (Clark 2007). The average standard of living during this period fluctuated but broadly hovered around subsistence, and life was, in the words of Thomas Hobbes, "poor, nasty, brutish, and short." The decisive break from subsistence started after the Middle Ages, culminating in the Industrial Revolution of the late 1700s. The profusion of technological innovation that allowed people to extract energy from nature transformed civilization (Clark 2007). This Industrial Revolution created also the "great divergence" whereby the West—the United Kingdom and its western offshoots—embarked on a trajectory of consistently upward improvement in living standards while the Rest lagged behind. The great divergence marked the second phase of human economic history and continued, with some exceptions, until World War II.

The third phase starting after the war witnessed another break from the preceding era. A group of countries started growing faster in per capita terms than rich countries, allowing them to narrow the gap in living standards (the level of per capita GDP) with those richer countries. In other words, they started to catch up with the frontier. The first cohort included war-ravaged Germany and Japan and other industrial countries. But the experience of these countries was thought to have limited relevance because prior to the war many of them were already reasonably rich and close to the frontier. Their postwar performance was a reversion to recent history.

What marked this third phase, however, was the performance of another cohort, whose growth took off between 1950 and 1970. This cohort comprised countries that had been poor for several centuries, including Taiwan, Korea, Singapore, Hong Kong, Malaysia, Indonesia, Thailand, Brazil, Chile, Tunisia, Botswana, and Mauritius. This cohort of high and converging performers was then followed by the two largest countries—China and India—with the potential to become systemically important. In some ways, China and India were latecomers to the catching-up process.

---

1. For reasons largely related to demographics and the consequential impact on growth, it seems more natural to focus on the BIICs than the BRICs, which excludes Indonesia and includes Russia. The contrast between Russia's expected negative population growth of nearly 0.5 percent a year between 2010 and 2030 and Indonesia's increase of 0.8 percent is likely to favor strongly Indonesia's prospects going forward.

Table 4.1 Convergence and growth rates over time, 1870–2008

	Data source			
	Maddison (2010)	Penn World Table	Penn World Table	World Bank, World Development Indicators
	1870–1960	1960–2000	2000–07	2000–08
US GDP per capita growth rate (CAGR) (percent)	1.7	2.5	1.3	1.1
World GDP per capita growth rate (CAGR) (percent)	1.3	2.8	3.2	2.3
Number of nonoil, nonsmall, developing countries with CAGR above US CAGR[a]	2	21	75	76
Average excess over US CAGR (percent)	0.02	1.53	3.25	3.01
Total number of nonoil, nonsmall developing countries in sample	38	72	103	89
Total number of countries in sample[b]	63	110	186	168

CAGR = compound annual growth rate

a. For the period 1870–1960, Venezuela's growth exceeded that of the United States but is excluded on the criterion of being an oil-based economy. The classification is from the IMF's *World Economic Outlook*. Small economies are classified as those with a population below 1 million in 2001.
b. The 1870–1960 sample excludes a number of countries classified as small by Maddison (2010).

It is possible that the world has now entered a fourth phase of economic history. In the decade and a half preceding the recent global economic crisis, a much greater number of countries in Europe, Africa, Latin America, and Asia have started growing much faster than in the past and much faster than the industrial countries. In other words, convergence is broadening and accelerating.

Table 4.1 illustrates the expanding membership in this convergence club. During the period from 1870–1960, two nonoil, nonsmall developing coun-

Figure 4.1 Broadening convergence: Percent of all nonoil, nonsmall developing countries with GDP per capita growth rates above the US growth rate, 1950–2007

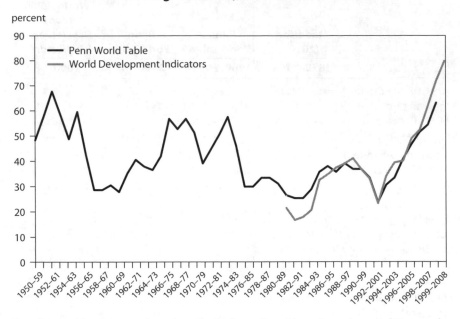

Notes: Rates are 10-year compound annual growth rates. Nonsmall countries are those whose population exceeds 1 million.

Sources: Penn World Table (version 6.3); World Bank, *World Development Indicators*.

tries (of a total of 38) grew faster, though barely so, than the United States (the benchmark for convergence analysis).[2] In the next phase (1960–2000), 21 of 72 countries converged toward US income levels, narrowing the gap at a rate of 1.5 percent per year. But in the period just preceding the recent crises, between 75 and 90 percent of developing countries (depending on the data source) grew faster than the United States, and at a faster clip, closing in by about 3 percent a year. Thus, something significant may have happened just prior to the crisis in terms of the breadth and speed of catch-up by the poorer parts of the world.

Figures 4.1 and 4.2 illustrate this phenomenon in more detail. Figure 4.1 computes the proportion of countries that have been converging—specifically growing faster than the United States—since 1950.[3] This proportion, which fluctuates around a declining trend, troughs in the 1990s and then

---

2. Oil-based economies and very small economies, whose population was less than 1 million in 2007, are excluded from the sample.

3. The sample is restricted to nonoil countries and those countries with a population exceeding 1 million. Two different sources of data are used—the Penn World Tables (version 6.3) and the World Bank's *World Development Indicators*—to compute the numbers.

Figure 4.2 Accelerating convergence: Average of excess of GDP per capita over US growth for all nonoil, nonsmall developing countries with growth above that of the United States, 1950–2007

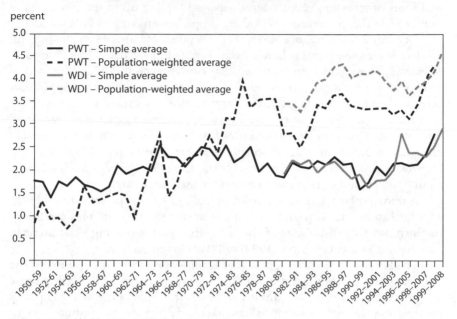

percent

PWT = Penn World Table; WDI = World Development Indicators.

Notes: Per capita GDP growth rate based on 10-year compound annual growth rate (CAGR). Nonsmall countries are those whose population exceeds 1 million.

Sources: Penn World Table (version 6.3); World Bank, *World Development Indicators*.

takes off decisively. Over the last decade and a half, an increasing number of countries have started to catch up with the United States, and just before the crisis nearly 80 percent of countries had embarked on catch-up.

Figure 4.2 computes the magnitude of catch-up. Specifically, it shows by how much the average growth rate in the catch-up group exceeded that of the United States. Since the 1990s there has been a sharp increase, and just before the crisis, catch-up seems to have been occurring at a rate of 3 percent per year (on an unweighted basis) and nearly 4.5 percent (on a population-weighted basis).

The picture that emerges from table 4.1 and the two figures in box 6.2 in chapter 6 is one of a strikingly positive and unprecedented change in the economic fortunes of humanity. Of course, there have been plenty of episodes of growth spurts in the past that have fizzled out after short periods of time (Hausmann, Pritchett, and Rodrik 2005). But while this has been true for individual countries, seldom in the last 50 years has one seen episodes where a large number of poor countries have simultaneously done as well as in the decade preceding the recent crisis.

In fact, if one checks for each of the four decades before 2000, the best collective performance was in the 1970s, when 38 of 87 countries exceeded US growth rates by an average of about 2.5 percent. Even that performance falls well short of what has occurred in the period leading up to the crisis. So the numbers for the most recent period are simply too striking to be ignored.

One cannot be sure, of course, that this phenomenon of broadening and accelerating convergence is here to stay. But as Robert Lucas (2000) argued, economic theory had long predicted that convergence should be the natural state of affairs for at least three reasons. First, poor countries are poor in part because they have small amounts of capital. But low capital levels imply big returns to capital because of investment opportunities that have remained unexploited. Hence, capital would flow from rich to poor countries, generate growth, and pull up the latter. Second, as Robert Tamura (1996) pointed out, knowledge produced anywhere benefits producers everywhere. Technology is a public good, and once created can be exploited anywhere.

A third explanation puts a political and policy interpretation on knowledge and spillovers: Governments in the unsuccessful economies can adopt the institutions and policies of the successful ones, removing what Stephen Parente and Edward Prescott (1994) call "barriers to growth."

The latter two points suggest that technology can be interpreted in the physical sense of converting inputs to outputs, but also in the policy sense of adopting good ways of running an economy by making sensible policy choices. And technology—both as hardware and software—is a public good, so once created it is available to all to use and replicate, which should also create a tendency for poorer countries to be pulled up toward the richer countries.

The surprise therefore is not why countries have started converging but why they had not done so earlier. Lucas (2000) notes that the Industrial Revolution was a revolution precisely because it overrode for more than 200 years this natural tendency toward convergence.

Conditional or Unconditional Convergence?

In the immediate post–World War II period, when the catch-up phenomenon was restricted to a few countries and had not become widespread—as seems to be happening in the most recent phase—economists characterized it as "conditional convergence." In other words, not all countries had been able to embark on a process of becoming rich and catching up with the standards of living of the rich countries. Only those that fulfilled certain conditions, or as Dani Rodrik (2009) puts it, those that did the "right things," had been successful. Development economics has been the locus of the most contentious and even acrimonious discussions about what those "right things" were. Were they strong institutions, geography, culture, political stability, lack of ethnic divisions, policies (and if so which policies), etc.? The newer consensus—such as it is—is about search and pragmatism rather than a ready-made of list of to-do's.

The fact that catch-up appears to be become more ubiquitous does not necessarily mean that it is now unconditional. It means simply that more and more countries are putting in place the basic conditions that allow faster growth to be realized. Two of those conditions are worth mentioning. First, the conviction that macroeconomic stability is a necessary condition for growth seems to be spreading. In a sense, if Paul Romer's (1994) emphasis on the role of ideas in growth is correct, one such idea that has taken hold is the need for and the ability to deliver macroeconomic stability, and a recognition that the failure to realize this stability lay behind the low and volatile growth performance of Latin America and sub-Saharan Africa in the 1980s and 1990s. The fact that a number of low-income countries survived the crisis of 2008–09 with minimal damage is in part a tribute to the embrace of the idea of macro-economic stability.[4]

A second condition seems to be the spread of new information and com-munication technologies, whose transformational role in low-income coun-tries is now being realized.[5] Neither of these conditions is a guarantee that low-income countries will grow at Chinese rates of growth in the future. What they do suggest is that on balance, more countries will catch up rather than lag behind the frontier in the years ahead.

A third factor that seems to have come into play is what might be called a "growth begetting growth" dynamic. If countries grow for some period of time, growth itself seems to create positive change, reinforcing subsequent growth. One good example is in India, where growth has increased the return to education so much that the demand for education has increased, forcing supply to respond. As a result, dramatic improvements have occurred in edu-cational outcomes.[6]

Thus, the numbers presented here are certainly not inconsistent with the possibility that the diffusion of technology and information (including how to manage or rather not manage economic policy at macro and micro levels) may be proceeding so rapidly that catch-up—though not necessarily at a frenetic and uniform pace—is now becoming the norm rather than the excep-tion that it has been until recently. The "new normal"—to borrow Mohamed

---

4. The irony, of course, is that industrial countries seem to have forgotten the importance of, and preconditions for, attaining macroeconomic stability, which might itself merit the label of a "great reversal" of ideas.

5. Jensen (2007) and Aker and Mbiti (forthcoming) highlight the role of mobile telephones in improving the functioning of markets in developing countries. Kenny (2011) discusses the impact of the telecommunication revolution in the spread of ideas and hence in improving development outcomes such as increased female autonomy.

6. Other examples illustrating this growth-begetting-growth dynamic are in my article in the *Fi-nancial Times*, "India's Weak State Will Not Overhaul China," August 16, 2010. And it is precisely this possibility of organically driven change that underlies the "modernization" hypothesis: that political change and democratization will result from economic development and the consequent demand for greater political freedoms (Lipset 1959).

Figure 4.3 Per capita GDP of the "populous poor" relative to the economic frontier, 1500–2008

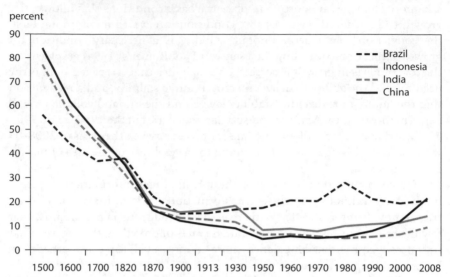

Note: The "frontier" country is the United Kingdom until 1900 and the United States thereafter.

Source: Maddison (2010).

El-Erian's (2010) phrase—could turn out to be what should always have been the old normal.

Convergence of the Populous, Previously Poor

While the broader phenomenon of convergence provided the background for analyzing shifts from the West to the Rest, from the perspective of dominance I am particularly interested in the performance of large and populous countries.

The phenomenon of the "great divergence" discussed above was in some ways and for some countries—especially today's large ones—actually one of "great reversal" (Acemoglu, Johnson, and Robinson 2002; Diamond 1997; Pritchett 1997; Morris 2010). Around 1500 AD, Ming China, Mughal India, Ivan the Great's Russia, Aztec Mexico, and Melaka (loosely what is now Indonesia) were among the more prosperous and populous places on earth. Data on urbanization, which is a reasonable proxy for levels of development, show that these countries were much better off than the United States, Canada (which Voltaire derisively described as "acres of snow"), Australia, or New Zealand. In addition, China was a technological leader and home to many of the world's important inventions, including the horse collar, gunpowder, the printing press, cast-iron tools, shipping, and the magnetic compass (Morris 2010).

Then the great reversal of economic fortunes happened. China imposed extensive prohibitions and regulations on foreign trade, allowed its technological excellence in long-distance maritime navigation (spearheaded by a Muslim eunuch sailor Zheng He) to fade, and more broadly turned inward as a result of internal struggle. India fell behind as the Mughal empire disintegrated, opening itself up to colonization. This was followed by colonization of the New World and Asia. Western Europe and its settler colonies raced ahead, especially after the Industrial Revolution in the mid-1700s, while the other regions stagnated, leading to the developed-developing dichotomy that has characterized much of the 20th century.

This history can be traced by looking at today's four most populous developing countries: Brazil, India, Indonesia, and China. Figure 4.3 plots the average per capita GDP of these countries as a ratio of the per capita GDP of the frontier or the richest country—the United Kingdom until 1900 and the United States thereafter. From 1500 to about 1960/1970, these countries were on a steady decline, slipping farther and farther away from the frontier. In 1500, the average person in India and China was nearly as rich as the person in the United Kingdom, but nearly 500 years later that average person's standard of living in these countries was a fraction (less than 10 percent) of their richer counterparts. A similar trend with slight differences in timing is evident for Brazil and Indonesia.

Then in the mid-20th century a historic "reversal of the reversal" starts occurring, with these most populous countries starting to grow faster in per capita terms than the rich countries, allowing them to narrow the gap in living standards (the level of per capita GDP). For China, India, and Indonesia the turning point occurs in the late 1970s, after which these countries started growing rapidly. For Brazil, it begins around the 1950s.

For the purposes of discussions about future economic dominance, the key question is whether the convergence in these large countries will continue over the next 20 or 30 years. The main argument of this book—the strong likelihood of shifts in economic dominance toward emerging-market countries and China in particular—is dependent on convergence continuing. The specific projections will be discussed later, but the broader phenomenon provides a backdrop for the discussion to follow. How can one be confident in this assumption of ongoing convergence, especially for the larger countries such as China and India?

It is impossible to be absolutely certain, of course, but the facts of the Chinese and Indian growth turnarounds offer confidence. They have grown respectively at about 8.5 percent and 5 percent per capita for 30 years, and their growth miracles are now entering their fourth decades.[7] During this period, they have decisively shed their dependence on agriculture and have be-

---

7. It is well known that China's turnaround occurred in 1978. Less well known is that India's growth turnaround occurred around 1980, even though the policy paradigm shifted in 1991 (Rodrik and Subramanian 2004).

come powerhouses in manufacturing (China) and services (India). They have also increased their share of trade substantially and mostly followed prudent macroeconomic policies, avoiding inflation and currency and financial crises. And all the while, they have remained politically stable.

There have been other examples of such rapid growth in recent history, but many have been followed by stagnation. Venezuela grew at above 7 percent per capita for 30 years after oil was discovered there in the early 1920s, but experienced a substantial and sustained decline in living standards, from a peak of $11,250 per capita in 1977 to $7,000 in 2003. Venezuelan growth was extraordinarily oil-dependent and its politics were always highly unstable. Brazil grew at about 4.75 percent per capita for 30 years between 1950 and 1980 and built up its manufacturing sector, but then endured nearly 20 years of stagnation from 1980 to 2000. Brazilian growth never approached Chinese levels, never achieved China's large increase in trade, and was perennially prone (until recently) to macroeconomic instability.[8]

In sum, few countries in economic history have grown as fast and for such a long time period, structurally transformed their economies to such an extent, and remained as politically and macroeconomically stable as China and India—and yet not become at least half as rich as the frontier country.[9] Any precipitous slide in the fortunes of China and India cannot be ruled out, of course, but history is more on their side than against them.

Projecting Numbers: Background Analytics

Bases for Projections: Convergence and Gravity

The previous chapter noted that economic dominance in the years ahead is likely to be shaped by the wealth, trade, and external capital of nations, especially the performance of large countries such as China, India, Brazil, and Indonesia, and especially in relation to the performance of currently dominant nations such as the United States. How rich will those growing countries become? How much will they trade with other nations? How much capital will they export or import? These are the numbers that need to be projected in order to assess future dominance.

The future is unlikely to indulge one's whim for prognostication but economic theory and history provide some guidance for gazing into the crystal ball. The projections of economic wealth (strictly speaking, GDP) will rely on

---

8. Argentina is cited as the classic case of reversal after attaining a relatively high standard of living. But Argentina never grew at the pace of China and India. Russia also grew rapidly at about 4 percent per capita for 30 years beginning just after World War II, and then famously witnessed an economic collapse because of highly dirigiste policies that had to be abandoned.

9. The significant exceptions are a number of oil-exporting countries—Oman, Libya, Gabon, Saudi Arabia, Equatorial Guinea—that have often seen rapid growth associated with exploiting new discoveries of oil or sharp price increases for their exports. But these countries have then slipped considerably when the oil exploitation has slowed down or oil prices have declined.

the phenomenon of convergence already discussed. For projecting trade, too, economic theory and evidence offer guidance. Just as the force between two objects in physics depends on the product of their masses and the distance between them, so trade between two countries is thought to depend on their economic mass (GDP) and all the frictions affecting trade, including transport costs and policy barriers.

The theoretical foundations of this so-called gravity model have been solidified in recent years (Anderson and van Wincoop 2003; Eaton and Kortum 2002; Helpman, Melitz, and Rubinstein 2008). Unlike economic convergence, which worked in theory but played out in the real world incompletely and tardily, gravity as a determinant of trade has been robustly and consistently vindicated in practice. The gravity model has consistently produced one of the most robust results in empirical economics and therefore has impeccable credentials in the field.[10]

One feature of the projections here is therefore an internal consistency between the growth and trade projections, because the key driver of trade in the gravity-model-based projections is GDP. Thus, the well-known but empirically contested phenomenon of convergence and the underrecognized but reliable phenomenon of gravity will be the two key drivers of future economic dominance, which is the subject of much of this book.

Baseline Scenario: Convergence

While the principles of convergence and gravity serve as the basis for deriving numbers of future GDP and trade, forecasting is inherently uncertain. So a range of possible outcomes must be considered. The focus is on the baseline, or what might be called the "convergence" scenario, predicated on the assumption previously discussed that the gap in GDP levels between the rich and poor will be narrowed over time. Details are provided in appendix 4A. It must be emphasized that the pace of catch-up will neither be rapid nor uniform around the developing world.

As a robustness check, I consider alternative scenarios. To avoid a proliferation of scenarios and numbers here, these alternative scenarios are taken up in the postscript and focus on the two countries contending for stakes in dominance. The scenarios quantify the impact of how economic dominance will evolve under differing assumptions not of absolute growth rates but of the difference in growth rates between the United States and China.

The basic growth projections for the convergence scenario are presented for the important countries and groups of countries in table 4.2. Projections of economic growth rates for industrial countries between 2010 and 2030 draw on the assessments of several experts at the Peterson Institute for In-

---

10. For recent applications, see Subramanian and Wei (2007), who estimate the impact of the WTO on trade; Helpman, Melitz, and Rubinstein (2008), who extend it to account for new theoretical developments; and Frankel and Rose (2000), who analyze the impact of currency unions.

Table 4.2   Growth projections in a convergence scenario, 2010–30

Country/group	GDP growth rate (PPP dollars)	GDP growth rate (dollars)	Per capita GDP growth rate (PPP dollars)	Per capita GDP growth rate (dollars)	Population growth rate (percent)
United States	2.5	2.5	1.7	1.7	0.8
EU-27	2.0	2.0	1.9	1.9	0.1
Japan	1.5	1.5	1.9	1.9	−0.4
China	5.9	6.9	5.5	6.5	0.4
India	7.6	8.9	6.5	7.8	1.0
Korea	3.5	3.9	3.4	3.8	0.1
Africa	7.4	9.0	5.3	6.9	2.0
Egypt	5.5	6.1	4.1	4.7	1.4
Pakistan	6.4	7.2	4.5	5.2	1.8
Iran	3.8	4.1	2.9	3.2	0.9
Middle East	5.2	5.9	3.2	4.0	1.9
Mexico	4.6	5.2	3.9	4.5	0.7
Chile	3.7	4.1	3.0	3.3	0.7
Brazil	3.7	4.0	3.1	3.5	0.5
Rest of Latin America	5.4	6.3	4.3	5.1	1.1
Indonesia	6.3	7.3	5.5	6.5	0.8
Rest of Asia	6.7	8.1	5.6	6.8	1.1
Russia	1.6	1.7	2.1	2.1	−0.4
Rest of Europe	4.7	5.5	4.5	5.3	0.2
Total	**4.3**	**4.1**	**3.4**	**3.2**	**0.9**
BRICs (Brazil, Russia, India, and China)	5.6	6.3	5.0	5.7	0.6
Populous countries (Brazil, India, Indonesia, and China)	6.1	6.8	5.3	6.1	0.7
Asia excluding Japan	6.3	7.3	5.4	6.4	0.8
Emerging and developing countries	5.6	6.4	4.6	5.3	1.0

Notes: Estimate in "dollars" refers to valuation based on market exchange rates. Estimate in "PPP dollars" refers to valuation based on purchasing power parity exchange rates.

Sources: IMF, *World Economic Outlook*; and author's calculations.

ternational Economics. They broadly take the view that the global crisis will not significantly affect medium-run growth rates in industrial countries. The United States is projected to grow at 2.5 percent, or 1.7 percent in per capita terms (over long time periods going back to 1950, the United States has grown at about 2.2 percent per capita); the European Union countries (which includes 27 countries) at 2 percent; and Japan at 1.5 percent. Within emerging and developing economies, China is projected to grow at 6.9 percent, which amounts to per capita PPP-based growth of 5.5 percent; for India, the corresponding numbers are 8.9 and 6.5 percent respectively; and for Brazil, 4 and 3.1 percent.

The assumption that postcrisis growth rates will be similar to those before the crisis suggests that the output decline (in the case of rich countries) suffered by industrial countries and the growth decline (suffered by developing countries) will not be recouped going forward. In other words, the crisis will have imposed a one-off but not permanent cost. This is also the conclusion drawn by the IMF based on analyzing previous episodes of crises (IMF 2009).

Before discussing the projections, however, some issues relating to measurement need to be reviewed.

Measuring GDP Level and Growth Rates: Purchasing Power Parity Estimates

Recall that the projections for GDP and trade are necessary inputs in computing and forecasting economic dominance. Further, the index requires levels of GDP at both market exchange rates and at PPP exchange rates. This means that growth too has to be projected at both market-based and PPP-based exchange rates.[11] How can this be done?

Most projections for GDP and GDP growth rates, including Goldman Sachs's (2003) renowned report on the BRICs (Brazil, Russia, India, and China) report and the more recent study by Citigroup (2011), project one or the other. For example, the Goldman Sachs report values GDP at market-based exchange rates, while the recent Citigroup report uses PPP for valuing GDP. As discussed in box 4.1, both cannot be right, so which one is? Neither of these reports makes the distinction between PPP and market exchange rates for growth projections (Johnson et al. 2010), and thus neither employs this distinction as a basis for projections. This book projects both.

Thus, two methodological innovations in this study are to project (1) PPP-based GDP and market-exchange-rate-based GDP and (2) long-run trade consistent with the GDP projections. There are very few predictions of long-run aggregate trade and fewer of bilateral and regional trade because of uncertainty about how to model trade flows. This is surprising because the gravity model of trade provides a simple and theoretically consistent way of doing so (see appendix 4B for details).

Before presenting the results, I draw attention to an important matter of measurement in box 4.2 that leads to an upward revision of China's PPP-based GDP estimate for 2010 of about 47 percent.

Results

According to the projections, between 2010 and 2030 emerging markets and developing economies will increase their share of world GDP (at market-based

---

11. Throughout this book "dollar GDP" or "dollar GDP growth" refer to values based on market exchange rates; correspondingly "PPP GDP" or "PPP GDP growth" refer to values based on PPP exchange rates.

Box 4.1 Goldman Sachs or Citigroup: Whose growth projections are right?

The rationale for using purchasing power parity (PPP) estimates to compare standards of living across countries at a point in time is well understood. Statistical, institutional, and intellectual apparatuses are in place to achieve that objective. What is less well understood is that GDP growth rates and growth projections should also take account of purchasing power parity considerations.[1]

Take, for example, the renowned Goldman Sachs BRICs (Brazil, Russia, India, and China) report and the more recent Citigroup report on growth in emerging markets.[2] Both project "real" per capita GDP growth rates. But Goldman Sachs applies these growth rates to the market-exchange-rate-based level of GDP ("dollar GDP") while Citigroup applies them to the base year GDP but valued at purchasing power parity ("PPP GDP"). Goldman Sachs's GDP projections are thus in dollars while Citigroup's are in PPP dollars. Which "real" growth rate is the right one? Because both cannot be.

The rationale for using purchasing power parity to estimate growth rates is broadly the same as that to estimate levels of GDP. If the market exchange rate was incorrect in valuing the GDP of the United States in 2005 relative to that of India in 2005 because some services were cheaper in the latter than in the former, so too the market exchange rate is likely to be incorrect in comparing India in 2030 with India in 2005 because these same services will be more expensive there in 2030 than they were in 2005 (this is the dynamic Balassa-Samuelson effect). What is true across countries at a point in time is likely to hold across time within countries.

A key point is that while market exchange rate based estimates of the level of GDP understate the real standard of living in poorer countries, market-exchange-rate-based growth projections, particularly those for longer periods, will overstate improvements in such living standards over time.

The best way to understand this point is to think in terms of the terminal condition. A poor country today has a higher level of PPP GDP than dollar GDP. At some point in the future, with growth and development, these different ways of valuing GDP must converge (as they have for most industrial countries). So the growth rate between these two points will necessarily be lower in purchasing power parity terms than in dollar terms.

A generous interpretation is that Goldman Sachs essentially interprets "real" growth as based on dollars while Citigroup interprets it as PPP dollars. Neither is strictly speaking wrong. But both are oblivious to the distinction and are therefore both limited and incomplete. The Goldman Sachs procedure cannot project PPP GDP and the Citigroup procedure cannot project dollar GDP.

exchange rates) by a whopping 19 percentage points and by 15 percentage points at PPP exchange rates (table 4.3). China's share of world GDP (in PPP dollars) will increase from 17 percent in 2010 to 24 percent in 2030, and India's share will increase from 5 to 10 percent. China's economy (in PPP dollars) will be more than twice that of the United States by 2030. Measured in PPP terms, the Rest, which account for half of world GDP today, will account for about 67 percent by 2030.

In incremental terms, the shift in the world economy will be even more dramatic: 68 percent of the increase in world GDP at market exchange rates between 2010 and 2030 will emanate in the emerging and developing world; the comparable figure in PPP terms will be about 79 percent. In other words, the dynamo for the world economy will be what are today the poorer parts of the world.

According to table 4.4, which shows the relative ranking of the world's largest industrial and emerging-market countries, China overtook the United States in 2010 if GDP is measured in PPP terms. By 2013, India will overtake Japan to become the world's third largest economy. Brazil will become the world's fifth-largest economy by 2012. In other words, before the middle of this decade three of the world's six largest economies will be what are now considered emerging-market countries. And other emerging-market countries—especially Indonesia and Mexico—will start climbing up the ranks of the world's largest economies, with Indonesia overtaking all the industrial economies except the United States and Japan.

Table 4.5 depicts the same relative rankings but based on the dollar value of GDP. By 2030, China and India will become the world's second and third

Box 4.2 Is China already number one?

The projections in this book involve applying growth projections for 2010–30 to levels of GDP in the base year (2010).[1] Data for this base year are from the October 2010 edition of the International Monetary Fund's *World Economic Outlook*. That publication contains the IMF's own purchasing power parity (PPP)–based estimates for 2010, but they are problematic in two important respects for China. First, the GDP number for 2005, which is the starting point for all the PPP-based calculations, is understated; and second, the price increases between 2005 and 2010 are overstated, which further reduces the GDP number for 2010.

When the World Bank published its PPP-adjusted estimates for GDP per capita based on disaggregated data collected by the International Comparison Program (ICP) in 2005, a number of commentators expressed doubts about them, especially because the estimates for China ($4,091 per capita) and India ($2,126) were revised downward by 40 percent relative to the pre-ICP estimates. The IMF uses this lower number for 2005 (in part because the World Bank does so).

Surjit Bhalla (2008) argued that the number for China was unrealistic. Suppose, he said, the revised number was extrapolated backward, using China's growth rate between 1952 and 2004 of 5.52 percent. It would imply a level of GDP per capita in 1952 of $153 (in 1985 prices) that was well below the threshold value of $250 that Pritchett (1997) has argued is the minimum required for subsistence. In Bhalla's evocative description, the revisions meant that there were few living Chinese in 1952.

The validity of doing this backward extrapolation is questionable because, as pointed out by Johnson et al. (2009), purchasing power parity growth rates and market exchange rate based growth rates are not identical and cannot be used interchangeably.

Nevertheless, Bhalla's point is correct, albeit for slightly different reasons, as argued by Angus Deaton and Alan Heston (2010). They suggest that China's PPP GDP was underestimated (by the ICP and by the World Bank) because of the urban bias of the price sampling in ICP 2005. Data on prices were collected for 11 cities and their surroundings, but no rural prices—which are typically substantially below urban prices—were collected (or rather allowed to be collected by the Chinese authorities).

Version 7 of the Penn World Tables released in February 2011 has corrected these biases, which results in an upward revision for China's PPP-based GDP by about 27 percent and for India by about 13 percent for 2005.[2] The projections in this book use the new Penn World Table corrections as the starting point for computing new estimates for PPP-based GDP and GDP per capita.

A second correction relates to developments between 2005 and 2010. For this period, if the IMF data are taken at face value, they suggest an increase in the real

Box 4.2 Is China already number one? *(continued)*

cost of living in China relative to that in the United States (which is equivalent to a real appreciation of the Chinese currency) of about 35 percent. This seems implausible because three alternative ways of assessing currency changes point to a much smaller appreciation.

First, most real exchange rate indices computed for China (e.g., those of JP Morgan and the Bank for International Settlements) point to an appreciation during this period of between 12 and 20 percent. Analysis by the IMF in its 2010 Article IV consultation report for China shows that productivity differentials between China and its trading partners, and between tradable and nontradable sectors within China, would also imply an appreciation of the renminbi of no more than 10 to 15 percent.

Third, one could ask what currency appreciation would be implied for China if it behaved like the average country. Here, Martin Ravallion's (2010) work is important. It is the only study that estimates the effect of market-exchange-rate-based GDP per capita growth on the changes in the price levels (the real exchange rate) across two different ICP reports (those in 1996 and 2005). In effect, this is the first accurate estimate of the dynamic Balassa-Samuelson effect, the changes over time within a country of the real exchange rate in response to growth. The other important point emerging from Ravallion's work is that, on average, estimating price level changes across time using relative inflation differentials—as the IMF appears to do—is distinctly inferior to a procedure using per capita growth differentials. Using the latter also yields estimates of about 10 to 15 percent for Chinese currency appreciation.

If a currency appreciates, the movement is akin to an increase in the average cost of living. So, taking 15 percent as the best estimate of the currency appreciation, rather than the 35 percent estimated by the IMF, requires adjusting China's 2010 GDP upward by 20 percent (because the increase in the cost of living has been overstated by 20 percent). To be conservative, the analysis here has not adjusted GDP up by the entire 20 percent.[3]

These two adjustments increase China's GDP from the current estimate of $10.1 trillion to $14.8 trillion (an increase of 47 percent, of which 27 percent is due to the revision in the 2005 estimate, with the rest due to smaller-than-assumed increases in the cost of living between 2005 and 2010). This $14.8 trillion figure exceeds US GDP of $14.6 trillion. It must be emphasized, of course, that the difference is small enough to be within the margin of error.

Applying the same adjustments to GDP per capita increases the estimate for China from $7,518 (the IMF estimate) to $11,047. The GDP per capita (the average

(box continues next page)

largest countries, so using this measure, China does not displace the United States as the world's largest economy. Brazil also surpasses a number of G-7 countries but will remain behind the United States, Japan, and Germany.

Finally, it is worth noting that GDP per capita growth rates for China and India are lower at PPP-based exchange rates than at market-based rates; the differences are about 1 percent per year. This highlights the importance of incorporating PPP factors into long-run GDP projections. Put differently, if PPP factors are ignored, there is the risk of overstating the improvements in real living standards: Over a 20-year period, the overestimate can be as much as 27 percent for a country such as India. In other words, if one does not take account of the PPP effects over time, the conclusions for the shift in economic weight would be even more dramatic than suggested above.

The shifting pattern of economic weight in the future is obviously of considerable interest. But the shifts in trade and trading patterns are of interest as well, particularly in terms of economics. If trade is indeed a source of dynamism, where will the future growth poles be? And what could be the implications for the role of currencies in the future? Shifts in trade are also of interest for politics and international political institutions: How should weight and influence be rearranged to reflect new trading power and trading relationships?

From an analytical perspective, it is important to note that the shifts in trade are likely to be a direct consequence of the shifts in the economy via the "gravity" effect (see appendix 4B for details). The results are shown in table 4.6 for selected countries and in table 4.7 for selected regions and trading groups.

If gravity exerts its expected force, the effects will be striking, indeed even more striking than the effects on GDP. China, which accounted for 9.8 percent of world trade in goods in 2010, will account for nearly 15 percent in 2030. Its trade will be more than twice that of the United States and more than nearly four times that of Germany, both of which will see a decline in their shares of

Table 4.3 Economic weight in 2010 and 2030 under the convergence scenario

Country/group	2010				2030				Change from 2010 to 2030	
	GDP per capita (PPP dollars)	GDP (billions of dollars)	Share of world GDP (dollars, percent)	Share of world GDP (PPP dollars, percent)	GDP per capita (PPP dollars)	GDP (billions of dollars)	Share of world GDP (dollars, percent)	Share of world GDP (PPP dollars, percent)	Dynamism: Share of incremental GDP (dollars, percent)	Dynamism: Share of incremental GDP (PPP dollars, percent)
United States	47,284	14,658	23.5	16.8	66,519	24,019	17.2	11.8	12.1	8.0
EU-27	32,615	16,282	26.1	18.7	47,683	24,195	17.3	11.9	10.2	6.8
Japan	42,820	5,459	8.7	6.3	62,374	7,352	5.3	3.6	2.4	1.6
China	11,303	5,878	9.4	17.4	32,980	22,440	16.1	23.5	21.4	28.0
India	3,795	1,538	2.5	5.3	13,373	8,422	6.0	9.8	8.9	13.1
Korea	23,961	1,007	1.6	1.3	46,753	2,172	1.6	1.1	1.5	1.0
Africa	2,633	1,437	2.3	2.8	7,425	8,075	5.8	5.0	8.6	6.7
Brazil	16,684	2,090	3.3	3.7	30,874	4,624	3.3	3.3	3.3	2.9
Indonesia	7,890	707	1.1	2.1	23,022	2,917	2.1	3.1	2.9	3.8
Russia	23,803	1,465	2.3	3.8	35,782	2,058	1.5	2.3	0.8	1.1
Total	**12,844**	**62,452**	**100.0**	**100.0**	**24,963**	**139,766**	**100.0**	**100.0**	**100.0**	**100.0**
BRICs (Brazil, Russia, India, and China)	9,112	10,972	17.6	30.2	24,063	37,544	26.9	38.7	34.4	45.1
Populous countries (Brazil, India, Indonesia, and China)	8,325	10,213	16.4	28.5	23,539	38,402	27.5	39.6	36.5	47.8
Asia excluding Japan	7,417	11,129	17.8	31.5	21,376	45,234	32.4	45.7	44.1	56.4
Emerging and developing countries	7,906	21,355	34.2	52.5	19,369	74,060	53.0	67.4	68.2	78.6

Notes: Estimate in "dollars" refers to valuation based on market exchange rates. Estimate in "PPP dollars" refers to valuation based on purchasing power parity exchange rates.

Sources: IMF, *World Economic Outlook*; and author's calculations.

Table 4.4 Relative rankings of countries under the convergence scenario with GDP measured in purchasing power parity dollars

Country	United States	Japan	Germany	France	United Kingdom	Italy
China	2010	b	b	b	b	b
India	—	2013	b	b	b	b
Brazil	—	—	2012	b	b	b
Russia	—	—	b	b	b	b
Indonesia	—	—	2025	2019	2015	2010
Pakistan	—	—	—	—	—	—
Nigeria	—	—	—	—	—	—
Bangladesh	—	—	—	—	—	—
Mexico	—	—	—	—	2029	2026
Korea	—	—	—	—	—	—

Notes: Year in a given cell is the year when the country in that row overtakes the country in that column in terms of economic size.

"b" denotes that the overtaking occurred before 2010; — denotes that overtaking will not occur by 2030.

Sources: IMF, *World Economic Outlook;* and author's calculations.

Table 4.5 Relative rankings of countries under the convergence scenario with GDP measured in dollars

Country	United States	Japan	Germany	France	United Kingdom	Italy
China	—	2010	b	b	b	b
India	—	2029	2022	2018	2016	2015
Brazil	—	—	—	2021	2014	2010
Russia	—	—	—	—	—	—
Indonesia	—	—	—	—	—	—
Pakistan	—	—	—	—	—	—
Nigeria	—	—	—	—	—	—
Bangladesh	—	—	—	—	—	—
Mexico	—	—	—	—	—	—
Korea	—	—	—	—	—	—

Notes: Year in a given cell is the year when the country in that row overtakes the country in that column in terms of economic size.

"b" denotes that the overtaking occurred before 2010; — denotes that overtaking will not occur by 2030.

Sources: IMF, *World Economic Outlook;* and author's calculations.

Table 4.6   Share of world trade under the convergence scenario, selected countries, 2010 and 2030

Country	Trade (billions of dollars) 2010	2030	Growth rate (percent) 2010–30	Share in world trade (percent) 2010	2030	Trade to GDP (percent) 2010	2030
United States	3,224	5,827	3.0	10.6	7.3	22.0	24.3
Japan	1,460	2,586	2.9	4.8	3.2	26.8	35.2
China	2,972	11,972	7.2	9.8	15.0	50.6	53.4
India	539	3,907	10.4	1.8	4.9	35.1	46.4
Korea	892	2,617	5.5	2.9	3.3	88.5	120.5
Brazil	384	991	4.9	1.3	1.2	18.3	21.4
Indonesia	136	993	10.5	0.4	1.2	19.2	34.0
Russia	648	890	1.6	2.1	1.1	44.3	43.3
Germany	2,318	2,918	1.2	7.6	3.7	89.7	76.0
World	30,387	79,905	5.0	100.0	100.0	48.7	57.2

Source: Author's calculations.

Table 4.7   Exports between countries as a share of total world exports, 2008 and 2030

Country grouping	Exports (billions of dollars) 2008	2030	Growth rate (percent) 2008–30	Share in world exports (percent) 2008	2030
Transatlantic	7,911	11,001	1.5	2.3	0.9
EU-27 + EFTA	6,193	7,953	1.1	29.3	9.7
NAFTA	2,004	3,738	2.9	6.7	3.7
BRICs (Brazil, Russia, India, and China)	2,212	9,155	6.7	1.0	2.2
Populous countries (Brazil, India, Indonesia, and China)	1,889	9,340	7.5	0.8	2.6
Sub-Saharan Africa	314	2,485	9.9	0.2	1.4
All Asia	3,808	18,965	7.6	9.6	22.6
Asia excluding Japan	3,074	17,589	8.3	9.2	19.2
World	15,228	44,107	5.0	100.0	100.0

EFTA = European Free Trade Association; NAFTA = North American Free Trade Agreement

Source: IMF, *Direction of Trade Statistics.*

world trade. India will nearly triple its share of world trade, but starting from a low base of 1 percent.

One of the subtler implications of the gravity model is that trade between two dynamic countries will grow exponentially faster than trade between less dynamic ones because trade benefits from the gravity exerted by the income of *both* countries. This effect is reflected in table 4.7. The share of intra-European trade, which comprised about 29 percent of world trade in 2008, will decline to about 10 percent in 2030. In contrast intra-Asian trade, which today is about a third of intra-European trade, will surpass intra-European trade well before 2030. In other words, not only will the world's economic center of economic gravity shift to Asia, so too will the center of *trade,* with China as the focal point or even the hub.

With China having become the largest economy in PPP terms by 2010, and with it projected to become the overwhelmingly largest trader by a factor of three over its nearest competitor by 2030, the implications for the renminbi's status as a potential reserve currency could be strengthened, as discussed in detail in chapter 5.

Caveat

A number of doubts can be raised about these projections. It could be argued that the collective precrisis performance of emerging-market and developing countries was an aberration based on a favorable external economic environment marked by three special factors prior to the recent financial crisis: large flows of capital to the poorer countries; rapid growth in trade; and the ability of some poorer countries to run mercantilist policies entailing large current account surpluses, which required a willingness by some large countries such as the United States to run current account deficits. In a postcrisis world, cross-border flows of capital and trade could decline, and deficit countries might be less inclined to continue running deficits and sustaining global imbalances. In short, a weaker external economic environment would dent the growth prospects of the Rest, including the larger emerging-market countries.

There are two counters to this skepticism, however, one theoretical and one empirical. The theoretical view is that long-run growth over the horizons considered in this study—and particularly growth rates in the richer countries—is driven by policies in the countries themselves rather than in the external economic environment. As Rodrik (2009, 11) puts it:

> While slower growth in the advanced countries would be bad news, its implications on the developing world would be largely indirect. When rich nations grow more slowly (or not at all) the stock of knowledge and technology that is available to firms in poor countries is not reduced. The potential for productivity enhancement and catch-up remains fully in place. From an economic standpoint, the rate of growth of developing countries depends not on the speed at which rich countries grow, but on the difference between their and rich nations' income levels—that is, the 'convergence gap.' The former does affect the latter, but only slowly and over time.

Empirical support for the limited and declining impact of rich-country growth on poor-country growth can be found in Akin and Kose (2007). Fig-

Figure 4.4 Impact of OECD growth on non-OECD growth

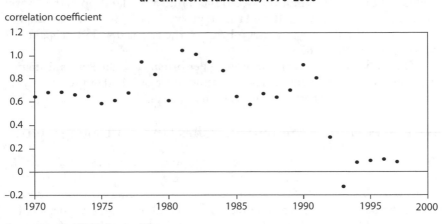

a. Penn World Table data, 1970–2000

correlation coefficient

Source: Penn World Table (version 6.3).

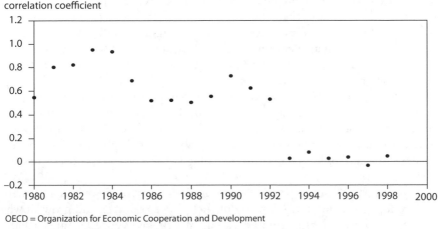

b. World Development Indicators data, 1980–2000

correlation coefficient

OECD = Organization for Economic Cooperation and Development

Source: World Bank, *World Development Indicators.*

ure 4.4 captures this changing impact, using data from both the Penn World Tables and the World Bank's *World Development Indicators* database. It plots the responsiveness of developing-country growth to growth in the rich countries.[12] Before the mid-to-late 1980s, a 1 percent change in rich-country growth

---

12. For every year since 1970 in the case of data from the Penn World Tables, and since 1980 for data from the *World Development Indicators,* the average growth of nonoil, nonsmall, non-OECD developing countries for that year and the nine subsequent years is regressed on average growth of OECD countries (so each regression is for a 10-year time period).

increased developing-country growth by between 0.8 and 1 percent; after that it dropped sharply to 0.6 in the early 1990s and to less than 0.2 in the late 1990s and early 2000s. Akin and Kose (2007) find a similar drop in the impact of growth in what they call the North on growth in the Emerging South: For the period 1973–85, the correlation between the two is 0.43 but drops to .07 for the period after 1985.[13,14]

On this view, whether the improving performance of the Rest is sustained depends less on growth in rich countries and more on whether the underlying determinants of that performance will remain in place.

Back to History: Economics Catches Up with Demographics

Recall that figure 4.3 shows that today's populous countries—Brazil, China, India, and Indonesia—have started to reconverge toward the rich world in terms of their standard of living. However, there is an alternative way of looking at the past and at the projections presented above. Table 4.8 depicts the share in world GDP (PPP-based) and share in population for these four countries individually and collectively from 1500–2010 and projected to 2030. For the period from 1500 to 1960, the table uses data compiled by Angus Maddison (2010). In 1500, demographic and economic weights for these countries were in balance: That is, their share of world population was identical to their share of world output. Since then, economic weight has fallen behind demographic weight at an accelerating pace, reaching a low in 1960, when, for these countries, the share in GDP was about a quarter of that in population. Since 1960, however, this process has started to reverse itself. Brazil has already attained parity between economics and demography and the projections presented here indicate that by just after 2030, three of the four most populous emerging-market economies will revert to the situation last seen in 1500, with near-parity once again between economics and demography. In other words, perhaps one can look forward to the "revenge of the populous" over the next 20 to 30 years.

During the postwar period large populations were viewed as a burden on development, and, indeed, many of these large countries did grow slowly (except for Brazil, which enjoyed rapid growth between 1950 and 1980). But since then, Brazil, China, India, and Indonesia have all grown despite,

---

13. The authors argue that one reason could be the changing nature of trade and growth in the North and South, leading to changing linkages and spillovers. The traditional framework was one of unidirectional dependence of the South on the North as a source of demand for goods and services. But the fact that the South has grown in economic and trading size, that its export base has diversified, and that it accounts faor a larger share of intraindustry trade means that the traditional patterns of dependence may have changed significantly.

14. A more recent World Bank study (Canuto and Guigale 2010) finds similar results, specifically that while output growth in developing and developed countries is correlated cyclically (i.e., over short periods), the growth rates of their respective trend outputs (i.e., over longer periods) have decoupled substantially since the mid-1990s and especially during the early 2000s.

Table 4.8 Demographic and economic weight of the populous poor, 1500–2030 (percent)

Country	Share of world GDP (measured in PPP dollars)					Share of world population		Ratio of economic to demographic weight				
	1500	1870	1960	2010	2030	1500	2030	1500	1870	1960	2010	2030
Brazil	0.2	0.6	2.0	3.7	3.3	0.2	2.6	70.6	82.0	84.2	129.9	123.7
India	24.4	12.2	3.9	5.3	9.8	25.1	18.2	97.1	61.3	27.2	29.5	53.6
Indonesia	2.4	1.7	1.2	2.1	3.1	2.4	3.4	99.8	66.5	36.5	61.4	92.2
China	24.9	17.1	5.2	17.4	23.5	23.5	17.8	105.9	60.9	23.9	88.0	132.1
Total	51.8	31.6	12.3	28.5	39.6	51.3	41.9	101.2	61.7	29.4	64.8	94.3

Note: "PPP dollars" refer to valuation based on purchasing power exchange rates.

Sources: Maddison (2010), United Nations, and author's calculations.

or perhaps because of, demography (Bloom and Canning 2001), related to their populations' favorable age structures in terms of the working young. With high growth, of course, population adds economic heft—at least from a comparative power perspective (more on this in the next chapter)—rather than economic drag. So convergence may have changed the way one looks at population and size. Except that this change in view once again represents a reversion to an older, long-held view about the important and positive effects of population, expressed by John Maynard Keynes (1919, 12–13):

> The great events of history are often due to secular changes in the growth of population and other fundamental economic causes, which escaping by their gradual character the notice of contemporary observers, are attributed to the follies of statesmen or the fanaticism of atheists . . . [The Russian revolution] may owe more to the deep influences of expanding numbers than to Lenin or to Nicholas; and the disruptive powers of excessive national fecundity may have played a greater part in bursting the bonds of convention than either the power of ideas or the errors of autocracy.

Conclusion

Subject to the important caveat that long-term projections can be highly uncertain, it seems that the world in 2030, especially if the forces of convergence and gravity take hold, will be unrecognizably different from the world of 2010 in economic and trade terms. The Rest will be in the ascendant. This ascendancy is highly likely and it is only the pace that is uncertain: In a world where convergence takes hold, the economic rise of the Rest will be faster; and in a world where things go wrong, these countries will still make strides but at a slower pace. The recent global financial crisis may end up accelerating some of these trends, but the crisis will not be the underlying cause for the shifts. They have been under way for some time. A key message is that the dominant West will have to start readjusting to the new reality of relative but not necessarily absolute decline. This, of course, will not just be true of groups of countries, but also individual ones. In particular, the economic dominance and hegemony of the United States will be under challenge from a rising China.

Appendix 4A
Projecting GDP Growth Based on Purchasing Power Parity and Market Exchange Rates

Per capita GDP growth (PPP-based) is first projected for countries in the convergence scenario according to the following simple formula:

Per capita growth$_i^{2010-30}$ = γ (Log per capita (PPP) GDP$_i$ ^{2010} – Log per capita (PPP) GDP$_{US}^{2010}$)

This equation says that the poorer the country is relative to the United States in 2010, the faster its growth rate per capita will be between 2010 and 2030. And the pace of this growth, which determines how fast a country will catch up to US standards of living, is determined by γ, the convergence coefficient. Based on historical experience, I vary this value across countries, with larger values for countries that have sustained growth for a longer period of time.

Note that a convergence framework by definition yields a growth projection that is in PPP terms (because the right hand side variables in the formula above are in PPP terms). In order to derive growth at market exchange rates, I make use of the dynamic Penn effect: namely, that for any developing country over time, the prices of nontradables will rise so that improvements in living standards (compared with other countries) will be slower than conveyed by the growth in the economy when measured in dollar terms.

For industrial countries, I assume that there is no dynamic Penn effect, so growth in constant dollar and PPP terms are identical. For other countries, I take the price level (P_i) of real GDP in 2010 (which is the ratio of GDP at constant and PPP prices). This price level is really the inverse of the real exchange rate.

Now the cross-sectional Balassa-Samuelson effect is estimated as:

$$\text{Log } P_i = \alpha (\text{Log } Y_i - \text{Log } Y_{us}), \tag{4A.1}$$

I estimate this equation using data for 2005 because that is the year for which the disaggregated prices are collected under the International Comparison Program (ICP), and hence the year for which GDP and price level measurements are most accurate. I obtain a value of α of 0.212.

Rewriting equation 4A.1 in terms of changes yields:

$$\Delta \text{ Log } P_i = \alpha (\Delta \text{ Log } Y_i - \Delta \text{ Log } Y_{us}), \tag{4A.2}$$

where Y_i is a country's per capita GDP measured in dollar or market-exchange-rate terms and Y_{us} is the per capita GDP of the reference country, namely the United States.

I also know by definition that the price level of GDP is the ratio of GDP at market rates to that in PPP terms. Thus,

$$P_i = Y_i / Y_i^{PPP}, \tag{4A.3}$$

so that

$$\Delta \text{ Log } P_i = \Delta \text{ Log } Y_i - \Delta \text{ Log } Y_i^{PPP}. \tag{4A.4}$$

I am interested in finding Δ Log Y_i, the growth rate of per capita GDP in dollar terms. Combining equations (4A.2) and (4A.4) yields:

$$\Delta \text{ Log } Y_i = (- \alpha \, \Delta \text{ Log } Y_{us} + \Delta \text{ Log } Y_i^{PPP})/(1 - \alpha). \tag{4A.5}$$

I have an estimate for α, I have projected the per capita PPP GDP growth rates (Δ Log Y_i^{PPP}), and for the United States, the growth rate of per capita GDP (Δ Log Y_{us}) is the same in dollar and PPP terms. Hence I can calculate Δ Log Y_i.

A final point worth noting relates to the difference between the PPP and dollar-based growth rates. Combining equations (4A.2) and (4A.4) and re-grouping differently yields:

$$\Delta \text{ Log } Y_i - \Delta \text{ Log } Y_i^{PPP} = \alpha \, (\Delta \text{ Log } Y_i - \Delta \text{ Log } Y_{us}). \tag{4A.6}$$

Equation (4A.6) illustrates that the dollar GDP growth rate will exceed the PPP growth rate. But the magnitude of the difference will relate to the difference between a country's growth rate and that of the United States. Convergence implies that this difference will be greater the poorer the country is to begin with. Hence, the difference between the PPP and dollar growth rate will be greater for poorer countries.

Appendix 4B
Trade Projections Based on the Gravity Model

Just as the force between two objects in physics depends on the product of their masses and the distance between them, so trade between two countries is thought to depend on their economic mass (GDP) and all the frictions affecting trade, which are typically proxied by distance.[15] As noted in the text, the theoretical foundations of the gravity model have been solidified in recent years and its empirical applicability has been robustly demonstrated. This model is the basis for projecting trade going forward.

I take the GDP projections shown in table 4.2 as the raw data. Bilateral trade data for the most recent period (2008) are compiled from the IMF's *Direction of Trade Statistics*.

The basic gravity equation is:

$$T_{ij} = (Y_i Y_j)^\alpha \times (D_{ij})^\beta, \tag{4B.1}$$

where T_{ij} is the trade between two countries i and j; Y_i and Y_j their respective incomes (not per capita incomes and not income measured in PPP dollars); and D_{ij} is the distance between them, which is a proxy for all the costs (the "frictions") associated with trade.

Taking logs yields:

$$\text{Log } T_{ij} = \alpha \left(\text{Log } Y_i + \text{Log } Y_j \right) + \beta \text{ Log } D_{ij.} \tag{4B.2}$$

Now, to project T_{ij} I need to project the Y's only (assuming that all the frictions that affect trade will not change significantly over the next 20 years).[16] Every bilateral trade pair is projected according to the following simple formula:

$$\Delta \log T_{ij} = \alpha \left(\Delta \log Y_i + \Delta \log Y_j \right), \tag{4B.3}$$

where the left-hand side is the growth in trade between two countries i and j; and the right-hand side expresses the sum of the growth rates of the incomes of the two countries. I need an estimate of the parameter alpha for these bilateral projections. The gravity model has consistently and robustly yielded a value of one for this parameter. Thus, the growth in bilateral trade is simply

---

15. The author thanks Alan Deardorff and Bill Cline for help in clarifying important issues relating to the use of the gravity model for projecting trade.

16. This is a restrictive assumption, but two distinct issues arise here. On the one hand, it is possible that technology reduces trade-related frictions for all trading pairs, in which case I will be understating the growth in trade for all countries. On the other hand, as Feyrer (2009) shows, technological changes will affect some trading pairs positively and others negatively. For example, if technological progress affects shipping costs, trade between countries reliant on shipping will increase while trade between countries that rely more on air transportation might actually decrease. These relative shifts are difficult to project over time.

the sum of the GDP growth rates (not GDP per capita) of the two countries involved in that trade.

However, I need to make one adjustment to equation (4B.3). This equation is usually estimated in the cross-section, that is, for a group of countries at a point in time. If I used it literally for projections across time, equation (4B.3) would yield the result that a country's trade-to-GDP share would grow without limit at the rate of (average) partner country growth. Deardorff (1997), the study that was the intellectual precursor to the full theoretical elaboration of the gravity model in Anderson and van Wincoop (2003), provided a simple theoretically consistent gravity equation that helps adapt equation (4B.3) so that it can be used for the purposes of projections.

In a simple frictionless world of gravity or even under a more realistic setting, trade between two countries is given by $T_{ij} = Y_i Y_j / Y_w$, where Y_w is aggregate world income. In more sophisticated formulations, more determinants of trade are added on the right-hand side but they all retain the term for world income in the denominator. When the gravity model is estimated as in equation (4B.2), the term Y_w is absorbed in the constant term. But this term cannot be ignored for projections purposes. Thus, a modified equation (4B.3) to reflect this term (and using a coefficient value of 1 one for the gravity coefficient) looks as follows:[17]

$$\Delta \log T_{ij} = \Delta \log Y_i + \Delta \log Y_j - \Delta \log Y_w. \qquad (4B.3)'$$

I then aggregate all the bilateral pairs to obtain trade projections not just for countries as a whole but also for selected groupings that might be of interest from an economic and policy perspective. Thus:

$$\Delta \log T_i = \Sigma^n_{j=1, \neq i} \Delta \log T_{ij} \qquad (4B.4)$$

where T_i is country i's aggregate trade and j refers to the n partner countries; and

$$\Delta \log T_r = \Sigma^k_{i=1, \neq j} \Sigma^k_{j=1, \neq i} \Delta \log T_{ij} \qquad (4B.5)$$

where T_r is intratrade within a regional grouping, comprising k countries.

---

17. Note that this adjustment to equation (4B.3) will not change relative growth rates of trade because all bilateral growth rates will be adjusted by the common factor of world growth rates.

5

Projecting Economic and Currency Dominance

The dollar will end up on history's ash heap, along with sterling, the guilder, florin, ducat, and if you chose to go way back, the Levantine bezant.

—Charles Kindleberger (1985)

Among all forms of mistake, prophecy is the most gratuitous.

—George Eliot, *Middlemarch: A Study of Provincial Life*

Having described and quantified the determinants of economic and currency dominance in chapters 2 and 3, respectively, and having projected the future evolution of these underlying determinants over the next 20 years in chapter 4, this chapter projects the course of future economic and currency dominance. In particular, the chapter examines the basis for the view that economic power might be shifting, as it did in the early 1900s. Back then, the United Kingdom was losing its imperial sway to the economic powerhouse of the United States. The question is whether a similar and imminent transition is under way from the United States toward China both in terms of economic dominance and reserve currency status.

The main conclusion is not just that there is indeed such a shift but that the shift away from the United States toward China is more imminent, more broad-based, and greater in magnitude than is currently anticipated or contemplated. Indeed, reasonable projections suggest that the relative economic dominance of China by 2030 could resemble that of the United Kingdom around 1870 or the United States in the aftermath of World War II. A similar conclusion emerges in relation to currency dominance: The renminbi could rival or even overtake the dollar as the primary reserve currency as soon as the early years of the next decade. Whether this happens will depend to a large extent on whether China maintains a reasonable amount of growth momentum.

Economic Dominance in the Future

Chapter 3 suggested that the index of economic dominance presented here appears to pass the smell test in terms of its ability to track the history of such dominance since 1870. Even Germany, Russia, and Japan make their brief appearance and quick retreats at the relevant points in time. The important next question is: What does the index reveal for the future leading to 2030?

Recall that chapter 4 generated projections under a "convergence" scenario for economic size and trade for 2030, so I have most of the numbers to project the index. How, though, does one project countries' future creditor/debtor positions, or more specifically, their future current account balances?

There is no theoretically satisfactory or empirically well-established basis for projecting this variable. In fact, as noted in Prasad, Rajan, and Subramanian (2008), actual net flows of capital in the last decade have been perverse in defying the theoretical prediction that they should flow from rich to poor countries. Instead of theory, I rely on the IMF's latest projections for current account positions for the period from 2010 to 2015. It is assumed that these numbers will persist through 2020. For the period beyond, I make an assumption that has the effect of understating China's possible economic dominance in the future.

It is assumed that for the period 2020–30, China will on average post a current account surplus that will be considerably reduced from today's levels. Specifically, in the second decade of the projection, it is assumed that China will get close to following Polonius's advice to "neither a borrower or lender be" to the rest of the world, and post an average surplus of 2 percent of GDP. This is based on one reading of Chinese policy intentions described in detail in chapter 4, namely that China will move toward internationalization of the renminbi. If this is correct, it would necessarily imply opening up China's capital account, reversing the repression of its financial sector, and hence an appreciation of the currency. With a currency that is forced to be flexible, it is likely that China's current account surplus will be considerably reduced over the 20-year horizon.[1]

Figures 5.1 and 5.2, which are based respectively on the IMF and reserve currency weighting schemes, suggest a dramatic possibility.[2] They portray a picture by 2030 not of relative American decline leading to a multipolar world,

---

1. Reserve currency status puts certain constraints on economic management. A reserve currency country will experience large and rising international demand for its assets as a store of value and as a means of payment. Satisfying this demand is incompatible with maintaining a closed capital account. But it would still be possible for the reserve currency country to run a current account surplus, since foreigners could obtain the currency needed to purchase its assets by selling their own assets (financial or physical) to the reserve currency country. In fact, the United Kingdom typically ran current account surpluses and accumulated net foreign assets during sterling dominance, as did the United States in the aftermath of World War II.

2. The two figures again correspond to the different weights assigned to income, trade, and finance.

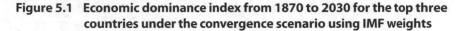

Figure 5.1   Economic dominance index from 1870 to 2030 for the top three countries under the convergence scenario using IMF weights

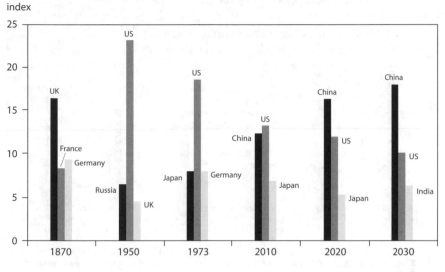

IMF = International Monetary Fund

Notes: This index is a weighted average of the share of a country in world GDP, trade, and in world net exports of capital. The index ranges from 0 to 100 percent (for creditors) but could assume negative values for net debtors. The weights for this figure are 0.6 for GDP (split equally between GDP measured at market and purchasing power parity exchange rates, respectively); 0.35 for trade; and 0.05 for net exports of capital.

Source: Author's calculations.

but of a near-unipolar world with Chinese economic hegemony. The first reason is that in 2030 economic size will have shifted dramatically in favor of China, which will account for nearly 20 percent of world GDP (average of PPP and market exchange rate shares) compared with 14.5 percent for the United States (table 5.1). Note that China's per capita GDP will be about half that of the United States by 2030 (in sharp contrast to the belief that China will remain extremely poor).

The second reason is that China, according to the gravity projections presented here, will account for 15 percent of world trade—twice that of the United States (table 5.2). And, by assumption, the projections have understated China's dominance from net creditor status (table 5.3). Appendix 5A shows that these results are robust to alternative weighting schemes.

Three points are worth underscoring. First, if these projections are reasonably accurate and if the index is plausible, Chinese ascendancy is much more imminent that currently believed. Indeed, on one measure of dominance (figure 5.2), China has already surpassed the United States, with the gap between the two rising rapidly over time.

Second, China's ascendancy will be much more broad-based than recognized. China will be larger than the United States and other countries in

**Figure 5.2   Economic dominance index from 1870 to 2030 for the top
three countries under the convergence scenario using
reserve currency weights**

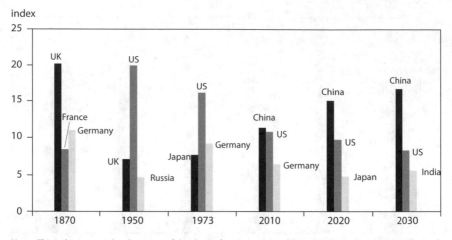

Notes: This index is a weighted average of the share of a country in world GDP, trade, and world net exports of
capital. The index ranges from 0 to 100 percent (for creditors) but could assume negative values for net debtors.
The weights for this figure are 0.6 for trade; 0.35 for GDP (split equally between GDP measured at market and
purchasing power parity exchange rates, respectively); and 0.05 for net exports of capital.

Source: Author's calculations.

**Table 5.1   UK, US, Chinese, and European shares of
world GDP measured in purchasing power
parity dollars, 1870–2030** (percent)

Year	United Kingdom	United States	China	EU-27
1870	9.0	8.9	17.1	
1913	8.2	18.9	8.8	
1919	6.9	18.2	7.7	
1929	5.6	18.8	6.1	
1939	6.7	19.2	6.3	
1950	6.5	27.3	4.6	
1973	4.2	22.1	4.6	
1990	4.0	24.0	4.7	27.83
2000	3.9	26.7	8.0	23.89
2010	3.1	20.1	13.4	22.37
2020	2.6	17.5	16.8	18.47
2030	2.2	14.5	19.8	14.59

Note: Starting in 1990, average share of GDP in PPP and current dollars.

Sources: Maddison (2001); IMF, *World Economic Outlook,* April 2011; and
author's and calculations.

Table 5.2   UK, US, Chinese, and European shares of world trade, 1870–2030 (percent)

Year	United Kingdom	United States	China	EU-27
1870	24.3	5.0	2.8	
1913	18.5	9.0	2.0	
1929	15.1	14.4	3.0	
1950	13.3	14.6	2.1	
1973	6.0	12.8	1.0	
1990	5.8	13.0	1.6	
2000	4.8	15.6	3.6	15.3
2010	2.7	10.6	9.8	9.3
2020	1.9	8.8	12.1	8.3
2030	1.4	7.3	15.0	7.0

Sources: Maddison (2001); World Bank, *World Development Indicators;* OECD Statistics; IMF, *World Economic Outlook,* April 2011; and author's calculations.

Table 5.3   UK, US, Chinese, and European shares of world net capital exports, 1870–2030 (percent)

Year	United Kingdom	United States	China	EU-27
1870	49.8	−0.7		
1900	40.2	10.2		
1913	55.8	0.6		
1929	22.6	35.6		
1939	−20.8	27.5		
1950	−62.8	34.0		
1973	0.9	17.1		
1980	−4.7	−0.2		
1990	−7.3	−52.6	0.0	
2000	−5.7	−50.4	4.1	
2010	−4.3	−50.8	17.5	−2.7
2020	−2.2	−31.6	40.1	−0.9
2030	−1.7	−22.3	17.5	−0.7

Sources: Maddison (2001); Taylor (2002); IMF, *World Economic Outlook,* April 2011; and author's calculations.

terms of economic size, substantially larger in terms of trade, and also likely dominant in finance (as a net supplier of capital). Put differently, this disparity between China and the rest of the world is quite robust to how I weight the different economic attributes in terms of their importance in determining power. The weighting scheme will matter little because on all the underlying attributes, China will be ahead of the United States (appendix 5A shows that the projection on dominance for 2030 is robust to different weighting schemes).[3]

Third, in terms of not only timing and scope but also magnitude, the gap between China and its closest competitor—the United States—could be far greater than currently supposed.[4] Joseph Nye's (2010, 2) invocation of the National Intelligence Council, which he cites as projecting that in 2025, "the U.S. will remain the preeminent power, but that American dominance will be much diminished" seems an unduly optimistic assessment of US economic prospects. The estimates here suggest that the gap between China and the United States will be similar to that between the United States and its rivals in the heyday of American hegemony in the mid-1970s (approaching the magnitude of American dominance circa 1950), and greater than that between the United Kingdom and its rivals during the halcyon days of empire.[5]

Is There a Role for Prosperity in Determining Dominance?

In the index of economic dominance, prosperity, as measured by a country's per capita GDP, does play a role in determining dominance. The variable measuring the share of a country in world GDP is nothing but the product of a country's per capita GDP multiplied by its population (expressed as a share of world GDP). So the higher a country's standard of living, the bigger its value on the index. But there is a subtler problem created by the index. A poor country with a very large population is treated similarly to a rich country with a smaller population.

Historically, the contenders for dominance—the United Kingdom, United States, Germany, France, and Japan—were all among the richest countries. Going forward, China contending for the dominance stakes creates problems for measurement because of the fundamental question of whether middle-income countries can in fact exercise dominance.

---

3. One possible counter is that technological dynamism and the capacity for innovation should be included in the determination of economic power, and doing so would make the United States look less vulnerable and threatened in the future. In other words, the ability of the United States to continually innovate and set the technology frontier will confer power beyond that captured in measures of GDP. There is some validity to this argument. However, here too the numbers do not necessarily run in favor of the United States. According to estimates produced by the National Science Foundation, the number of science and engineering undergraduates in China (about 912,000) was nearly twice that in the United States. Over time, this differential is only likely to grow. Even adjusting for quality differentials, the picture is not one of US dominance.

4. It bears emphasis that I might be understating China's economic dominance to the extent that I have been conservative about projecting its future creditor status and current account positions.

5. All these comparisons would shift even more in China's favor if I use PPP-based GDP in computing the index instead of including both measures of GDP.

Supposing one takes seriously the argument that prosperity is an independent source of dominance. How seriously would that affect or reverse the projection of Chinese economic dominance depicted in figures 5.1 and 5.2? One way to take account of prosperity is to correct for the bias in the measurement of GDP by adding per capita GDP as an independent and additional variable in the index of economic dominance. This raises complicated issues of measurement and weighting, but the bottom line is that prosperity would have to receive an unreasonably high weight relative to the other dominance determinants—aggregate resources, trade, and external finance—to reverse the basic projection of rising Chinese economic dominance. In effect, one would have to say that notwithstanding China being one-and-a-half times the size of the United States in terms of GDP and two-and-a-half times larger in terms of trade, and being a net creditor to the United States while the latter is a net debtor, the simple fact of China being only half as rich as the United States would preclude it from being dominant. Whether a country can be a "premature" power, as Martin Wolf has dubbed China, is discussed in greater detail in the next chapter.

Europe?

The projections have thus far not considered Europe as a potential candidate for dominance. It is true that on trade policy, Europe (or strictly speaking the EU-27) can be considered a single entity because policy is decided centrally. On monetary and currency policy, the euro area countries, with a common European Central Bank, can also be considered a single entity (as they are in the discussion of currency dominance below). And in response to the recent financial crises, greater European-level authority has been instituted in relation to financial and economic crisis resolution. But on financial sector, fiscal, and political issues, Europe is still a sort of halfway house, with decisions taken both at national and European levels. Europe is yet to demonstrate that it is a fully integrated political entity with clear authority for key decisions. Henry Kissinger's famous question—"To whom should the telephone call be made in Europe in the event of a political or security crisis?"—remains unanswered.

The recent crisis in Europe has raised questions about the optimality of a common currency for the entire euro area, hinting at the possibility of a two-speed Europe between the richer northern core and the poorer southern periphery. But the predominant impulse seems to be one in favor of deeper integration and greater centralization of economic and political authority within Europe. At least the possibility that this impulse will be translated into greater centralization in the future cannot be ruled out. Accordingly, the projections here of economic dominance for the next 20 years consider Europe (or rather the EU-27) as a single entity capable of wielding economic dominance.

How does Europe as a single entity fare on the index of dominance in the future? Figures 5.3 and 5.4 plot the index for China, Europe, and the United States between 2010 and 2030. The EU-27, but not the current euro area, ranks

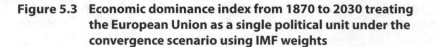

Figure 5.3   Economic dominance index from 1870 to 2030 treating the European Union as a single political unit under the convergence scenario using IMF weights

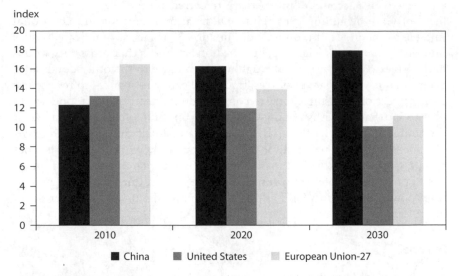

IMF = International Monetary Fund

Notes: This index is a weighted average of the share of a country in world GDP, trade, and in world net exports of capital. The index ranges from 0 to 100 percent (for creditors) but could assume negative values for net debtors. The weights for this figure are 0.6 for GDP (split equally between GDP measured at market and purchasing power parity exchange rates, respectively); 0.35 for trade; and 0.05 for net exports of capital. An important point is that when Europe is considered as one unit, its trade flows refer to those with the rest of the world, that is, excluding intra-EU flows.

Source: Author's calculations.

slightly higher than the United States on the index. The European Union and the United States are projected to account for broadly similar shares of world GDP and trade (extraregional trade in the case of the European Union) and it is only because the United States is projected to be a slightly larger net debtor to the world that their indexes differ. The bigger point though is that both the United States and the European Union would remain substantially less dominant than China by 2030.

The Future of the Dollar and the Renminbi

What about currency dominance? This section draws on the analysis in chapter 3 to project the future in terms of the magnitudes and timing of any transition between the dollar and the renminbi. That analysis suggested that economic dominance in a broad sense (comprising GDP, trade and net creditor status) is the key determinant of reserve currency status but that there is persistence so that reserve currency shifts occur after those in broader economic dominance.

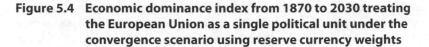

Figure 5.4   Economic dominance index from 1870 to 2030 treating the European Union as a single political unit under the convergence scenario using reserve currency weights

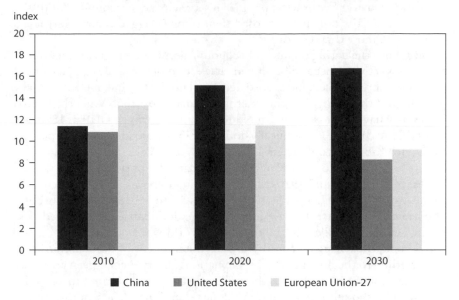

Notes: This index is a weighted average of the share of a country in world GDP, trade, and in world net exports of capital. The index ranges from 0 to 100 percent (for creditors) but could assume negative values for net debtors. The weights for this figure are 0.6 for GDP (split equally between GDP measured at market and purchasing power parity exchange rates, respectively); 0.35 for trade; and 0.05 for net exports of capital. An important point is that when Europe is considered as one unit, its trade flows refer to those with the rest of the world, that is, excluding intra-EU flows.

Source: Author's calculations.

But how long are these lags? History provides some clues. In what follows, I will use the projections of future economic dominance, apply the lags between economic and currency dominance from history, and thereby project the timing of future currency dominance.[6]

The history of reserve currencies shows that there are in fact two transitions: the rise of a currency from anonymity to being the dominant reserve currency status, and the demise of a once-dominant reserve currency. Persistence tends to delay both transitions: A new currency becomes the reserve currency after the rise to ascendancy of the economy of that currency, and a currency remains a reserve currency, even if not the dominant one, well after the economy of that country declines. As Paul Krugman (1992, p. 1973) puts it: "The impressive fact here is surely the inertia; sterling remained the first-ranked currency for half a century after Britain had ceased to be the first-ranked economic power."

---

6. Appendix 3A in chapter 3 elaborates on the procedure for projecting currency dominance.

But persistence in relation to the first transition seems to have been over-stated. The conventional view on persistence is based on comparing the period when the United States became the largest economy (in the early 1870s) and the period when it became the premier reserve currency (around World War II). The rise of the dollar is supposed then to have lagged the rise of the US economy by more than 60 years.

But both the dating points—for economic dominance and currency domi-nance, respectively—need to be altered. The econometric analysis in chapter 4 suggests that reserve currencies are determined not just by income but crucially by trade and the strength of the external financial position. While the United States may have overtaken the United Kingdom in terms of GDP in 1870, the United States became economically dominant in the broader sense, surpassing the United Kingdom, only around the end of World War I (figures 2.3 and 2.4). As late as 1929, the United Kingdom was a larger exporter than the United States, and until the mid-1920s, the United Kingdom was a larger net creditor to the world than the United States (see tables 5.1 to 5.3). So, for the purposes of currency dominance, the relevant economic dominance clock started tick-ing in favor of the dollar around the end of World War I not 1870.

Second, the dating of World War II as the moment of durable transition from sterling to the dollar is also problematic. As Barry Eichengreen and Marc Flandreau (2008) have argued, the dollar first eclipsed sterling in the mid-1920s, and although sterling and the dollar shared near equal status during the interwar years, the persistence of sterling during this period was driven to some considerable extent by the politics of the United Kingdom as a colonial power. In 1932 at the Ottawa Conference, preferential trading between Britain and its colonies and dominions received fresh impetus, and toward the end of the 1930s, the sterling area was created. Both these politically-driven develop-ments played a role in prolonging sterling's international use.

In fact, if one looks at evidence for the demand for dollars from interna-tional private sources, it appears that the dollar not only overtook sterling in the early 1920s (as Eichengreen and Flandreau point out) but retained that status in the inter-war years. Figure 5.5, based on data from Reinhart (2010), plots the share of sterling relative to the share of dollars in cumulative issu-ance of international bonds by Argentina, Brazil, and Chile, three countries that were actively raising money internationally. The figure shows that prior to World War I, nearly all issuance was in sterling. Thereafter, an overwhelm-ing share was in dollars.

Thus, correcting the relevant dates, the lag between the rise to economic dominance of the United States (the end of World War I) and the establish-ment of the dollar as the premier reserve currency was considerably less than the 60-plus years conventionally believed and closer to 5 to 10 years (from about 1919 to the mid-to-late 1920s).

Let us apply this to the current situation. These facts and the implications for the possible timeline of a future handover based on the historical experi-ence are depicted in figure 5.6.

Figure 5.5 Share of sterling relative to dollars in bond issuance by Argentina, Brazil, and Chile, 1870–1939

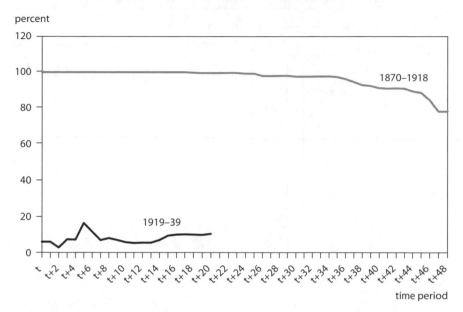

percent

Note: Annual bonds issued are converted to dollars and deflated by the US consumer price index. These annual values are added for all three countries. For the top line, bond issuance is cumulated beginning in 1870. For the bottom line, cumulation begins in 1919. The plot shows that share of sterling-denominated bonds in total (sterling- and dollar-denominated) bonds, where for each year both the numerator and denominator are cumulative amounts.

Source: Reinhart (2010).

Looking at the index of economic dominance that is based on using reserve currency weights, one finds that the index for China surpassed that of the United States in 2010 (figure 5.2). Therefore, unless some extraneous noneconomic factor intervenes (like it did for the sterling area), history suggests that the renminbi could be in a position to rival the dollar within the next ten years. If this sounds implausible, it is worth adding that the differential between the index of dominance of China and the United States in 2020 will be similar to, or even slightly greater than that between the United States and the United Kingdom in the mid-1920s, when dollar eclipsed sterling. Of course, there is considerable uncertainty surrounding all these calculations. But what they hint at is the possibility of a more accelerated rise of the renminbi, and a possible eclipsing of the dollar as the premier reserve currency.[7]

---

7. There is an alternative way for projecting future currency shares described in the appendix to chapter 3. This method suggests that, the share of dollars and euros in overall currency holdings will each decline by about 20 to 25 percentage points in 2030. Since, these declines will have to be mirrored in increases in the shares of other currencies, and since the renminbi is likely to be the main candidate, one could indirectly project that the share of the renminbi will rise to about 40 to

Figure 5.6   History and possible timeline of future reserve currency transition, 1870–2022

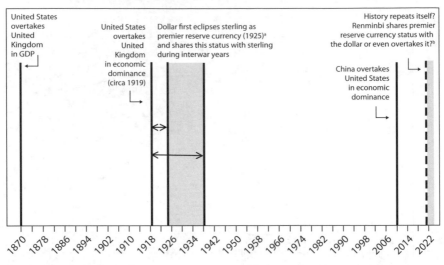

a. The difference in the economic index between the United States and the United Kingdom is approximately 5 to 8 percentage points in 1929.
b. The difference in economic dominance index between China and the United States is approximately 5 to 7 percentage points in 2020.

Sources: Eichengreen and Flandereau (2008); Lindert (1969); Kennedy (1989); Triffin (1961); and International Monetary Fund, Currency Composition of Official Foreign Exchange Reserves (IMF COFER) database.

Of course, there is one key difference between the possible handover today and the sterling-to-dollar handover. At its ascendancy, the United States had an open capital account, whereas China's is closed, its financial markets are still rudimentary judged against the requirements of a reserve currency in today's world of ultra-sophisticated financial markets, and the renminbi less convertible. This would delay the transition beyond the 5 to 10 years suggested by history. There is also the bigger question of whether a nondemocratic country can inspire the basic trust in rule of law that might be necessary for spreading internationalization of a currency.

The key finding that trade is a significant determinant of reserve currency status combined with China's growing trade dominance portend strongly for the yuan. And it is likely that the route to renminbi internationalization will be via its increasing use as a currency within Asia because trade links between China and Asia are increasing especially rapidly as suggested by the trade projections in chapter 4. Rising trade will then increase the advantage of using

50 percentage points (from virtually zero today). The share of the dollar will decline to about 40 percent, rendering the renminbi the world's premier reserve currency by 2030. This method yields projections that are not very different from the method described in the text.

the renminbi in Asia, which might engender policy changes such as Asian countries linking their exchange rates to the renminbi, which would further increase the use of the renminbi and so on. Thus, it looks likely that the road to renminbi internationalization is likely to occur via renminbi regionalization within Asia.

The historical experience of the other transition—from dominance to demise of sterling—is also instructive. On the one hand, the handover was difficult for the United States for reasons of history, namely the inheritance of the sterling area from the era of empire. This inheritance became difficult to eliminate because of the weakness of the UK economy. Any move on the part of holders to diversify out of sterling balances raised the prospect of devaluation (because the United Kingdom did not have enough dollars as reserves to meet the diversification demands), which caused problems for the British government (Schenk 2010a).

On the other hand, the United Kingdom and United States were allies, and there was a conscious and concerted effort by governments to minimize the costs of the transition to the United Kingdom and internationally (Schenk 2010a). These included lines of credit extended by other central banks to the United Kingdom to minimize the impact of any move away from sterling.

Today, the environment is quite different. There would likely be less cooperation between the governments of the United States and China if there were a similar need to manage the transition. On the other hand, the scale of private flows today so overwhelms official flows that transitions are likely to be endogenous and market-driven, with governments, individually or collectively, less able to exert control or influence.

Before the eyebrows go up at the magnitudes and timing implied by either of these scenarios, one must be careful about their interpretation. These numbers are suggestive about the medium run and about the eventual impact of fundamentals, and they are conditional. Many policy changes will need to occur before these fundamentals can prevail.

Conditions

A prominent role for the renminbi as a reserve currency may still be a ways off. The key point is that the renminbi still remains inconvertible for many international transactions, which means that foreigners can only use it to purchase goods from China itself. There are restrictions on use of the renminbi for capital account transactions. Foreigners cannot easily buy Chinese assets, and Chinese citizens' access to foreign assets is also limited. Foreign central banks cannot use the renminbi to intervene in foreign exchange markets.

The heart of the problem, of course, is that China's current growth strategy—heavily reliant on export growth, which in turn is fostered by a competitive, even undervalued exchange rate—relies in part on a closed capital account, which is to say, on limiting the use of renminbi by foreigners and for international transactions.

Eichengreen (2009, 65) lists the prerequisites for use of the renminbi as an international reserve currency:

> Markets must first become more transparent. Banks must be commercialized. Supervision and regulation must be strengthened. Monetary and fiscal policies must be sound and stable, and the exchange rate must be made more flexible to accommodate a larger volume of capital flows. China, in other words, must first move away from a growth model of which bank lending and a pegged exchange rate have been central pillars.

Put differently, internationalization of the renminbi necessarily requires meeting the demands of foreigners for it: There must be a net flow of renminbi from China to the rest of the world via the current account (running deficits and hence reversing currency undervaluation) or the capital account (through convertibility). In short, there are many reasons to believe that China is far from attaining reserve currency status.

On the other hand, there is no mistaking China's plans, reflected above all in its actions.[8] It is seeking a dominant role for its currency and working gradually but consistently toward it.[9] The strategy toward internationalization of the renminbi might be described as typically Chinese in two respects. First, highly interventionist means are used. The opening is controlled, discretionary, and micromanaged, even if the ends are liberalizing. One might describe this aspect of the Chinese currency internationalization strategy as "interventionist opening," targeting transactions, countries, and companies rather than liberalizing across the board as some European countries did in the 1960s.

Second, there is an uncanny resemblance to the strategy adopted in trade, where islands of openness to trade and foreign direct investment were created in the form of special economic zones (SEZs): One might call this "liberalization via enclaves." Once the SEZ experiment was seen as successful, it was gradually extended to the rest of the economy. Similarly, China intends to use Hong Kong and Shanghai as islands where the experiment to open the capital account and internationalize the renminbi will be attempted. For example, Shanghai is slated to become an international financial center by 2020 and Hong Kong has always been more open to use of the renminbi. It is envisaged that these experiments will be gradually extended to the rest of the mainland.

---

8. China's latest five-year plan states the goal of expanding the international use of the renminbi and gradually realizing its convertibility. It also states the goal of supporting Hong Kong in becoming an offshore renminbi business center.

9. Statements by Xiaochuan Zhou, governor of the People's Bank of China, in favor of the SDR in late 2009 are now widely interpreted as an aberration and not as a signal of China's true intentions.

Consider the various actions already taken to internationalize China's renminbi, which are coming so fast and so furious that it is becoming difficult to keep up with them.

In 2009, China issued renminbi-denominated sovereign bonds amounting to RMB 6 billion to offshore investors in Hong Kong in a move to provide foreign investors with an attractive means by which to hold renminbi and to create an offshore market to set the benchmark "risk-free" interest rate for renminbi debt instruments, thereby paving the way for further issuance by mainland borrowers in the offshore bond market. And in April 2011, Singapore announced that transactions could be settled in renminbi, paving the way for further internationalization of the Chinese currency. As of this writing, gross bond issuance in renminbi is expected to reach between $180 billion to $230 billion in 2011, from virtually nothing just a few years ago.

There have been other actions as well. China has entered into a host of swap agreements with Argentina, Belarus, Iceland, Indonesia, Malaysia, Singapore, and South Korea (as well as Hong Kong). China is also reported to be considering a similar currency swap arrangement with Pakistan and Thailand, which would make the total currency swap amount to more than renminbi 800 billion. The currency swaps allow China to receive renminbi instead of dollars for its exports to those economies, thereby expanding the use of the renminbi as a settlement currency in its trade with the seven countries.

Recently, seeking to further liberalize the use of renminbi by foreign entities for settlement of transactions in China, the People's Bank of China enacted rules allowing foreign entities to open bank accounts that can be used to accept and make payments in renminbi. The Administrative Measures on Renminbi Bank Settlement Accounts Opened by Overseas Entities (Measures on Renminbi Accounts of Overseas Entities), which were enacted on September 29, 2010, establish rules nationwide for the administration and oversight of renminbi bank settlement accounts owned by overseas entities. By enabling foreign entities to accept and make payments in renminbi—rather than having to convert to a foreign currency—the new measures should make it somewhat easier and more efficient for foreign entities to do business in China.[10]

China has also explored with Brazil ways of using the renminbi in bilateral trade. The renminbi can already be used in selected cross-border trade (such as with its neighbors, like Mongolia, Vietnam, Cambodia, Nepal, and North Korea, and with the special administrative zones of Hong Kong and Macau) even if only for selected companies.

In sum, United States policymakers while not unaware of the big shifts that are likely to occur in the fundamental determinants of reserve currency

---

10. According to a *Financial Times* article (Kevin Brown, Robert Cookson, and Geoff Dyer, "Malaysian Bond Boost for Renminbi," September 19, 2010), Malaysia decided to hold renminbi bonds as part of its reserves. The news story also speculates that the transaction had accompanied or been followed by purchases by other Asian central banks.

status, are nevertheless overly sanguine in recognizing the competition, and its imminence, posed by the renminbi to the dollar. Applying the historical experience of broader economic dominance to today's situation, it appears that the renminbi could actually surpass the dollar towards the end of this decade or early part of the next decade The historical experience, properly analyzed and quantified, suggests that persistence in matters of reserve currency status is somewhat overstated: The rise of the dollar and its eclipsing of sterling as the primary reserve currency was quicker than recognized and would have been even quicker (relative to fundamentals) had politics and history not intervened: The empire-instigated sterling currency bloc created in the 1930s led to some considerable "involuntary" holding of sterling reserves by the British colonies.

The Renminbi When the Chips Are Down

Skeptics of these projections will concede that size and policies are important determinants of reserve currency status but would argue that the deepest determinant is confidence and trust in the government issuing the reserve currency, especially in hard times. Their telling question will be: In a crisis, when the chips are down, will investors feel secure that their money is safer in China than in the United States or at least safe enough against expropriation or nationalization by China's government?

Of course, broader political developments—especially Chinese political stability accompanied by transition toward greater democracy and freedoms—will be important in providing reassurance to investors. But there are grounds for believing that China, regardless of the political transition, is unlikely to act in a manner that should worry investors. These reasons are elaborated in greater detail in chapter 8. But the essential point is that China is demonstrating through its actions that it seeks reserve currency status for the renminbi not least because it offers policymakers the political exit from their current mercantilist strategy. Combined with a broader stake in openness, it seems unlikely that China would undermine tomorrow what it is working toward today.

Conclusion

In the last few years, the world has witnessed the subordination and near elimination of the G-7, the ascendancy of the G-20 (not to mention the quiet demise of the G-77, the group of developing countries). C. Fred Bergsten (2008) has argued that de facto world decision-making is located in a G-2, comprising the United States and China. Underlying economic trends suggest that one should not rule out the future possibility of a G-1, with that one not being the United States of America. China in solitary dominance is a possible, sobering, and not-too-distant reality.

Chinese economic dominance is more imminent and more broad-based—encompassing, output, trade, and currency—than is currently recognized.

China's economy will be larger than that of all its rivals and its trade could be nearly twice as that of the United States. By 2030, this dominance could resemble that of the United States in the 1970s and the United Kingdom around 1870. And this economic dominance will in turn elevate the renminbi to premier reserve currency status much sooner than currently expected.

Projections of Chinese economic and currency dominance are of course conditional. But what the numbers do suggest is that if—and it is not a small if—China's policy regime moves in the direction of liberalizing the use of its currency and opening and deepening its financial markets, the economic fundamentals are in place to sustain a rapid bolstering of the reserve currency status for the renminbi. Recall that these fundamentals include not just a large economy but levels of trade and an external financial position that resemble the United Kingdom at the peak of the British empire; and these levels of trade were never matched by the United States at the peak of its economic dominance.

These fundamentals—growth and trade—are largely China's to determine. As important is the fact that the other conditions for currency dominance—deep and liquid financial markets and greater political freedoms, which investors might view as critical during a crisis—are also China's to determine.

It is therefore also misleading, and symptomatic of the insular perception among some that the United States is an undislodgeable superpower, to think that the fate of the dollar or economic dominance more broadly is in the hands of the United States rather than China. Indeed, there might even be an asymmetry. Faltering US performance could hasten the transition away from the United States and dollar dominance. But strong performance may do little to arrest the move in China's favor of economic and currency dominance.

The funny thing about currency dominance, of course, is that it is not an unalloyed blessing. It might even be a poisoned chalice. Public professions of ambivalence about currency dominance notwithstanding, American policymakers, during Pax Americana, have not resisted drinking from this chalice. China is unlikely to do, or want to do, otherwise. China will drink and sooner than most think.

Appendix 5A
Robustness of the Index of Economic Dominance

Are the projections of economic dominance in this study driven by the choice of weights used for the three underlying determinants? I used two weighting schemes and found that the results do not change materially, but might there not be other weights that could produce significantly different results? There is a simple way of checking the robustness of the results.

To test the robustness to alternative weighting schemes, from my two weighting schemes I assign minimum weights on the three variables of .35 for GDP, 0.35 for trade, and .05 for net capital. I then find values of the index of economic dominance for all possible combinations of weights subject to the constraint that these minima be respected. The weights are allowed to change by increments of 0.01. I get 75 possible combinations of weights and express the resulting values of the indexes in the form of a range of possible values, going from +2 standard errors to –2 standard errors and traversing the mean (shown in the middle). This range is depicted for the two leading countries for 2030 in figure 5A.1.

The figure shows that the entire distribution of outcomes for China lies above that for the United States, suggesting that the index is robust to alternative weights assigned to the determinants of dominance. The intuition is simply that China outperforms the United States on all the underlying determinants—GDP, trade, and finance—so that weighting can affect the magnitude, but not in a way as to change the relative ranking of the two countries. Also, the figure shows that the mean difference in the indexes is about 10 percentage points.

Figure 5A.1 Robustness of economic dominance index to weighting, 2030

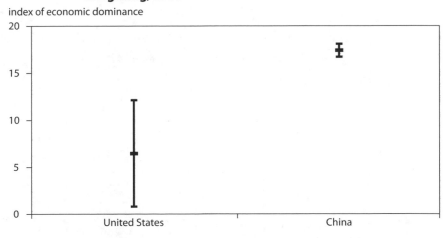

Sources: Author's calculations.

6

A Historical Perspective on China's Distinctive Dominance

The Way of Heaven holds good for you as us ... the Celestial Empire shares with others only its good things, such as rhubarb, tea and silk ... but [there is] a poisonous article manufactured by certain devilish persons subject to your rule who tempt the people of China to buy it.

—Governor Lin Zexu of Canton in a letter to Queen Victoria
in the run-up to the first opium war

If something resembling the projections in the previous chapter comes to pass, China's economic dominance will be assured. The question is: How will China compare with the United States and the United Kingdom in their rise to economic dominance? China will, of course, be distinctive in that its rise will occur under a nondemocratic political system, unlike the United States and the United Kingdom, where the franchise, although by no means universal, was constantly being extended during the period of their economic ascendancy. China's rise will also be distinctive in a number of economic dimensions.

This chapter makes a historical detour to make that comparison, highlighting in particular the distinctive nature of two paradoxes: first, China being a superpower while still not being amongst the richest countries; and second, China being highly open and highly mercantilist at the same time.

Precocious or Premature: Can a Not-the-Richest China Be Dominant?

Martin Wolf has used the term "premature superpower" to describe China and the uniqueness of its rise in the sense of wielding power despite being poor. But the projections in this book suggest that by 2030, China will not be so poor; indeed its per capita GDP (in PPP terms) will be more than half that of the United States, and certainly greater than the average per capita GDP in the world. China's economic dominance will still be unique, because historically, the dominant powers (the United Kingdom and United States) have been rich,

Table 6.1 UK, US, Chinese, and European GDP per capita, 1870, 1950, and 2030 (PPP dollars)

Year	United Kingdom	United States	China	EU-27
1870	3,190	2,445	530	
	3.67	2.81	0.61	
1950	6,939	9,561	448	
	3.29	4.53	0.21	
2030	48,888	66,519	32,980	47,683
	1.96	2.66	1.32	1.91

Notes: Measured in purchasing power parity (PPP) dollars (1990 prices for the 1870 and 1950 data and 2010 prices for the 2030 estimates). The multiples of the world average are in italics.

Source: Maddison (2010).

indeed amongst the richest relative to their competitors, when they have been dominant. Table 6.1 shows that the United States and the United Kingdom at their peaks had per capita GDPs that were more than three times the world average. In China's case that will not be so. But neither will it be a case of a poor country wielding power. China will be a middle-income or upper-middle-income country. So perhaps China's future economic dominance should more aptly be described as that of a "precocious" rather than "premature" superpower.

But this raises the question: Can a country be dominant even while not being among the richest countries?

History is clearly on the side of those who believe that dominance requires a high standard of living. But before accepting this proposition, it is worth delving deeper to ask why this might be the case. One can think of at least four reasons why dominance cannot be wielded by a poor country.

First, a poor country might be inwardly focused because the tasks of maintaining social stability and achieving a higher standard of living—which might be a precondition for social peace—are the government's major if not exclusive preoccupation. In this case, projecting power internationally will have to be subordinated to addressing more pressing domestic challenges. Internal fragility sits uneasily, or is just downright incompatible, with external dominance. As Thomas Friedman put it: "China is rich nationally but still dirt poor on a per capita basis and, therefore, will be compelled to remain focused inwardly and regionally."[1]

Second, a poor country might not be able to raise the resources—at least on a sustained basis—for the projection of power internationally. The classic example is military resources. These will have to be financed. But the poorer

---

1. Thomas Friedman, "Superbroke, Superfrugal, Superpower?" *New York Times*, September 4, 2010.

a country, the more difficult it might be to tax the people to raise resources. As Richard Cooper (2003) has noted, tax revenues generally rise with the level of development. Russia sustained military dominance for some time beyond its underlying economic potential, but eventually economics caught up with geopolitics. North Korea is a more extreme example of external power being incommensurate with internal stability and wealth. North Korea can be a nuisance, a country that can cause trouble, but hardly one that can exercise international dominance.

A third reason why a poor country cannot project dominance is that it may not have the "soft power" attributes—such as democracy, open society, and pluralistic values—for dominance. Put differently, the leadership that comes with dominance is only really possible if it inspires followership. And followership comes when the dominant country stands "for" something that commands universal or near-universal appeal.

The fourth reason, related to the previous attribute, is that only a rich country—which by definition is at the frontier of economic and technological possibilities—can be a fount or source of ideas, technology, institutions, and practices for others to follow and absorb. A poor country is less likely to be such a model worthy of emulation and an inspiration to follow.

Clearly dominance is inconsistent with being extremely poor, but if one reflects on these points, it is worth noting that with some exceptions, neither does dominance necessarily require being among the richest countries. There is, for example, no reason why internal cohesion, the ability to raise resources for external purposes, the possibility of being democratic, or possessing some emulation-worthy national narrative or values or ideals is inconsistent with being a middle-income power as China is likely to be by 2030.

Moreover, one knows, not from speculation but from recent experience, that China's current low per capita GDP is entirely consistent with different forms of the exercise of dominance. Chapter 1 described all the different ways China has been exercising power through its economic weight. So two possible conclusions suggest themselves. A form of dominance that naturally inspires followership and which might be necessary to create or build systems and institutions—as the United States did after World War II—might possibly elude China for some time, especially if it is unable to make the political transition. But other forms of dominance—to undermine, thwart, and above all inflict systemically negative externalities, undermining the spirit of the current open economic system—are already being exercised to some extent by a China at low levels of income. These manifestations will only grow as China becomes richer and attains a level of per capita GDP by 2030 that is half that of the United States.

China's Trade and Openness Outcomes in Historical Power Perspective

If something close to these trade projections—based in turn on the GDP projections—were to materialize, how distinctive would China's achievement be compared with its two economically dominant predecessors? One metric for comparison is a country's trade expressed as a ratio of the country's GDP, shown in column 1 of table 6.2. China's trade-to-GDP ratio in 2008 was about 57 percent, its export-to-GDP ratio was 32 percent, and its import-to-GDP ratio about 25 percent. China's trade ratios exceed by a large magnitude those of the United States and the United Kingdom (e.g., in 1975 the trade-to-GDP ratio for the United States was about 13 percent compared with 57 percent today for China).

But this comparison is not entirely valid because the nature of the relationship between trade and GDP has itself been changing over time: The ratio of global exports to GDP was about 4 percent in 1870 according to Maddison (2001) and 12 percent in 1960 and 33 percent in 2008 according to IMF data. China could be trading more just because every country today is trading more than in the past because transport and communications costs have fallen worldwide. The best way to do the comparison is to assess how much a country is trading relative to other countries at a given point in time (which takes account of the previous objection) and then compare the degrees of under and overtrading across time.[2] That is, we compare the degree of under/overtrading for the United Kingdom relative to other traders in 1870, United States in 1975, and China in 2008. The time periods chosen roughly correspond to the heyday of dominance for the United Kingdom and the United States.

But even in assessing how much a country trades relative to others we need to take account of the well-established regularity that small countries trade more than larger countries. This regularity derives from the fact that the economic and political costs of trading over longer distances across countries are greater than trading over shorter distances within a country (because of distance and trade barriers). If it is easier and cheaper to sell over short distances than over longer distances, more of GDP will be internally rather than externally traded. This is captured in the empirical regularity that a country's trade-to-GDP ratio is negatively correlated with size (Balassa and Noland 1989, Pritchett 1994). There is also the possibility that China is a large trader because poor countries, on average, trade more as a share of their GDP, especially if their economy is resource-based or relies on imports to satisfy a large portion of domestic needs.

Taking into account these two factors of size and level of development, how does China compare with the United States and the United Kingdom during their respective heydays? The results are presented in columns 2 to 4 of table 6.2. The margins of overtrading and undertrading for exports, imports, and total trade as well as their statistical significance are reported in columns 2 to 4 in table 6.2.

---

2. Instead of asking whether Roger Federer would have defeated Rod Laver in a direct contest, we ask how good each player was relative to his own contemporaries, say, by comparing how many Grand Slams each won. These Grand Slam victories then serve as the basis for comparison across time between Federer and Laver.

Table 6.2 Trade patterns of economically dominant powers in history

	Actual trade (percent of GDP)	Percent overtrading controlling for size[a]	Percent overtrading controlling for size and income level[a]	Percent overtrading controlling for size, income level, and oil-based economies[a]
United Kingdom, 1870 (sample = 26 countries)				
Exports	12.2	339.3***	84.0*	n.a.
United States, 1975 (sample = 121 countries)				
Exports	6.7	−16.5	−49.8***	−48.3***
Imports	6.5	−38.7***	−39.6***	−47.5***
Total trade (exports plus imports)	13.3	−29.7***	−45.3***	−47.5***
China, 2008 (sample = 136 countries)				
Exports	31.6	73.5***	67.7**	99.0***
Imports	24.9	56.3***	56.4***	39.5**
Total trade (exports plus imports)	56.5	70.7***	68.6***	74.1***

n.a. = not available

a. Negative value denotes undertrading. ***, **, and * denote statistical significance at the 1, 5, and 10 percent confidence levels, respectively. No asterisk denotes that overtrading/undertrading is not statistically significant.

Source: Maddison (2010); World Bank, *World Development Indicators*.

The United Kingdom was clearly a very significant exporter (column 2 suggests overtrading of about 340 percent). But it turns out that in the days of empire, unsurprisingly, richer countries traded more. Once the United Kingdom's income level is taken into account, the degree of overexporting shrinks significantly to about 84 percent.

In contrast, the United States in 1975 was a sizable undertrader in terms of exports, imports, and total trade. Columns 3 and 4 suggest that the United States undertraded by between 40 and 50 percent, with undertrading a little more pronounced on the import side than the export side. The United States, thus, has always been, in trade terms, an insular economic superpower.

China, in contrast, is even today a ferocious trader, with levels of trade much greater than typical for a country of its size and level of development. Specifically, China exports more than is warranted by its size and level of development by a factor of about 70 percent (column 3). In light of Chinese mercantilism and undervalued exchange rate policies over the last decade, this finding will come as no surprise.

But China also imports much more than a country of its size and level of development should. Overtrading on the import side amounts to about 55 percent, which is somewhat less than the overtrading on the export side but not by a substantial margin. As a result of its export and import performance, China turns out to be a large trader. This is the paradox of China being mercantilist but also highly open, as defined in terms of trade outcomes, not in terms of policy barriers to trade, which remain higher in China than in the industrial countries (a theme discussed further below).

Note the striking contrast between the United States and China as traders: The United States undertraded by about 50 percent and China overtrades by about 70 percent, a net difference of about 120 percent. Note too that these numbers involve comparing China in 2008, not yet at its peak as an economic and trade superpower, with the United States and the United Kingdom at their peaks. Over time, the contrast could become even more stark. Indeed, if China's growth remains strong, it may only strengthen its position as a hub in Asia, which will further sustain its trade momentum.

An open China could have important implications for the international system and prospects for trade cooperation, which will be discussed in chapters 8 and 9.

Chinese Mercantilism in Historical Perspective

Consider, first, history and the parallels between Chinese mercantilism today and its counterpart of the early 1800s. Then, like today, China was running large trade surpluses and accumulating reserves, not in the form of dollars but silver. Then, like today, the deficit country was agitated by the imbalance and the resulting outflow—which then took the form of silver—and threatened action. Unlike today, the action taken by the United Kingdom was effective and unconscionable. To redress the bilateral imbalance, the United Kingdom flooded the Chinese market with opium grown in India.

So successful was the policy that China's surplus turned into a deficit within a short period, the flow of silver was stopped, even reversed, and levels of opium addiction rose alarmingly. The resulting ban on opium by the then "drug czar," Governor Lin Zexu of Canton, followed by the machinations of the British superintendent of trade at Guangzhou, Captain Charles Elliot, led to the opium wars and inaugurated the "century of humiliation" for China that is etched in the collective Chinese DNA (Keay 2009).[3]

---

3. As the opium ban took hold, Elliot persuaded traders to give up seventeen hundred tons of their opium to Governor Lin, promising them, without authority, that the British government would reimburse their losses. Under pressure from the financial interests in the tea trade and Parliament, the British prime minister, Lord Melbourne did indeed pay up. But he sent an expedition to recover this money (2 million pounds) from the Chinese government for the opium that had been handed over by the traders to Governor Lin. The famous opium wars followed (Morris 2010).

Table 6.3 Comparing mercantilist outcomes and instruments of economic powers in history

Power	Outcome		Policy	
	Current account surplus?	Surplus in the hands of government?	Mercantilist policies pursued?	Which policies?
United Kingdom	Yes	Yes	Yes	Trade/commercial
United States	Yes	No	No	None
China	Yes	Yes	Yes	Exchange rate; closed capital account

Table 6.3 provides a guide to understanding Chinese mercantilism today with its historical counterparts practiced by the previous two superpowers, the United Kingdom and the United States. (Box 6.1 discusses some of the confusion that has arisen in discussions about mercantilism.) All three powers have presided over mercantilist outcomes, involving trade and/or current account surpluses. There the commonality ends.

The first difference relates to where these surpluses end up. Like the mercantilism of yore, China's mercantilism is aimed at and results in the accumulation of foreign exchange reserves (the modern day equivalent of specie), and, crucially, accumulation in the hands of the government or near-government agencies, including sovereign wealth funds. This accumulation in the hands of government is achieved by maintaining undervalued exchange rates and by the central bank intervening to buy up the dollar surpluses. As with the British empire, the Chinese surpluses are used to project power internationally, as when China's government or state-owned firms provide aid to Africa, build roads, develop natural resource sectors, buy assets overseas, buy US treasury bonds, or offer to prop up Greek and Irish bond markets.

In this key sense, China's current account surpluses are similar to the experience of imperial United Kingdom but different from the surpluses run by the United States since the 1920s or by Japan and Germany more recently. In the latter examples, surpluses led to increased wealth in the hands of the private sector, and by definition this wealth is more dispersed. China's surpluses lead to concentrated acquisition of resources in the hands of the state.

The second big difference relates to the instruments used to achieve mercantilism. As box 6.1 described, mercantilism in the past, with a few exceptions, had to be achieved through trade policy. In the modern era, mercantilism can, of course, be implemented via trade policy or active exchange rate policy. An undervalued exchange rate is the combination of an import tariff and an export subsidy and is hence the ideal mercantilist policy to increase exports minus imports (or $X - M$). And that is what China has done: It has used

Box 6.1   Mercantilism and mercantilist confusion in history

Mercantilism has always been intimately associated with economic dominance. Often, though, mercantilism and protectionism are used interchangeably, so that these two are in turn seen as opposed to free trade and openness. But mercantilism is also used to describe the accumulation of specie then and current account surpluses today. So what is mercantilism really about? Table 6.3 provides a guide to understanding different discourses around mercantilism.

An important distinction is between the objectives and instruments of mercantilism. Historically, mercantilism was about objectives and specifically the objective of maximizing power. Mercantilists believed in the pursuit of national power and considered the acquisition by governments of specie (gold and silver) as the basis for such power. As Jean-Baptiste Colbert, one of the original mercantilists, put it: "It is simply, and solely, the abundance of money within a state [which] makes the difference in its grandeur and power."

Since specie was to be acquired from abroad, the only way to a carry out acquiring it was to run trade surpluses, which led to inflows of specie. In the mercantilist perspective, this had the added advantage that the acquisition of specie was at the expense of trading partners (and rivals) and hence led to increased power at the expense of the power of others: the enrichment of the acquirer of specie was because of the impoverishment of the country losing specie. Thus, in its original conception, the objective of mercantilism was to maximize exports (*X*) *minus* imports (*M*) or the trade balance.

In *The Wealth of Nations,* Adam Smith's refutation of mercantilism and advocacy of free trade was founded on his view that a society's key objective was to maximize the interests of the consumer (what in today's parlance might be called consumer welfare). Mercantilism, in his view, was inefficient because the consumer was being taxed (in the form of higher prices and hence lower real wages and living standards) to promote the interests of the producer:

> Consumption is the sole end and purpose of all production, and the interest of the producer ought to be attended to, only so far as it may be necessary for promoting that of the consumer. The maxim is so perfectly self-evident, that it would be absurd to attempt to prove it. But in the mercantile system, the interest of the consumer is almost constantly sacrificed to that of the producer; and it seems to consider production, and not consumption, as the ultimate end and object of all industry and commerce.

But mercantilism was also about the instruments used to achieve key objectives. And because historically countries were on the silver/gold standard, exchange rates were largely fixed and generally unavailable as instruments of mercantilism. Mercantilism as objective had to be achieved through trade and commercial policy. But that is where the confusion about mercantilism—with the conflation of means and ends—set in. This confusion is captured by Smith:

Box 6.1 Mercantilism and mercantilist confusion in history
  (continued)

Though the encouragement of exportation, and the discouragement of importation, are the two great engines by which the mercantile system proposes to enrich every country, yet with regard to some particular commodities, it seems to follow an opposite plan: to discourage exportation and to encourage importation. . . . It discourages the exportation of the materials of manufacture. . . . And to enable them to undersell those of other nations in all foreign markets; and by restraining, in this manner, the exportation of a few commodities, of *no great price*, it proposes to occasion a much greater and more valuable exportation of others. It encourages the importation of the materials of manufacture, in order that our own people may be enabled to work them up more cheaply, and thereby prevent a greater and more valuable importation of the manufactured commodities.

The confusion was this: If the opposition between mercantilism and free trade were posed in terms of objectives (producer versus consumer), that did not translate clearly and uniquely to the methods to be used. Mercantilism required some promotion of free trade and some subsidization and restriction of trade. And this is what Britain did.

As Ronald Findlay and Kevin O'Rourke (2007, 347) point out, Britain's trade policy, especially before the Napoleonic wars, was perfectly targeted at mercantilism and maximization of value addition: the country had low or zero tariffs on imports of raw materials (empire actually enabled it to access these raw materials very cheaply) and it banned and imposed high tariffs on the import of foreign manufactures. On the export side, exports of manufactures were allowed duty-free, and the export of key raw materials such as wool were banned. And of course Britain forced its colonies to have no restrictions on the imports of manufactured products such as clothing, which in effect improved the terms of trade and market access for British high-value-added manufacturing (a move that Indian nationalists would complain led to India's de-industrialization).

Modern day theory allows us to reconcile the apparent conflict between free trade and mercantilism both in terms of objectives and instruments. Mercantilism is about increasing the size of trade and current account surpluses, exports *minus* imports $(X - M)$. Openness, on the other hand, focuses on increasing total trade, exports *plus* imports $(X + M)$.[1] On instruments, undervalued exchange rates, which amounts to an export subsidy and import tariff, are the best way of achieving mercantilism. But if trade instruments are to be used, modern day trade theory has shown that mercantilism and value addition are about increasing what is called "effective protection," which requires: on the import side, imposing high tariffs on imports of final goods and zero tariffs on intermediate inputs; and on the export side, subsidizing final goods and imposing restrictions on intermediates.

(box continues next page)

Box 6.1   Mercantilism and mercantilist confusion in history
(continued)

In others words, the distinction between free trade and mercantilism is not clear-cut nor, for the same reason, is protectionism synonymous with mercantilism.[2]

Finally, although historically, trade policies were the means to achieve mercantilism because rigid adherence to the gold standard neutered the exchange rate as a policy instrument, there were exceptions. Two such arose in the late nineteenth century.

Some countries chose to go off the gold standard (such as Argentina in the late 1800s) or devalued against gold (as Chile did in response to a drop in the price of copper before World War I). A second exception arose around 1870 with a wave of silver discoveries, which reduced the price of silver by as much as half against gold. Countries such as China and India, which were on the silver standard, experienced a weakening of their currencies, thereby enjoying a competitive advantage in the export of commodities.

In 1896, when William Jennings Bryan, taking up cudgels on behalf of the "toiling masses," thundered with evangelical fervor that they should not be crucified "upon a cross of gold," it was viewed as a reaction against the tight money and deflationist policies that increased the burden of debt-ridden agricultural interests already the victims of the global decline in commodity prices. The target of the speech was the domestic gold bugs. But it could also be seen as a reaction on behalf of American farmers who were the competitiveness victims of the active mercantilism of Argentina and the passive or unintended mercantilism of countries such as China and India. The unexpressed international concerns implicit in the cross-of-gold speech—the use or manipulation of the silver standard for mercantilist ends—were more clearly articulated by one member of the Populist movement in the United States that campaigned on behalf of the farming community in the late 1800s. He railed "that the yellow man using the white metal, holds at his mercy the white man using the yellow metal" (as quoted in Frieden 2006, 114).

---

1. That a tariff reduces imports is well known, but a tariff, in the long run, also reduces exports, which is the famous symmetry theorem of Abba Lerner. Hence a tariff is a tax on trade not just on imports. Similarly, an export tax is a tax not just on exports but on trade.

2. Another difference in practice between mercantilism and protectionism as trade policy is that the former focused as much on the instruments necessary to promote competitiveness of exports (such as export subsidies, export restrictions on raw materials, and duty-free access for imported raw materials) as on maximizing value addition in import-substituting industries, which has been the traditional focus of protectionism. France, under Jean-Baptiste Colbert, also attempted mercantilism. But lacking the naval dominance of Britain and Holland and thus the ability to influence export markets, France's main instrument of mercantilism became import tariffs and other forms of encouragement for domestic import substitution. Hence, Colbertian mercantilism became more associated with protectionism.

the exchange rate to achieve mercantilist outcomes while the United Kingdom used import and export policies.

Indeed, in the case of China, its accession to the World Trade Organization (WTO) is widely acknowledged to have led to considerable liberalization and hence to circumscribing China's ability to use trade policies for mercantilist purposes. Recall that China's export-focused development strategy began in the mid-1980s, but it did not start generating consistently large current account surpluses until the 2000s. It is not a coincidence therefore that China's mercantilism started to emerge after its accession to the WTO. One might compare the Chinese mercantilist experience with the knitting activities of Penelope, from the Greek myth *The Odyssey,* who kept her suitors at bay by unraveling at night all that she had knit during the day. China liberalized by joining the WTO and undid some of this through exchange rate undervaluation and mercantilism. Facing constraints as a result of WTO accession on the use of trade policy instruments (including tariffs, export and other subsidies, and local content requirements on foreign firms) that could sustain the export juggernaut, China turned to using policy instruments other than trade, namely the exchange rate.[4] An undervalued exchange rate not only sustained exports, it also conveniently generated surpluses.

The China undervaluation-after-WTO-accession example shows that there can be policy substitution in achieving mercantilism, what Daron Acemoglu et al. (2003) call the "see-saw effect" (if a government wants to achieve an objective, restrictions on the use of one instrument lead to the use of others). That is, mercantilism can be achieved through trade policies (as has been true historically) or through exchange rate policies (as in the case of China). The international trading system has managed to address the first but by no means the second. The General Agreement on Tariffs and Trade (GATT) and WTO place constraints on import tariffs and export subsidies—and did so in the case of China. But China's undervalued exchange rate, which is a potent and additive combination of both import tariffs and export subsidies and has the most egregious mercantilist impact, remains to be disciplined. Multilateralism to tame mercantilism is therefore long overdue (Mattoo and Subramanian 2008).

A related difference between China and its predecessors is that China's surpluses and net creditor status have been achieved despite being closed to inflows of capital. The United Kingdom had an open capital account for much

---

4. It is difficult to establish clearly causation from the straitjacket of WTO accession to the need for alternative instruments. Rodrik (2010) argues that an index of undervaluation of the currency shows the renminbi bottoming out in 2001 and rising steadily thereafter, tracking with remarkable timing the evolution of China's current account surplus. Also, as noted in chapter 1, Paul Blustein (2009) suggests that Chinese industry viewed WTO accession as highly constraining. Blustein also writes that China was highly disinclined to entertain any further tariff reductions in the Doha Round because "China's chemical and machinery industries had already endured steep tariff cuts a few years earlier as part of the WTO membership deal, and Beijing had promised those industries that their barriers would not be lowered again" (p. 271–72).

of its imperial past and the United States too was open to capital throughout the 20th century. China is the outlier. China's net creditor status seems to have been sustained through mercantilist exchange rate policies whose success has depended on remaining closed to foreign capital.

The other difference between the current surpluses run by the United States since the 1920s and those of the United Kingdom and China are that the former were not achieved through active policy. The United States had the highest import tariffs on manufacturing among advanced economies well into the 20th century, but mercantilism is not a charge leveled against the United States because aggressive dominance of export markets aimed at maximizing the trade balance was not a real national goal, strategy, or policy.

Thus, currency has been to China what colony was to the United Kingdom as an instrument for pursuing mercantilism. In that sense, it is the United States that is the outlier, having become a net creditor without recourse to mercantilist trade or exchange rate policies.

Third, China's mercantilism is distinctive in that it is less susceptible to the Adam Smith critique that consumers pay a heavy price for the enrichment of producers that results from mercantilism. Critics of China's policy point to declining consumption shares of GDP as evidence of the high welfare toll paid by consumers. But it must be remembered that Chinese mercantilism has delivered exceptional and historically unprecedented growth rates—not just production growth but crucially consumption growth. Per capita consumption has grown by nearly 7 percent a year during the period of acute mercantilism; indeed box 6.2 shows that it is during this mercantilist period of the 2000s when consumption of the average Chinese consumer grows the fastest and when China pulls ahead of other rapidly growing countries (at comparable stages of their growth experience) in delivering greater consumption opportunities for the average citizen. In other words, mercantilism worked, and not at the expense of the consumer.

Perhaps a move away from mercantilism would have delivered even more rapid consumption growth, but that is not an easy case to make. The burden is on the critics to prove that the pie would not have shrunk to offset the fact that consumers would have had a larger share of this pie. In any event, the case of the critics is not one that politicians would accept, especially if it entailed short-term adjustment costs as resources are reallocated away from tradable sectors. American politician Barney Frank has famously said that no politician ever won an election by claiming that things would have been worse without him. Similarly, no regime—not even an autocratic one—ever fomented revolution or restiveness because its population figured out that its consumption could possibly have grown 7.5 percent in counterfactual time rather than a blistering 7 percent in real time.

Finally, and perhaps most importantly, Chinese mercantilism has been unusual in that it has not made China a closed economy (where closed and open are measured in terms of trade outcomes rather than policy barriers). In fact, the biggest paradox about China is that it is at once the most mercantilist

Box 6.2 Has Chinese mercantilism shortchanged Chinese consumers?

China's growth story is widely acclaimed. But especially in the last decade, critics have conveyed the impression that its consumers may have been shortchanged because of the nature of Chinese growth, which has been highly reliant on investment and exports. Echoing Adam Smith's concern, it is alleged that mercantilism and production have trumped the interests of the consumer. Is this accurate?

Figure B6.2.1 plots GDP performance of six nonoil countries—Japan, Singapore, Hong Kong, Taiwan, Korea, and China—that have posted stellar growth performances during the period of their most rapid growth in per capita GDP (purchasing power parity–based).[1] The starting point is indexed at 100 for all countries. The starting point varies across countries and is indicated in the legend. For example, Japan's rapid growth episode begins in 1950, Taiwan's in 1959, Singapore's and Korea's in 1964, and China's in 1976. The figure merely highlights what is well known, namely that the Chinese growth performance matched that of Japan for about 25 years, and then surpassed it (as indeed it had surpassed the performance of the other Asian tigers) in the 2000s (corresponding in the figure to the years $t +$ 23 to $t + 33$ for China). In other words, it is in the era of mercantilism that China's growth performance literally went off the charts.

Figure B6.2.1 Per capita GDP (purchasing power parity) of selected economies during period of most rapid growth

index = 100 at starting point (in parentheses)

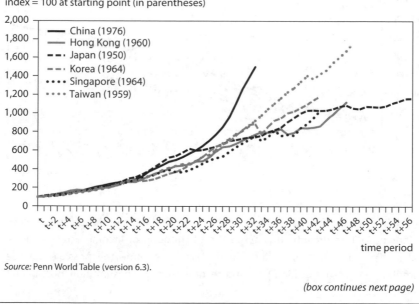

Source: Penn World Table (version 6.3).

(box continues next page)

Box 6.2 Has Chinese mercantilism shortchanged Chinese consumers? *(continued)*

Figure B6.2.2 is identical to figure B6.2.1 except that it plots per capita consumption (also in purchasing power parity terms) rather than per capita GDP growth. For this figure, consumption per capita is calculated from the Penn World Tables, which gives the share of consumption in GDP.[2] What this figure illustrates is that China's performance was less stellar in delivering consumption than in delivering GDP growth. Japan delivered more rapid consumption growth per capita than China in the first 25 years of their respective episodes of strong economic performance, and China's edge over other countries in consumption was less than its edge in GDP. But the striking facts are these: It is in the era of mercantilism (the 2000s) that the growth rate of consumption for the average Chinese is greatest; and second, it is in the era of mercantilism when China's average per capita consumption growth starts to pull ahead of the other countries at comparable stages in their growth trajectories. Mercantilism has not shortchanged the Chinese consumer.

Figure B6.2.2 Per capita consumption of selected economies during period of most rapid growth

index = 100 at starting point (in parentheses)

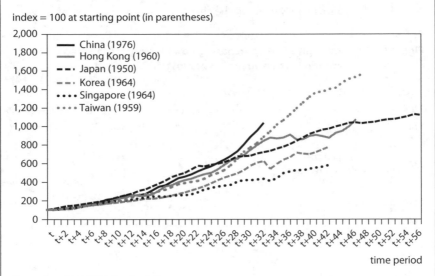

Source: Penn World Table (version 6.3).

Neither of the figures speaks to the very important question of the implications of China's growth strategy on the distribution of income across regions, skill levels, and sectors. Neither do the figures capture the possible adverse implications of mercantilism for future growth and consumption possibilities stemming from overreliance on investment and the attendant inefficiency of capital use. But if one focuses on average current performance, the figures suggest that mercantilism delivered not just for the producer but also the consumer. Caution is therefore warranted before hurling the casual criticism that mercantilism has been self-evidently bad for China and the Chinese consumer.

---

1. In the postwar period, only the following additional countries have grown at 7 percent or more for a period exceeding 20 years: Romania, Botswana, Equatorial Guinea, Bhutan, Maldives, and Iran. In the prewar period, there is only one country, Venezuela, that came close to matching the strength and duration of China's current growth. Venezuela's per capita GDP grew on average by 7 percent between 1919 and 1949. Its growth was all due to oil: Its first major oil discovery was in 1914, with one of the biggest strikes in the petroleum industry following in 1922.

2. The series "kc" in the Penn World Tables is the basis for the consumption estimates.

economy and among the most open economies. While it generates a lot of exports relative to imports (resulting in trade imbalances) it also generates a lot of exports *and* imports as discussed above. In some ways, this might be the contrast between Chinese mercantilism in its two incarnations.

In the incarnation of the early 1800s that led to the opium wars, China was mercantilist and closed. China's surplus was a consequence of unquenchable foreign demand for China's tea and rhubarb, combined with a closed door policy that virtually extinguished Chinese demand for foreign products. Put simply, China exported a fair amount and imported very little. In the 2000s incarnation, it is mercantilist and highly open. Both types of mercantilism can, evidently, trigger conflict of one sort or another. But it is a reflection of Chinese dominance today, that whereas about a hundred and fifty years ago, its mercantilism led to war, humiliation and partial foreign take-over, today Chinese mercantilism encounters sabre-rattling and weak threats of trade retaliation. That is a difference China will happily live with.

7

Guarding Against
Rash Prophesying

Fashionable and excessively ingenious theories that read deep-seated significance into contemporary conditions do not deserve quiet oblivion as soon as brute facts crush them; they should be remembered to permit recognizing their counterparts in the future.

—Leland Yeager (1966)

One pitfall of projections is the tendency to extrapolate the recent past because one assumes that the present is a much more serviceable guide to the future as John Maynard Keynes suggested. Subsequent events often quickly belie that notion, leading to a spate of wrong predictions. Is the projection of an economically dominant China a counterpart of hopelessly wrong calls in the past? Two such prognostications related to Russia and Japan.

When Nikita Khruschev famously pounded his shoe on the UN podium and declared that "we will bury you," he was making an economic prediction as much as brandishing a military and nuclear threat. Economic growth in the Soviet Union between 1946 and 1960 averaged about 7 percent per annum (Maddison 2010). The common belief that this dynamism would endure—together with the Soviet Union's military arsenal—led many to project a bipolar world of dominance shared between the United States and the Soviet Union.

Paul Krugman (1994) wrote that browsing through the issues of *Foreign Affairs* from the mid-1950s through the early 1960s, one discovers that "at least one article a year deals with the implications of growing Soviet industrial might." A 1957 article by Calvin Hoover concluded that "a collectivist authoritarian state" was inherently better at achieving economic growth than free-market democracies and projected that the Soviet economy might outstrip that of the United States by the early 1970s.

But within a decade after Hoover's article, the Soviet growth rate had slipped to less than 2.5 percent, which combined with military overstretch and later (during the 1980s) declining oil prices, created the conditions for the break-up of the mighty Soviet Union (Åslund 2007).

Fast-forward to the 1980s, and the predictions were the same with only the identity of the nation changed. With the Japanese economy operating at full steam, there was considerable enthusiasm for the Japanese model of capitalism, and a spate of writings forecast superpower status for Japan. The most famous of these was Ezra Vogel's *Japan as Number One: Lessons for America* in 1979. Vogel's thesis was that Japan had developed a system—close cooperation between business and government in addressing competitiveness, bureaucrats able to take a long view, establishment of communitarian values—that was better able at coping with challenges than the system in the United States.

Paul Kennedy (1989, 461) predicted that "Yet while it may be true that Japan's economic growth is slowing down as it enters a more mature phase . . . there nevertheless remain considerable substantive reasons why it is likely to expand faster than the other *major* powers in the future." These reasons included the ability of agencies such as the Ministry of International Trade and Industry to guide the economy to high-tech sectors, Japan's high level of savings, the fact that Japanese firms had guaranteed access to its home markets, and the very high quality of the Japanese workforce. For these reasons, Kennedy seemed to concur in the "many assessments [that] . . . the Japanese economy is still likely to expand 1½ to 2 percent faster than the large economies (except, of course, China) over the next several decades" (p. 467).

History, or rather the Japanese economy, has not been kind to those predictions. Japan has been in the throes of apparent secular decline since the asset price crash of the early 1990s, averaging economic growth of just over 1 percent per capita.

Although the mistakes on Japan and Russia were similar in the sense of assuming the continuation of economic dynamism that was evident for some extensive period of time (nearly three decades in the case of the Soviet Union and four decades in the case of Japan), the predictions were wrong for different reasons. In some ways, the optimism about the Soviet Union was perhaps more understandable because in the postwar period (and against the backdrop of the 1930s and the success of the New Deal), the lure of the welfare state and government intervention remained strong, the failures of excessive centralization were not yet evident, and the growth successes of alternative less-dirigiste policies such as those in east Asia had yet to come.[1] With hindsight, one knows that the Soviet growth story was based on a distorted and unsustainable pat-

---

1. What is ironic, though, is that Krugman (1994) and Alwyn Young (1993)—who used growth theory to show (retrospectively) that the Soviet model was always unlikely to succeed because it was based on "perspiration" (i.e., capital accumulation) rather than "inspiration" (productivity growth)—were not completely right in their predictions using the same logic about the east Asian successes such as Singapore, Korea, and Taiwan. That is, cheerleaders for the Soviet Union made a Type II error, accepting the false hypothesis that it would grow for a long time. In contrast, Krugman and Young, in trading cheerleading for skepticism about east Asian growth prospects, made a Type I error (rejecting a true hypothesis.)

tern of development that relied too much on capital accumulation and which allowed little room for markets, decentralized incentives, and dissemination of information (Åslund 2007).[2]

In the case of Japan, the optimism was unfounded not because the country had failed (as with the Soviet Union) but because it had been brilliantly successful. The key error was to overlook a central insight from growth theory. Within four decades after the war, the Japanese economy had caught up with the advanced countries, reaching as it were the economic frontier. In 1990, just before the collapse of the economy, Japan's per capita GDP was $26,4000 (PPP-adjusted in 2005 dollars) compared with $31,000 for the United States. Japan, in other words, had nearly caught up to the United States and was on the technology frontier.

Growth theory strongly predicts that countries at or close to the frontier grow relatively slowly compared with countries that are poor and well below the frontier. Historically, the United States has grown at roughly 2.2 percent per capita, which is what predictions for Japan should have converged around. And if demographic decline, which was apparent even then, had been taken into account, growth projections for Japan should have centered around 1.5 to 2 percent. Instead, growth was routinely forecast to be upwards of 3 to 3.5 percent for some considerable period of time.

The IMF was not immune to Japan boosterism and its flagship publication, the *World Economic Outlook* of October 1989, makes for interesting reading. A chapter on the impact of aging and the rising dependency ratio in this report argued that this demographic decline (which was a well-known future development even then) would actually contribute *positively* to GDP growth for about 20 years beyond the projection period (IMF 1989). The argument was that a rising dependency ratio would reduce savings and increase consumption, which would boost aggregate demand and growth. Thus, the IMF predicted in 1989 that demographic developments would boost economic growth in Japan for the four five-year periods beginning in 1996–2000 by 0.2, 0.6, 0.8, and 0.5 percent, respectively.

Today, when growth projections are made to reflect aging, the view is that the effect is generally negative because aging reduces labor force growth (leaving aside complications arising from participation in the labor force) and reduces domestic savings, both of which reduce the potential rate of economic growth. In other words, long-run projections today reflect supply-side factors. The IMF, on the other hand, was essentially but erroneously, using demand-side arguments (higher consumption) even for long-run projections. Either the IMF's analytics were faulty. Or, it was a case of strongly held priors in search of rationalizations.

---

2. Weitzman (1970), though, did anticipate in a low-key and analytical manner, the problems with the Soviet growth model and prospects.

China's Growth: Repeating Mistakes?

In the case of China, in particular, how can one guard against the mistakenly overoptimistic projections made regarding Russia and, especially Japan. Or put more bluntly, is the growth projection for China, which results in the dramatic shift in the pattern of economic dominance, reasonable?

Recall above all that the growth forecast for China does not require continuation of anything close to current growth rates. In the convergence scenario, China is projected to grow at 5.5 percent per capita, which is about 3 to 4 percentage points per capita slower than in the recent past (put differently, this scenario assumes a slowdown of the growth rate of close to 35 percent). In other words, despite China being well below the economic frontier—China's per capita GDP in 2010 is about a quarter of the comparable US number—the projections here are conservative in predicting China's future. Compared with the earlier Japan projections, there is conservatism twice over: Japan, which was close to the frontier, was projected to grow much faster than the frontier, whereas in the case of China the projections assume slower growth despite China being far away (three-quarters away) from the frontier.

The question can nevertheless arise whether even this very conservative forecast is itself reasonable. There are two ways of assessing this. The first is to look ahead and identify and analyze all those factors and shocks that could potentially derail China's growth by even more than that being allowed for here. The skeptical school on China typically focuses on three factors that could derail or set back China's growth: politics, prices, and people. Clearly, there are some scenarios involving each of these factors—political upheaval, distorted relative prices for capital, energy, foreign exchange, labor, and demographic changes that are leading to an aging of the population—in which growth could slip well below the projection.

There is very little to add to the voluminous literature that has assessed the likelihood of these potentially derailing factors being realized and their possible consequences. The political transformation question has been examined extensively (Bergsten and Lardy 2009, Chang 2001, Li 2011, Pei 2009, Perkins 2010, Shambaugh 2009, Yang 2010).[3]

The same holds true for the distorted prices. Adjustments to these prices will no doubt test the Chinese economic system. Realistic prices of capital, and the elimination of financial repression, might reduce growth and result in large declines in investment, which has been the engine of growth. In turn, this will cause severe banking system stress. Eliminating currency undervaluation and rebalancing the economy will create severe dislocations as the size of

---

3. For the purposes of this book, just two points are worth noting. Recent history has provided examples of political transitions that have been disruptive of economic growth (as in the Soviet Union and Indonesia) and other examples where the transitions have been smooth and not exacted a toll on economic performance (Czech Republic, South Korea, and Taiwan). And, of course, it goes without saying that any political upheaval will affect growth, and so all bets will be off in such an eventuality.

the traded goods sector shrinks and the nontraded sector expands. As Martin Wolf and others have pointed out, re-balancing growth from investment to consumption will be bumpy not least because the Chinese economy, driven by subsidized expansion of investment and capacity, will have to learn find ways of matching supply with demand. Similarly, realistic energy pricing will render some energy-intensive sectors uncompetitive. The key question in all these cases is whether the authorities have the political will to respond appropriately and in a timely fashion, and the fiscal ability to cushion the shocks. Reasonable people will disagree and there is not much that can shed new light on the question of whether and how any such shock will affect the 20-year forecast presented here.[4]

Nicholas Lardy (2010) argues that forecasts of sharp declines in GDP growth in China over the next 20 years are exaggerated. In his view, these projections are overly pessimistic and based on sharp declines in total factor productivity growth that overlook available sensible policy options.

> [T]he broader, systemic, and long-run explanations of China's hypothesized slowdown are far from fully convincing. They ultimately are based on a hypothesized dramatic slowdown in the growth of total factor productivity. But this may not occur in large part because China, for more than three decades, has been more open to foreign investment than other major east Asian economies that experienced sharply lower economic growth after their levels of per capita GDP exceeded $10,000–$16,000 in PPP terms in year-2000 prices. By the late 1990s foreign invested firms accounted for more than a quarter of China's output of manufactured goods. More and more evidence is accumulating that the resulting increased competition in the domestic market has caused indigenous Chinese firms to upgrade their technology, marketing, etc. to survive. As a result these indigenous firms become successful competitors with global firms at a much earlier stage of China's economic development than was the case historically in the development of Japan, Korea, and Taiwan. This is already documented in a study by Eric Thun and Loren Brandt for the automotive, construction equipment, and machine tool sectors. It is likely to also be the case in high-speed rail. China allowed the global industry leaders, including Germany's Siemens, France's Alstom, Japan's Kawasaki Heavy Industries, and Canada's Bombardier, to form joint ventures with state-controlled companies starting more than a decade ago. These joint ventures received contracts to produce 200 self-propelled electric multiple-unit trains for 200 km/h and 300 km/hr operation (Lardy 2010).

Looking Back

This chapter aims to shed new light on the growth forecast not by looking ahead—which is difficult because for every cautious optimist (e.g., Nicholas

---

4. Demographics represent less of a threat to my projections. It is now well documented that China's dependency ratio will eventually start rising very sharply and create a host of complications. But that will begin around 2025, which does not seriously overlap with the 20-year horizon (2010–30) that is the focus of this book.

Lardy) there is a skeptic (e.g., Yu Yongding)—but rather by looking back in history and adopting the growth and convergence perspective. How did countries fare that were at a stage comparable to China (and it is important to appropriately define comparability)? And what can one learn from them?

Dwight Perkins (2010) points out that all countries experience slower growth, 5 percent or less, once their per capita incomes (measured in PPP terms) reach $10,000 to $16,000 in year 2000 prices. He believes that China's GDP today is between $7,000 and $8,000 (not the higher $10,000 figure given in the Penn World Tables), giving China at most another decade of high growth. Consistent with this observation, a recent Asian Development Bank update pegs China's baseline growth over 2011–30 at only 5.5 percent (aggregate not per capita), barely more than half the average pace of the past 30 years (ADB 2010, 41).

While this is a useful way of setting up the comparison, it is not consistent with a growth and convergence perspective. Recall that growth predictions based on convergence-type effects do not depend on the absolute value of a country's per capita GDP. Convergence suggests that the speed of reaching the frontier depends on the distance from it (Lucas 2000 makes the same argument). It is that distance that matters.

The simplest way of measuring distance is in terms of a country's standard of living relative to that of the world's richest countries, typically proxied by the United States. The estimate here for China for 2010 puts its GDP per capita at roughly a quarter of that of the United States. One can turn to the postwar historical record to ask how fast countries have grown once they attained the same relative living standard. In other words, the comparison must be set up between China and its historical predecessors not in terms of an absolute standard of living but as relative to the frontier country.

Table 7.1 presents some evidence. The table calculates the average growth rate (over 20 years) of per capita GDP for all countries *after* their per capita GDP reached between quarter and 30 percent of that of the United States. Of a total of 25 countries or territories for which the threshold is applicable and data are available, eight—Japan, Hong Kong, Korea, Taiwan, Spain, Portugal, Greece, and Germany—grew faster than what I have projected China to grow over a comparable 20-year period. These growth rates (all per capita) varied from 5.2 percent for Portugal to 7.8 percent for Japan. Thus, my forecast for China of 5.5 percent per capita for the next 20-year period would not have to rely on China being especially unusual—or defying the general pattern. China could be a normal "fast" converger and yet achieve the growth rates forecast here.[5]

The historical comparison could also be set up in a different way. One could ask how many countries in China's situation today—having reached a quarter of the living standard of the United States—experienced a growth decline (relative to their recent history) greater than what is projected here for

---

5. The experiences of Japan and Germany may be less relevant for China because their rapid growth was a recovery from World War II.

Table 7.1 Twenty-year growth rate of selected economies after reaching 25 percent of US GDP per capita

Country	Start year	GDP per capita at start (PPP dollars)	Percent of US GDP per capita at start	End year	GDP per capita at end (PPP dollars)	Annual average rate of growth of per capita GDP over 20 years after reaching 25 percent of US living standards (percent)
Japan	1954	3,518	26.0	1974	15,806	7.80
Hong Kong	1960	3,849	26.1	1980	15,605	7.25
Germany	1947	2,436	27.4	1967	9,397	6.75
Spain	1950	3,527	27.1	1970	11,561	6.12
Taiwan	1979	6,321	25.2	1999	20,562	6.08
Greece	1951	4,078	30.3	1971	13,024	5.98
Korea	1983	6,512	25.8	2003	20,550	5.91
Portugal	1957	3,616	25.1	1977	9,888	5.16
Iran	1958	3,526	25.2	1978	8,815	4.69
Malaysia	1982	6,396	26.5	2002	14,456	4.16
Mexico	1950	3,270	25.2	1970	6,190	3.24
Cuba	1970	5,003	25.3	1990	9,219	3.10
Peru	1961	3,765	25.4	1981	5,749	2.14
Brazil	1971	5,197	25.6	1991	7,721	2.00
Iraq	1970	5,683	28.8	1990	7,540	1.42
Poland	1970	5,647	28.6	1990	7,195	1.22
Jordan	1954	3,456	25.5	1974	4,333	1.14
Algeria	1960	4,370	29.6	1980	5,190	0.86
Romania	1977	6,414	27.2	1997	6,089	−0.26
Bolivia	1950	3,397	26.2	1970	2,884	−0.82
Guinea	1960	3,702	25.1	1980	3,103	−0.88

Source: Penn World Table (version 6.3).

China. My projections for the next 20 years involve China's growth slowing by 3 to 3.8 percentage points per capita or about 40 percent relative to the growth average of the previous two to three decades.[6] What has been the experience of other countries in this regard in the postwar period?

Unfortunately, my sample is somewhat limited by the fact that for most countries, the year at which they are first observed to have 25 percent of US GDP is the first year for which data on them are available (so one cannot compute the growth rates prior to reaching this threshold). But for the countries for which there are some data, one finds that of six countries—Brazil, Korea, Taiwan, Malaysia, Peru, and Romania—growth after reaching 25 percent of US GDP per capita in four of them was either greater or similar to growth before that. In the case of Brazil, there was a slowdown of about 2.6 percent, which is similar to what is projected here for China. Only in the case of Romania does one see a significant drop-off in growth at a stage comparable to China's today.

The conclusion from each of these historical comparisons is that there are enough instances of countries having reached China's situation today that have continued to do well in line with my growth forecast. But there are also countries that have not. The question then is whether China will resemble Japan, Korea, Taiwan, Korea, and Malaysia and continue growing, or suffer collapse and stagnation like Nicolae Ceausescu's Romania, post-Stalin Russia, or Brazil between 1980 and 2000.[7]

It is worth comparing my projection for China to the analysis of Barry Eichengreen, Donghyun Park, and Kwanho Shin (2011) on the historical experience of growth slowdowns.[8] They argue that rapidly growing economies slow down in that their growth rate decreases by 2 percentage points per capita after they reach a per capita GDP of about $17,000, which China is expected to reach by 2015 (according to the authors). But, if slowdowns are measured not in terms of the absolute level of per capita income but in terms of relative incomes (as is appropriate for a convergence framework), slowdown occurs

---

6. For the 22-year period from 1989–2009, China's per capita growth rate was 8.8 percent, and for the 10-year period from 1999–2009, it was 9.7 percent. My 20-year projection is 5.5 percent per capita.

7. These historical comparisons also serve to address the so-called middle-income trap that China might fall into (Gill and Kharas 2007). The notion of this trap is based on the observation that between 1980 and 2000, countries with per capita incomes between $826 and $10,665 have grown less rapidly than countries that are richer and poorer. It is not clear whether this trap holds over longer periods of time and, moreover, why thresholds are defined in absolute terms rather than in terms of the distance to the frontier. The broader point is that growth in countries will slow down as they approach the frontier, and the comparisons that I have made speak to the issue of whether and to what extent China can continue growing as it approaches the frontier.

8. This analysis is different in one key sense from that presented here. In tables 7.1 and 7.2 the comparator used is all countries that have reached China's current level of per capita GDP relative to the United States. In the Eichengreen, Park, and Shin analysis, the comparison is with all countries that experienced growth as rapid as that of China's regardless of where they are in terms of their level of per capita GDP.

Table 7.2   Long-run growth rates of economies before and after reaching 25 percent of US GDP per capita (percent)

Country	Year threshold reached	Years in growth measurement period	Growth rate before threshold reached	20-year growth rate after threshold reached	Difference in growth rate (after – before)	Growth after as a ratio of growth before
Brazil	1971	20	4.58	2.00	–2.58	0.44
Korea	1983	30	4.82	5.91	1.09	1.23
Malaysia	1982	20	5.11	4.16	–0.95	0.81
Peru	1961	10	1.79	2.14	0.35	1.20
Portugal	1957	5	4.24	5.16	0.91	1.22
Romania	1977	15	8.57	–0.26	–8.83	–0.03
Taiwan	1979	20	7.34	6.08	–1.27	0.83
China (projection)	2010	30	7.95	5.50	–2.45	0.69

Source: Author's calculations.

when a country's per capita GDP is about 58 percent of that in the frontier country. China, according to the authors, is expected to reach this threshold in 2023 (after growing at about 9 percent between now and then).

China's other features—its aging, its high share of manufacturing, and its undervalued exchange rate policy—argue for a quicker slowdown. The central estimate of the authors is that there is about a 75 percent chance today of growth slowing by 2 percentage points per capita. My estimate for China is even more conservative than that of Eichengreen, Park, and Shin. It already factors in—with 100 percent probability—a growth slowdown of 3.5 percentage points per capita rather than the 2 percentage points that history appears to warrant.

More recent skepticism about China (e.g., Spence 2011) focuses on the stylized fact that only seven countries in the history of postwar growth have in a sense made it to high-income status. But this fact is less relevant for the China forecast upon which the dominance projections in this book are based. First, these projections do not require China to become an advanced or high-income country, but merely a middle-income one that attains half the standard of living of the frontier country by 2030. Second, the relevant projection is not an unconditional one, but rather one conditioned on the fact of China having reached a certain standard of living relative to the frontier, as captured in tables 7.1 and 7.2.

These distinctions are important because otherwise the probabilities conveyed are misleading. If the stylized fact about postwar growth—from the Spence analysis—were simply applied to China today, it would suggest crudely that China has a 7 in 200 chance of making it. With the two caveats proposed, Chinese chances of achieving the kind of dominance projected in this book are, again crudely speaking, 8 in 21 (if table 7.1 is the basis for comparison) or 6 in 7 (if table 7.2 is the right basis).

Finally, it must be emphasized that nothing about these forecasts precludes the possibility of China and other emerging markets experiencing a major financial crisis over the next 20 years. The projections implicitly assume that over a 20-year period these economies will be resilient enough to emerge from these crises and register rates of economic growth close to those assumed in this book.

Realism of Trade Projections

The projections of economic dominance presented here will depend not just on the realism of the growth projections but also on the realism of the trade projections. In some ways, my projections for trade are even more dramatic in the shifts that they imply. For example, China's share of world trade, which is currently similar to that of the United States, is projected to be two times that of the United States by 2030.

The trade projections could go wrong for two reasons: because the growth projections are flawed or because the gravity model for converting the growth numbers into trade numbers is faulty. I have already discussed the first possibility. What about the gravity model?

One way of testing the gravity model is to ask what one would have predicted for 2008 (the latest year for which trade data are available) had one carried out the same exercise based on the gravity model in 1988 (i.e., over the same 20-year horizon that I am forecasting). That is, if I had forecast correctly the GDP growth rates of the United States and China between 1988 and 2008, would the gravity model have produced estimates for the relative global trade shares for these two countries that resemble the actual shares in 2010?

The answer is yes. The gravity model suggests that the difference in the growth rate of trade of two countries is roughly the same as the difference in their GDP growth rates. Between 1988 and 2008, trade (nominal merchandise imports and exports) for the United States and China grew annually at 7.75 and 17.5 percent, respectively. Their respective GDP growth rates were 14.4 and 5.35 percent, respectively. The difference was 9.1 percent broadly the same as the difference in the growth rates of their GDP (a difference of 9.75 percent). Up to first order, the gravity model produces plausible estimates.

But China's future trade could slow down considerably. To see why, consider figure 7.1. Prior to its reforms, China started as a closed economy shut off to the world. Since the late 1970s, it has used trade as an engine of growth with a vengeance. As a result, between 1980 and 2010, China's openness ratio, which was substantially lower than that of the world, has over time grown to equal that of the world in 2010. This is the reason why it has become an overtrader, as discussed in chapter 6. Between 1980 and 2007 (just prior to the global financial crisis), China's trade-to-GDP ratio increased faster than

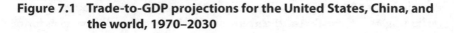

Figure 7.1 Trade-to-GDP projections for the United States, China, and the world, 1970–2030

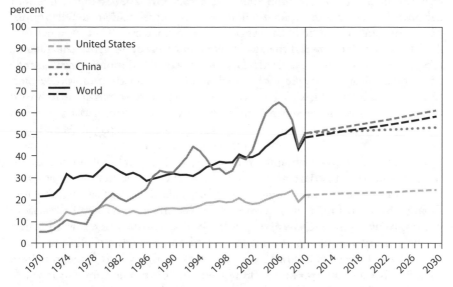

Notes: Dashed lines in the projection horizon assume that "gravity" holds. The dotted line is China's actual trade forecast to allow for slower trade growth than implied by gravity.

Sources: Maddison (2001); World Bank, *World Development Indicators*; IMF, *World Economic Outlook,* April 2011; and author's calculations.

the world average by about 1 percentage points each year (from 20 percent in 1980 to 62 percent in 2007).

Going forward, this trend could be projected to (1) continue so that China continues to sees its openness outstrip world openness; (2) reverse itself so that China sees its openness merely keep pace with that of the world; or (3) reverse itself so that sees its openness decline relative to the world. In this last scenario, China starts the process of "catch-down" to become a normal trader rather than remaining the unusually large trader that it is today.

The first projection would err on the side of optimism (and commit the cardinal error of extrapolating the recent past). The second would be defensible because it would entail a correction of recent trends. Notwithstanding these considerations, and to be conservative, I have assumed that China's trade-to-GDP ratio will grow more slowly than that of the world so that China starts the process of becoming a normal trader.[9] The speed and duration of this process is difficult to predict, but one can use the gravity model and the quantitative exercise in chapter 6 to pin down the end point. That chapter

9. Some of this reversion to normalcy will be occasioned by the decline in importance of China's manufacturing relative to services.

calculated that China's openness ratio of 57 percent in 2008 amounted to an overtrading margin of about 70 percent, suggesting a "normal" openness ratio of between 35 and 40 percent in 2008. Extrapolated to 2030 to take account of the growth in the world's trade-to-GDP ratio, a normal trade-to-GDP ratio for China for 2030 would be in the range of 43 to 50 percent.

It is difficult to predict the pace at which China will revert to this normal ratio. But four factors suggest that over the next two decades, China's trade will remain buoyant, arguing for a more gradual rather than rapid reversion to normalcy. First, China's GDP will continue to grow faster than the world average and growth dynamism generates trade dynamism. Second, China's trade will still be based for some time on it being an assembly hub, so its exports are likely to be import-intensive, which would sustain a large volume of trade. Third, and very importantly, China's pattern of trade will continue to shift toward countries, largely in Asia and Africa, that will themselves be growing rapidly, which will also tend to offset any decline from mean reversion. Finally, this shift in the pattern of trade toward Asia and Africa will lend an important and subtle upward bias to trade. The shift to trade toward faster-growing countries will also be a shift toward more geographically proximate countries, effectively reducing the average distance that China's trade will have to "travel" and simulate the effects of a decline in transport costs for goods traded from China. This too will tend to shore up trade, forestalling the effects of any secular decline toward normalcy.

Thus, taking into account, on the one hand, that China's trade will have to revert to normal, but on the other, that there will be forces continuing to shore up trade, I assume that by 2030 China's openness ratio will decline to about 53 percent, or by about 9 percentage points relative to where gravity might have taken it, and crucially, about halfway back to some long-term "normal" trade-to-GDP ratio. Thus, the trade projections have been conservative in not extrapolating the very recent trends and in correcting for China's unusual past trade performance.

So, going forward, my projections assume that China will be catching up to attain a higher (and more normal) level of income, and catching down to attain a lower (but more normal) level of trade.

Conclusion

If one leaves aside the rhetoric that tends to dominate geopolitical discussions and focus on the economic determinants of power and influence, one is in for a surprise. The current consensus is that although US economic dominance will decline in relative terms, the world in the near future will still be a place where the United States dominates, with China a close rival and competitor.

Yet the previous chapter showed that China's economic dominance is imminent (if not already at hand), likely to be broad in scope, and substantial in magnitude. And this chapter showed that these basic trends are quite robust. Mindful of the false positive predictions of the past—in relation to the Soviet

Union and Japan—I am conservative in my growth and trade projections for China. The basic picture of dominance does not require China to grow at anything close to current rates: It can grow substantially slower (by 3 to 4 percentage points per capita or 35 to 40 percent relative to its recent past) and still attain dominance.

To be sure, several roadblocks—unsettled politics, distorted prices, and unfavorable demographics—might derail current growth rates. But a lot would have to happen to make China grow at half the current pace (say below 5 percent per year). History may not be overwhelmingly on China's side, but it is at least not overwhelmingly against it. There are enough examples in the past of countries (Japan, Germany, Korea, Taiwan, Spain, and Portugal) with income levels at one time similar to that of China (and being as far away from the technology frontier) and yet posting the 5 to 5.5 percent growth rates that are necessary for the picture of a dominant China to be realized. And few countries in the postwar period have experienced growth slowdowns greater than what I am projecting at a comparable stage for China.

8

Economic Cooperation with a Rising China

There is only one law in economics:
every purchase [import] is a sale [export] and vice versa.
—Nobel Prize–winning economist Robert Solow[1]

If China does indeed become dominant by the end of the next decade along the lines projected in this book—the G-1 in 2030—what kind of superpower or hegemon will it be? A lot will depend on the big questions of whether China will make the transition to becoming genuinely democratic and whether there will be checks, notably through effective civilian control, on the Communist Party and the army. The more China becomes like the West as a society, the more confidence it will inspire in the continuation of an open, rules-based economic system. If these transitions do not occur, a post-2030 hegemonic regime without clear values may be based much more on bilateralism, discrimination when it seems expedient, and opaque and ad hoc rules rather than transparent, universal ones.

The questions addressed in this chapter relate not to 2030 but to the transition from now to then. How can one characterize this period of transition for the multilateral economic system from a historical perspective? How might China's rise affect this system? The next chapter considers the question of what can be done, if anything, to ensure that possible future Chinese hegemony or quasi-hegemony does not lead to a serious departure from today's open, rules-based trade and financial system.

How Many Country Groupings Are There in 2011? Historical Parallels

What has been the history of cooperation and leadership in history and how might today's world be characterized in relation to that history? Table 8.1 tries

---

1. The words in brackets are an adaptation of the original quote to trade.

to encapsulate schematically the history and the present conjuncture. Restricting ourselves to the last 100 plus years of history instead of going farther back to the rise of Britain in the late 1600s or to Dutch, Spanish and Portuguese dominance before that, three possible historical parallels suggest themselves: the period between 1870–1914; the interwar years; and the period after 1945.

It is interesting that China and Chinese scholars have themselves seen and spoken about these parallels if only to repudiate them. For example, the Chinese scholar and Communist Party theorist Zhen Bijan said that China "would not follow the path of Germany leading up to World War I or those of Germany and Japan leading up to World War II, or of the great powers vying for global domination during the Cold War" (quoted in Kagan 2008, 26).

Prior to World War I, the world's economic system was shaped by a G-1, the United Kingdom, which dominated trade, set the currency standard (via gold), ensured the flow of capital, and kept trade flows open (subject to the constraint of empire). So, the analogy between today and the pre-World War I period would draw on the possible similarities between the rise of China and that of Germany after the Franco-Prussian War, with the similarity being the assertiveness and/or possible territorial ambitions of the two countries. There is also the same uncertainty about whether the rising power buys into the values of the existing international order: broadly, the fact that China is still not a democracy just as Germany remained nationalistic and, in Henry Kissinger's (1994) words, "unleavened by democracy" despite adult male suffrage.

The interwar years (the "lull between catastrophes" as Anthony Lane of the *New Yorker* described it) could be characterized as being a G-0, with the complete breakdown of the economic system. Charles Kindleberger's theory that the world needed hegemony to provide stability was born of his observation that "The 1929 depression was so wide, so deep and so long because the international economic system was rendered unstable by British inability and American unwillingness to assume responsibility for stabilizing it" (Kindleberger 1973, 292).[2]

The analogy between today and the interwar years would draw upon these similarities: that the existing power had been significantly diminished by war and overconsumption (the United Kingdom), not unlike the situation that the United States finds itself in today thanks to a combination of overconsumption (the housing bubble) and some military overreaching (Iraq and Afghanistan). The then rising or risen power—the United States—was, to use Isaiah Berlin's phrase, "in isolationist disregard of the outside world, " retreating from, and being inattentive to, the demands of the world stage, initially as a reflex reaction to World War I and its messy aftermath, and later because of domestic economic problems. The case could be made that while the United States is increasingly unable to take on international responsibilities, China,

---

2. By 1934, the United States had started to reverse the effects of the infamous Smoot-Hawley tariffs by negotiating reciprocal tariff reductions combined with a most favored nation clause that ensured that the fruits of opening were shared beyond the signatories to such agreements.

Table 8.1   Who is in charge? 1870–2030

Type of leadership	Period				Beyond 2030?
	1870–1914	Interwar years	1945–2010	2010–30?	
G-0		Absence of a hegemonic power because the United Kingdom was unable, and the United States unwilling, to exercise leadership		1. Lack of hegemonic power and presence of multiple veto players—reflected in impasse in Doha Round on global imbalances and climate change—results in a G-0 minus 2. Despite lack of clear leadership resulting in a G-0 plus, the world economic system is able to cooperate, at least in response to major crises, as in the case of the 2008–10 financial crisis	China as the G-1?
G-1	United Kingdom as a hegemonic power with a rising Germany (and United States)				
G-2			1. United States and Soviet Union as Cold War rivals in the security sphere 2. United States and Europe jointly steering the trading	China and the United States steering the world system?	

(table continues next page)

Table 8.1 Who is in charge? 1870–2030 *(continued)*

Type of leadership	Period				
	1870–1914	Interwar years	1945–2010	2010–30?	Beyond 2030?
			system, with the United States as leader, resulting de facto in a G-1 plus 1		
G-other			United States and other G-7 countries (Japan, Germany, France, and the United Kingdom) managing macroeconomic and exchange rate cooperation, but with the United States as *primus inter pares*, resulting in a G-1 plus 5/6	G-20 as the world's new "steering committee?"	

Source: Author's analysis.

too, because of being overwhelmingly preoccupied with the domestic task of promoting development and raising living standards, is insufficiently mindful of the international consequences of its actions (e.g., on the exchange rate or climate change).

At the end of World War II, the United States was the uncontested economic hegemon that shaped the international economic architecture. On trade issues, too, the creation of the European Union meant that the United States did not have unrivaled monopoly in setting the terms of the trade system, although it was highly influential—hence the characterization as G-1 plus 1 rather than a G-2, suggesting that the United States was at least *primus inter pares* if not more dominant in the trading system. On broader economic issues, the United States, Japan, and the larger countries of Western Europe were joint stewards of the system, again though with the United States as a kind of leader with the others as important followers. The G-7 that ran the world until the recent global financial crisis could thus be better described as a G-1 plus 6.

The similarity between today and 1945 would be that of a bipolar world, with two military superpowers facing each other off. Then it was between the United States and the Soviet Union, with security, ideology, and politics the major theaters of engagement and potential conflict, whereas today economic issues are as salient. In other words, it was, to use C. Fred Bergsten's (2008) characterization, a G-2 then as it is a G-2 now, with only the areas of conflict and cooperation differing.

Of course, all these historical parallels are incomplete or even misleading. China today has the size to be globally dominant in a way that Germany prior to World War I could only aspire to in Europe, but not in the world. The implicit power hand-off in the interwar years was between two allies that shared a vision about organizing society that comprised the Fukuyaman end-of-history ingredients of democratic politics and market-based and market-driven economics supported by some safety nets (Fukuyama 1992). Today the relationship between the two powers, while not adversarial, has elements of rivalry and conflict. Further, they do not, at least as yet, share the same societal vision. Moreover, the world is also much more globalized today than it was in the interwar years, when all the major countries turned protectionist for substantial periods of time. And there is no analogue today to the rise of Nazi Germany.

Finally, 2011 is not 1945 in some major ways: No global conflict has bequeathed a *tabula rasa*, a blank slate on which to write the new rules of economic engagement. To the contrary, China enters a global economic order that is highly elaborated if not always particularly effective. Just as important is the fact that never in history—not before World War I, during the interwar years, or after World War II—has there been a globally dominant or rising economic power whose standard of living has been substantially lower than that of the status quo power and lower than that of many other countries.

Furthermore, today's world has a plurality of dominant actors even compared with the post-1945 period. When Europe speaks with one voice and because India and Brazil have important roles in certain areas, there are today more centers of power and certainly more veto points than perhaps ever before.

In terms of cooperation, though, one might describe today as a G-0 positive because even though leadership is diffused and veto points abound, the world has shown the capacity to cooperate in the most testing of times in two major ways—through collective acts of commission and omission.

First, at least in the face of the recent financial crisis, all the major countries undertook a mutually consistent and coordinated macroeconomic response, loosening monetary policy and injecting public demand to prevent the crisis from turning into another Great Depression.

Second, the collective act of omission was that countries refrained from beggar-thy-neighbor policies that would have undermined the open economic system. Despite the unprecedented collapse in trade—matching that during the Great Depression—few countries resorted to protectionist exchange rate or trade policies. For sure, there were big currency swings, but these were mostly market-driven—except in the case of China, where the hand of policy in manipulating competitiveness has been more evident. It is also true that several countries raised trade barriers. But these were small in magnitude, limited in geographic scope and product coverage, and mostly consistent with World Trade Organization (WTO) rules. The exception was the large-scale assistance to the financial and auto sectors, especially in the United States, supported at least by the extenuating argument that the assistance was aimed at averting extinction rather than providing a competitive boost. Overall, however, there was a general forswearing of beggar-thy-neighbor policies, stemming in large part from the awareness of their devastating consequences. Of course, this positive response to the crisis can also be assigned to the effectiveness of the newly created G-20 as the world's de facto steering committee.

Of course, with the passing of the crisis and the urgency brought by it, the world seems have reverted to a kind of G-0 negative because the lack of clear leadership has rendered cooperation difficult on a host of issues such as climate change, trade, and exchange rates.

The truth is one is in a fuzzier, more muddled world with history supplying only imperfect analogies and providing limited guidance. Whether G-2, G-0 plus, G-0 minus, or G-20, it is time to narrow in on China's incentives and interests in, and attitudes to, cooperation as it becomes dominant.

Prospects for Cooperation Leading Up to Chinese Hegemony

Drawing on some of the key findings in the previous chapters, prospects for cooperation can be captured in the following sequence of propositions:

(1) Yes, Chinese dominance will mean that China's actions will be largely beyond the ability of outsiders to influence and that China will subordinate external imperatives to domestic interests.

(2) However, Chinese mercantilism, a source of today's conflict, will likely be phased out over time, which . . .

(3) . . . would leave behind a China that is highly open to trade, with an unprecedented stake in maintaining an open trade and financial system, which in turn . . .

(4) . . . would make the WTO, not the International Monetary Fund (IMF), the key arena for international cooperation involving China, which is not necessarily bad because . . .

(5) . . . in the postwar period, the WTO and not the IMF has been the most legitimate multilateral institution and the only forum that has had a modicum of success in mediating relationships between the large and dominant countries.

Before elaborating on these five propositions, it should be emphasized that the analysis will not assess the scope of political and security cooperation between the major countries and China. Nor will it examine the very important questions of whether and when China will become democratic and the role of the military in domestic Chinese politics. All these questions might shape China's attitude toward multilateral economic engagement. But the broad thrust of the discussion below will, hopefully, remain relevant for most likely realizations of noneconomic outcomes.

The Demise of "Chimerica:" Self-Interest Rather than External Influence

The first and most obvious implication for cooperation from a rising Chinese dominance must be emphasized. This is captured by Niall Ferguson's term "Chimerica," which has been taken to connote the mutual dependence of the United States and China. But it is increasingly coming to mean that China is beyond the scope of influence of the United States and outsiders more broadly, especially when influence is wielded through sticks. Several recent examples illustrate this. The United States has had limited success in changing China's exchange rate policy, and it has not been able to meaningfully change China's stance on the Doha Round or climate change.

Consider some conventional sticks and carrots. Trade sanctions are proving less effective or even ineffective because of the possibility of China's retaliation, which in turn reflects the relative economic size and trade of China and the United States, which is now roughly at parity. If China's market is important to US firms, whose business China has facilitated by letting them invest heavily in the country, then that will diminish the US government's leverage over China. This is the dynamic at work in the exchange rate discussions, where the US trade stick has had to be wielded so tentatively—because US companies were at best ambivalent about China's policy—as to not be very credible as a threat. In terms of financial carrots it is China, as the bankroller, rather than the United States, as the bankrollee, that has the upper hand.

So "Chimerica" and the rise of China mean that international cooperation will be successful only when each of these two countries perceives cooperation to be in its own interest. That interest will not be significantly determined by the carrots or sticks that the other can deploy. It is not that external ideas and values—such as democracy—will not be an important factor in influencing domestic politics or represent a challenge to the legitimacy of the Chinese government. But external power cannot be wielded to significantly change the incentives facing Chinese policymakers. If there is a clash of interests over key issues such as exchange rates or technology protection, securing cooperation will be less easy, more prolonged, and messier or simply prove elusive.

It is not that China will never change some of its more problematic polices. China will no doubt change its exchange rate policy because of the need to curb rising inflation, to reduce export dependence, or to internationalize the renminbi, but not because of threats by the US Congress to deny China market access. China might take action on climate change because it sees competitive advantage in being the leader in green technology or because the retreat of the Himalayan glacier threatens its supply of water. But it will not take action because the United States demands that China as the world's largest polluter contribute its fair share to mitigating climate change. China also might eventually move away from or beyond technology protectionism, but only because it has itself become an exporter of technology, not because US firms complain about indigenization and intellectual property theft and piracy. In this sense, China will be no different than the United States has been in the last 50 years, when it seldom subordinated important domestic objectives to international ones, as discussed in chapter 1. The key point is that the China of 2011 and beyond will be very different from the China that agreed to comprehensively open up its economy as part of WTO accession not much more than a decade ago in part because of the sticks wielded and carrots offered by the United States and other trading partners.[3]

The Likely Demise of Mercantilism

From the current vantage point, Chinese exchange rate policy seems like it is undermining the spirit—and some would argue the letter—of international

---

3. As noted earlier, Chinese leadership in the late 1990s used the WTO as an external anchor to pursue domestic reforms.

trading rules.[4] This portends badly for the future of international cooperation with China in the ascendant.

The international implications or the beggar-thy-neighbor consequences of Chinese mercantilism are undeniable. But looking ahead, it is quite possible, albeit not inevitable, that Chinese mercantilism will pass. As described in chapter 5, all the signs are that China has embraced the objective of internationalizing the renminbi and embarked on a process to achieve it.

The political economy of Chinese exchange rate policy pits export interests, which have become accustomed to the de facto subsidy from an undervalued exchange rate, against two other constituencies: the central bank and the fiscal conservatives who worry about the large quasi-fiscal losses that will accrue from the eventual and inevitable rise of the renminbi (Yu 2010). The more reserves that are accumulated, the greater the eventual losses, which could reach 20 to 25 percent of GDP.

There are also the elite policymakers who have taken away the lesson from the recent global financial crisis that export dependence came at the high cost of exposing a large part of the economy to external events: One estimate suggests that about 20 million people in China were under risk of dislocation from the downturn in the world economy. Severe dislocation was avoided because China's healthy public sector balance sheet allowed the government to step in and make up for the collapse of external demand. But this may not be easy or possible in the future. So China might sooner rather than later embrace a rebalancing strategy (advocated by Lardy 2007) that relies less on foreign demand and mercantilism and more on the domestic market to sustain long-run growth. Rising Chinese inflation will also strengthen domestic pressures for renminbi appreciation.

In this political economy struggle, export interests have been winning for standard reasons: They are more concentrated and the benefits they derive are tangible and clearly attributable to an undervalued exchange rate. In contrast, opponents of the current policy are few (the central bank and some policymakers) and the costs somewhat counterfactual (they would have been felt more acutely had the government not stepped in with the fiscal stimulus).

The way policymakers are tilting this calculus is through internationalization of the renminbi. As described in chapter 5, internationalization is proceeding in typically Chinese fashion—micromanaged, discretionary, selective, gradual, and enclave-based (as China did for its opening to trade and foreign direct investment via the special economic zones). One might call it interventionist liberalization. Not a day passes without some company, some country, or some transaction having greater access to the renminbi.

---

4. Article XV:4 of the GATT/WTO prevents countries from using exchange action to frustrate the intent and provisions of their trade obligations. Whether China's policy violates this clause is the subject of intense debate, although the weight of opinion comes down against such an interpretation (Hufbauer et al. 2006).

But internationalization of the renminbi cannot succeed without chipping away fundamentally at China's domestic financial repression and undervalued exchange rate, which underpin Chinese mercantilism. Internationalization of the renminbi will require the Chinese financial system to compete globally and offer attractive returns, including on banking system assets. Control of domestic interest rates and other restrictions on domestic banks cannot easily survive renminbi internationalization. For example, internationalization will mean that foreigners can hold domestic assets (and domestic residents, surely, can hold foreign assets). In that case, it will be impossible to subsidize domestic interest rates, because foreigners will then want to take advantage and borrow low-cost Chinese capital, while domestic residents will want to invest abroad in high-return currencies. Internationalization will be the death-knell for financial repression.

Similarly, as financial transactions increase, then speculative pressures will mount, and the costs of maintaining an undervalued currency will rise to the point where China will have to adjust the rate. In other words, foreigners seeking to invest in China and Chinese assets will put upward pressure on the currency, undercutting the ability to maintain undervalued exchange rates.

When the currency consequences of internationalization start affecting, and eliciting opposition from, export interests, the Chinese authorities will seek to overcome that by playing up the benefits of international reserve status of the renminbi. The calculus then will be that the economic losses (reduced exports and valuation losses) are matched by the gains to national prestige from encouraging the rise to reserve currency status of the renminbi. The trumpeting of symbolic and nationalist gains could serve to drown out the protests of those who might suffer substantive losses.[5]

To be sure, internationalization will proceed in a fashion much more slowly and messily than desired by outsiders, and much faster than can be countenanced by some domestic interests within China. But the process has been set in motion and might prove difficult to reverse. Above all there is—or appears to be—a plausible strategy to tackle the difficult political economy of the currency impasse that China has created for itself over the past decade.[6] "Renminbi rules" (and not the dollar) could be the slogan that China's policymakers use as they navigate their fraught exit from mercantilism.

A Reasonably Strong Chinese Stake in an Open Trading System

But a China that acts out of self-interest—at least on key issues—is not necessarily a China that will seek to roll back the open trade and financial system

---

5. Some might add the seigniorage gains from reserve currency status to the calculation, as well as the gains of running current account deficits and borrowing more cheaply, although China as a net borrower is not a near-term prospect.

6. Note that even if Chinese policymakers have embraced rebalancing as the right economic strategy going forward, they still need to overcome the political opposition to this strategy.

bequeathed by the United States after World War II. The case that China will broadly continue the current system over the next 20 years relies on one of the key findings in this book, namely the paradox that while China may currently be mercantilist, it is also highly open.

Taking account of China's size and the regularity that large countries tend to trade less than small countries, China is an exceptionally big importer and trader. Chapter 6 showed that the degree of China's openness, measured in terms of trade outcomes, is far greater than anything achieved by the United States in the postwar period and resembles the levels of openness achieved by the United Kingdom at the height of empire. To recap those numbers, the trade-to-GDP ratio for the United States rarely exceeded 15 percent during Pax Americana compared with China's current ratio of 57 percent. Even if this ratio trends down over time, China will remain a large trader.

Why is the fact of China's openness important? Chinese openness does not absolve Chinese mercantilism or eliminate its beggar-thy-neighbor consequences, especially for poorer countries. But a China that moves away from mercantilism will be a China that is an exceptionally large trader with strong stakes in maintaining an open trading and financial system.

US Secretary of State Cordell Hull famously said that where goods cross borders, armies don't, and that countries that trade goods don't trade blows. But historians and political scientists have argued that trade and the intertwining of interests that trade brings are no guarantee against economic or military conflict. They note that Germany just prior to World War I was a major trader. But there are two critical differences: China is trade dependent in a way that the United States or even Germany never were, and moreover, given China's low levels of income, its stake in openness might be greater because its rise to prosperity, which is still a way off and on which is predicated the legitimacy of its government, will depend on an open system.

After World War II, the United States fashioned such a system out of enlightened self-interest in which politics was perhaps even more important than economics. In contrast, China's interest in this system might be much more existential and stronger because of its low level of income. There will, of course be scores of skirmishes between China and its trading partners related to China's policies. But wholesale retreat into protectionism by China would create too much self-inflicted damage for it to be a serious policy option. Hence China's practical stake in keeping markets open.

One reading of China's exchange rate policy over the last few years is that undervaluation was seen a way of clawing back some of its trade opening concessions made as part of WTO accession, a kind of Penelope effect (discussed in chapter 6). Certainly, the timing of currency undervaluation—immediately following WTO accession—is consistent with this reading. With a decade of undervaluation and rapid growth behind it, China seemingly will be more willing to accept and abide by the terms of its WTO accession. In other words, the last decade was one when China revealed through its currency actions that it was still unwilling or able to abide by the rules, despite having de jure signed on to these rules. But going forward, perhaps one can be more confident that its stake in an open system will be more sustained.

There is another reason for believing that China's stake in an open system might deepen. The analysis above is that China is in fact promoting and seeking the rise of the renminbi, and the prediction in chapter 5 is that the fundamentals are moving in favor of such an outcome. If these are borne out, China is unlikely to act systematically in a protectionist and destabilizing manner. Such actions would undermine the reserve currency status of the renminbi that China seems to be seeking for external and domestic reasons. One would have to think that Chinese policymakers are unaware of the consequences and responsibilities of their aspirations for the renminbi. The steady criticisms and recriminations that have emanated from Beijing about the policies of the United States as the guardian of the major reserve currency suggest otherwise.

Arena of Cooperation: Trade Not Macroeconomics

Given the conjecture that exchange rate issues for China will become less salient over the next few years but trade will be of enduring importance, much of the focus of this chapter and the next is on international trade cooperation rather than macroeconomic cooperation. This might seem out of touch with current realities, especially considering that the Doha Round has been in a coma now for several years, while the recent global financial crisis and the effective response to it have rescued the IMF from nearly terminal irrelevance prior to the crisis. The public perception is one of a moribund multilateral trade system and a rejuvenated, relevant, and responsive multilateral economic and financial system, and almost all the policy discussion today focuses on reforms of the international monetary system.

However, the rationale here for focusing on international trade cooperation and neglecting monetary issues is twofold. First, it is likely that the vanes of taste and intellectual effort now pointing strongly in the direction of the IMF and the macroeconomic system will veer again toward trade and the trading system. That is likely not only because the rise of China will imply a shift toward trade issues, but also because there are greater limits to successful international monetary cooperation than to cooperation on trade. Put differently, the trading system has actually performed better than the macroeconomic system in two important respects: governance and as a forum of cooperation between the major players (which will be of relevance in thinking about China going forward).[7] Understanding why this is so will also explain

---

7. The appropriateness of comparing monetary and trade is itself controversial. Objections can come from opposite sides. One claim is that the same countries that sit around the table to discuss monetary matters also discuss trade matters, so there cannot be differences in cooperative outcomes across these areas. An entirely different objection to the comparison is that the theoretical rationale for macroeconomic cooperation is much less strong than it is for trade

the contention here that prospects for international monetary reform might not be quite as bright as they seem at the moment (box 8.1).

To project future cooperation involving China, historical parallels from the earlier half of the 20th century or the late 1800s may not be instructive, but there is the history of postwar economic cooperation between two superpowers in the trade arena (the United States and European Union) and to a lesser extent between the United States and various large countries such as Germany and Japan in relation to macroeconomic and exchange rate issues.

Of the three major multilateral institutions created after World War II—the World Bank, IMF, and the General Agreement on Tariffs and Trade (GATT), which subsequently became the WTO—the GATT/WTO is the one institution that has fared well in two key respects. First, its governance has evolved organically to keep up with changing economic (and political) realities. The international financial institutions (IMF and World Bank)—and it might be added the UN Security Council—suffer from a crisis of legitimacy in a way that is less true of the GATT/WTO. The IMF's outdated governance reflects the receded Atlantic-centered realities of 1945 rather than the ascendant Asia of the 21st century. Emerging-market countries have expressed skepticism about the role of the IMF and its credibility. In contrast, the GATT/WTO has changed its governance endogenously to broadly reflect changes in economic weight in the world economy. As explained below, these governance changes relate less to formal voting procedures (which have not changed substantially over time) and more to do with de facto governance, that is, perceptions of legitimacy and effectiveness that determine the fundamental incentives to cooperate, to agree to new rules and subsequently abide by them.

Second, in the postwar period the GATT/WTO was an important and effective mediator of trade relationships (especially of frictions and conflicts) between the major powers (notably the United States and European Union) in a way that the IMF seldom was in the macroeconomic arena. Macroeconomic issues have mostly been resolved through the G-5 or the G-7 industrial countries as in the Plaza and Louvre exchange rate accords of the mid-to-late 1980s.

What is the evidence for these two virtues—that capture two important dimensions of governance, legitimacy and effectiveness—of the GATT/WTO over the IMF? Take, for example, initiation of conflict resolution and compliance with rules.

The WTO has developed a reputation among its members as a forum for relatively impartial dispute settlement. Any country affected by the actions of others is able to complain to the WTO, bringing into play a well-established, frequently used, and generally respected system of dispute settlement. In fact,

---

cooperation, where the intellectual pedigree establishing the mutuality and magnitude of gains is time honored and well established. So comparison would not just be a case of comparing apples and oranges, it would also unfairly favor trade because of the clear expectation of benefits from cooperation.

Box 8.1   Limits to international monetary cooperation

Proposals for reform of the international monetary system are flying fast and furious around the globe. The key role played by the International Monetary Fund (IMF) in the crises of 2008–2011 has not only helped rescue it from the brink of irrelevance, it has raised the ambition for future systemic reform. This sense of possibility has also been fed by the return of the IMF as an intellectual player with its backing of un-IMF-like policies: fiscal expansion during the crisis and imposition of capital account controls more recently.

The prospects for any serious reform, however, remain slim because of the inherent limits to international monetary cooperation. Systemic threats arise from the policies of the largest countries, and in particular when polices pursued in self-interest conflict with the collective interest. But, by definition, it is difficult for the rest of the world to change the incentives of the large country to give more weight to the collective interest. Successful cooperation is fated to falter if not fail. This is in contrast to trade cooperation which can be reasonably effective even between the major players because of reciprocity and the exchange of concessions highlighted in the text.

Consider three of the major issues on the agenda of IMF reform: global imbalances, reserve currencies, and provision of emergency or crisis financing (the "global safety net"). Global imbalances are in part a manifestation of the asymmetric adjustment problem. Deficit countries have greater pressure on them to adjust via markets or via the leverage of financing that allows creditors to impose policy conditionality on debtors.[1] What leverage can be exerted over creditor countries, especially the large ones?[2]

If the world has found it difficult to persuade China to appreciate its currency and reduce its surplus, that is not the first instance of failure. As John Williamson (2011, 1) has noted: "It has been 80 years since John Maynard Keynes first proposed a plan that would have disciplined persistent surplus countries. But the Keynes Plan, like the subsequent Volcker Plan in 1972–74, was defeated by the major surplus country of the day (the United States and Germany, respectively), and today China (not to mention Japan or Germany) exhibits no enthusiasm for new revisions of these ideas."

The question to ponder is whether there is anything that the rest of the world could have done—by way of sticks or carrots—to have persuaded the US in 1944, Germany in 1973 or China in 2007 to change their positions or policies for the collective good.

On reserve currencies, the reform-related discussions have focused on creating official alternatives to the dollar by rehabilitating the special drawing rights (SDR). These discussions are a side-show because countries with reserve currencies—actual and aspiring—must be willing to actively take steps and make contribu-

Box 8.1   Limits to international monetary cooperation
  (continued)

tions to promote the alternative at the expense of their own currencies. It is like asking Coke to also tout the virtues of Pepsi in its ad campaigns.

Although the United States played a key role in the creation of the SDR in the 1960s that was in part an attempt to prevent a rush into gold, which would have jeopardized the role of the dollar. Its attitude to the SDR would have been quite different had the SDR become a serious rival to the dollar. China is likely to adopt a similar attitude to the SDR in the future. Natural market forces are inevitably, if slowly, working to elevate the renminbi to reserve currency status. China will have to undertake some key reforms to turn that possibility into reality. All the signs are that it is doing so because not a day passes without some foreign country, transaction or company gaining greater access to the renminbi. In these circumstances, why would China have any serious incentive to strengthen an SDR that might check the rise of its own currency? And if China decides to promote the renminbi, the rest of the world can do little to prevent or delay that as it has proved difficult to change the incentives for China to reverse its mercantilism.

A corollary of the observation that cooperation is least likely where the self-interest of the largest countries are at stake is that the prospects for successful cooperation are greater where these countries are less affected and when the demands on them are minimal. Building global safety nets via greater and more expeditious access to crisis financing is in fact one area where the greatest progress has already been made. The Fund's lending ability has been increased three-fold after the crisis and more may yet come. For the large countries, it is both desirable and effective to push for larger safety nets. The costs are relatively small, involving larger financial contributions rather than any major change of domestic policies. And the rewards are great because the system as a whole is strengthened while the individual clout of the large countries is increased.

The IMF will be what it always has been. It is a valuable provider of global public goods such as research, analysis and institution-building in member countries. And it is a very effective forum for "cooperation" between creditors and borrowers because of the clout that creditors can exercise. The IMF, with some exaggeration, stands for Insolvents Must Fawn, albeit with different insolvents having to fawn to different degrees. But the institution's dirty secret is that, outside this creditor-borrower context it has not really been successful in securing cooperation between the systemically critical players, in getting them to subordinate, in some

(box continues next page)

key instances, narrow self-interest over the collective good. That reality is unlikely to change materially. What is changing is merely the identity of the systemically critical players.

1. For debtors with reserve currencies these pressures might be attenuated.
2. It is true that the United States under President Richard Nixon in 1971 was able to get some surplus countries (including Germany) to revalue their currencies but it is worth remembering that that attempt: was directed against large but not the largest players, relied on trade sanctions not monetary or financial carrots and sticks, and in any event proved short-lived reflected in the break-down of the Bretton Woods system of pegged exchange rates in 1973.

disputes are the stuff of WTO proceedings, and it is not unusual to bring a dispute in the WTO, a possibility that is absent in the IMF.

The WTO's legitimacy is highlighted by the fact that bringing disputes in the organization has become much more of a two-way practice (in the sense of industrial and developing countries being both complainants and defendants). For example, the United States has been a complainant in 88 disputes and a defendant in 99 disputes. The analogous figures for India are 17 and 19; and for Brazil 23 and 14. Even China has initiated seven disputes in the WTO, of which five have been against the United States (Hufbauer and Woollacott 2010). Not only are the large developing countries active complainants, so are small countries. Tiny Costa Rica successfully challenged US trade practices. Tinier Antigua (with a population of less than 100,000) successfully challenged US gambling laws.

Effectiveness is illustrated by reasonably good (though not perfect) compliance with dispute settlement rulings. As of 2007, the compliance rate for all disputes was above 80 percent (Wilson 2007). Crucially, not just developing countries have complied. The major trading powers have exhibited good behavior. Of the 33 cases where violations were established, the United States has complied or is in the process of complying solely through administrative actions in 26 cases. The European Union has complied in nearly all the 16 cases where it was found to be violating WTO rules.[8]

One free-trade-oriented critique of WTO dispute settlement is that it is based on retaliation, which can be extremely dangerous. But instances of retaliation have been relatively few. Of the 109 cases surveyed, only in eight was retaliation requested and authorized. Compliance thus occurs mostly without actual retaliation, although some threat of it is always present and is perhaps even necessary. Experience suggests that the mere prospect of retaliation, as

---

8. There are, however, concerns about delays in compliance (Davey 2009).

well as the reluctance to be seen as a rule-breaker, are sufficient to ensure compliance, and there is rarely need for action.

The comparable picture for the IMF is dismal. In terms of legitimacy, the IMF has attempted periodically to revise its governance and decision-making structure by changing the allocation of quotas. Most recently at the G-20 summit in Korea, the IMF agreed to a further shift in quotas away from the United States and Europe toward the dynamic emerging-market countries. However, despite this effort and others, including the move to make money accessible at cheaper rates and with less conditionality, there is a fundamental problem with the IMF, captured in the stigma associated with borrowing from it. Ask any Asian country whether it would contemplate borrowing from the IMF in the foreseeable future and the answer is likely to be negative.

On effectiveness, especially where larger countries are involved, the IMF's record is poor. It should be remembered that while the IMF has been able to effect changes in member-country policies in the context of financial arrangements, it has not been influential without the leverage of financing. In its key surveillance function (where no financing is involved), there have been relatively few instances where IMF intervention has led to changes in the policies of large creditor countries even when such policies have had significant spillover effects on others. In other words, the IMF has not been able to persuade these countries to sacrifice domestic objectives for systemic ones. There seems to be an implicit "pact of mutual nonaggression," in IMF surveillance, as Bergsten and C. Randall Henning (1996) and long-serving IMF Economic Counselor Michael Mussa (2008) have argued.[9] The IMF has had a history and tradition of nonadversarial dialogue between its members in a surveillance context and has not had to develop a real dispute settlement system. There is no legal mechanism in the IMF for affected members to initiate action against the offending party.

And in fact, when serious problems have arisen—for example, over currency issues in the early 1970s (the break-up of the Bretton Woods System) and over the dollar and the yen in the mid-to-late 1980s—they were largely resolved outside the IMF, either bilaterally or through the G-5 and G-7. During the European Exchange Rate Mechanism crisis of the early 1990s too, Europe kept the IMF largely out of the discussions. And the IMF was involved in the recent turmoil in Europe largely because financial resources were at stake.

But the historical record is actually worse. It is also forgotten that the early years of the IMF were notorious for the major players largely ignoring the key IMF article requiring members to keep their exchange rates pegged and changing them only after consultation. Canada through much of the

9. Cohen (1998, 161–62) describes this asymmetric effectiveness well: "[T]he IMF's writ has come to run mainly to smaller and poorer member countries, where authority can be exercised through the organization's control of access to credit as well as through policy conditions attached to its loans. For larger and wealthier states, by contrast—arguably the most critical actors from a systemic point of view—the direct role of the IMF has dwindled over time . . ."

Bretton Woods period maintained a floating exchange rate. France devalued its exchange rate in 1948 and in 1969; and the United Kingdom devalued sterling in 1949 and 1967 and only nominally consulted the IMF. The Deutsche mark floated upward in 1962, in late 1969, and again in the early 1970s, which elicited the comment from the Canadian representative: "They'll have to build a bigger dog house now."

Except in rare instances, no erring country has been penalized.[10] Indeed, a cynical interpretation of the post-1973 IMF was that it reincarnated itself as a forum for soft cooperation based on surveillance because the harder form based on clear, hard obligations demonstrably failed.

Exchange and Reciprocity as Determinants of the Efficacy of the World Trade Organization

In order to examine how effective the WTO or WTO-type governance will be going forward, one needs to understand why the WTO works and whether these factors will persist over time and survive China's rise. There are two related reasons why the WTO has had more legitimate governance and been more effective in dealings between the rich countries than has the IMF.

First, trade inherently lends itself to exchange. If a country gets large, others automatically have an incentive to engage with that country in order to gain access to growing markets. The history of the GATT confirms this. In the seven bouts of tariff negotiations prior to the Uruguay Round and the formation of the WTO, only the industrial countries were meaningful participants in multilateral trade negotiations because only these markets were large (WTO 2007). They bargained among themselves to reduce trade barriers, while developing countries were largely left out of this process and had few obligations to liberalize. They availed themselves of the benefits of industrial-country liberalization, courtesy of the most favored nation (MFN) principle, but that defined pretty much the limits of their contribution to or benefits from the GATT. Industrial countries were content with this arrangement, in part because it alleviated the pressure on them to liberalize sensitive sectors such as agriculture and clothing, but perhaps more importantly because the markets of developing countries were not at that stage sufficiently attractive. It did not really matter enough to the industrial countries to exert pressure on developing countries to liberalize: The benefits were smaller than the costs of having to liberalize their own labor-intensive sectors (Wolf 1987).

As development and globalization proceeded apace through the 1980s, hitherto "small" developing countries started growing in size and becoming attractive to industrial-country exporters as markets. This "shock" of the economic transformation of a large number of developing countries (con-

---

10. France (1948), Czechoslovakia (1953), and Kampuchea (1978) were three early instances of countries having to face some kind of sanctions. Czechoslovokia was expelled from the IMF in 1954.

vergence) meant that the previous equilibrium whereby developing countries were left out of the GATT process needed to be revisited.[11]

The Uruguay Round was then precisely the required adjustment to this shock and established a new "equilibrium." The larger developing countries were brought into the fold because their markets started to matter, and they in turn had to take on many of the obligations of industrial countries. The two-tiered approach was abandoned to create a symmetry of obligations between all members.

The second reason the WTO works is reciprocity—the exchange of concessions to open markets. Robert Solow's demotion of the economics profession to accounting, quoted at the beginning of this chapter, nevertheless has powerful implications for trade. That one country's exports is another's imports and vice-versa creates the basis for reciprocity. This is the heart of the GATT/WTO process and one that ensures that all players feel that they have derived a fair political "bargain." Reciprocity ensures political buy-in to cooperation. What periodic negotiations have done in the GATT/WTO is to update this political contract between countries, redressing some old grievances and papering over others, with the implicit understanding that there will be a future occasion to take up the unsolvable problems of the day.

A consequence of reciprocity and the periodic updating of the political contract to cooperate, and another reason why the WTO works, is that this process creates the incentives to adhere to the dispute settlement contract. WTO dispute settlement is effective largely because countries feel that they have previously (and recently) made a reasonably advantageous, fair, and equitable bargain to which they must adhere. It is interesting here that a number of WTO rulings have gone against China, which it has not protested but rather chosen to implement. India, despite having strenuously opposed the introduction of intellectual property in the WTO, now complies with WTO dispute settlement rulings asking for changes to Indian intellectual property laws and practice. WTO governance works because negotiations to create the rules and agree on liberalization are perceived as fair and broadly equitable in outcome, which renders subsequent compliance with the rules and agreements possible.

From a governance perspective, whereas power in the Bretton Woods institutions was historically determined and has proved immutable (especially since the currently powerful have been reluctant to cede power), power and influence in the WTO evolve organically because they flow from market size. As China, India, and Brazil have grown rapidly, they have naturally and without any help from other countries become serious players in the trading system. They have commanded power. They have not needed it to be granted to them.

---

11. This underlay the loaded rhetoric during the Uruguay Round that developing countries were free riders in the system, extracting the benefits from MFN status and offering little by way of their own liberalization.

One important caveat to this glossy reading of the WTO is the contention that WTO rules never impinge on big and important policy issues such as exchange rates or monetary policy. Cooperation on everything from underwear to shirts and semi-conductor chips will always be easier than cooperation on exchange rates or monetary policy. This charge—that some issues are too big to negotiate or litigate in the WTO—might have some validity but should not be overstated. Agricultural subsidies, intellectual property laws, tax policies, and consumer safety are all issues that have major political implications domestically and have been addressed with some degree of success in the WTO.

If this analysis of the WTO's efficacy is valid—and to the extent that China feels that it has gained from WTO accession and its terms, and values an open rules-based trade system from which it has gained immensely—China will have a reasonable incentive to abide by existing WTO rules. In this sense, it is encouraging that China is becoming more of a routine participant in WTO dispute settlement proceedings both as an initiator of disputes and as a respondent. It is also encouraging that so far, China has largely agreed to comply with the terms of WTO dispute settlement proceedings. For example, of the eight cases brought by the United States, three have been resolved by a memorandum of understanding, two are pending decision, and in three China has claimed compliance with the decision of the Dispute Settlement Body. China's actual compliance will take some time to ascertain, and there is always scope for circumventing actions—especially in China's case given the vast amount of economic activity controlled or directed by the state. But all the indications are that China takes its WTO commitments seriously.

If an economically dominant China will have a reasonably strong stake in maintaining the current open trade and economic system and if the existing trade institutions can be reasonably effective in coping with such a China, what then is the problem for the world and for economic cooperation? What could go wrong?

9

China as the New Raison d'Être for Reviving Multilateralism

[Opium was] a mere incident to the dispute . . . the cause of the war is the kowtow—the arrogant and insupportable pretensions of China that she will hold commercial intercourse with the rest of mankind not upon terms of equal reciprocity, but upon the insulting and degrading forms of the relations between lord and vassal.

—US President John Quincy Adams, on China's attitude to trade

In 1910, Norman Angell, future Nobel Peace Prize Winner, published *The Great Illusion*, a pamphlet-turned-book that acquired cult status for propagating the view that Europe had become so interlaced economically through trade, credit, and finance that war was impossible (Ahamed 2009). Twentieth-century wars would be so economically devastating even to the aggressor that waging it would amount to self-inflicted folly.[1]

Notwithstanding the fact that Angell was proved so catastrophically wrong, one would have to maintain that the world today has once again become so, and so much more, intertwined that not just wars but even economic aggression by dominant powers must be very low probability outcomes. The world's trade-to-GDP ratio in 1913 was about 15 percent; today it is close to 50 percent. Global financial integration—measured as the stock of world external liabilities/assets to world GDP—amounted to about 20 to 30 percent in 1913; today it is closer to 200 percent.[2]

More broadly, there are many more active participants in, and beneficiaries of, globalized trade and finance than ever before. Further, prior to World

---

1. In the words of Lord Esher, who was Angell's most earnest disciple, the inevitable consequences of "commercial disaster, financial ruin, and individual suffering," would be "pregnant with restraining influences" (Tuchman 1962, 12).

2. The trade data are from Maddison (2001); financial globalization data for 1913 from Schularick (2006) and for 2009 from an update of Lane and Milesi-Ferretti (2007).

War I, while the world was globalized, the flows were mostly unidirectional: Capital and manufactured goods flowed from Europe (and to a lesser extent the United States) to the periphery, commodities the other way, and labor from Europe to the United States. In contrast, modern trading and financial relationships, notably the slicing up of the value-added chain and foreign direct investment (FDI) have created greater two-way flows of capital, goods, and ideas—leading to the phenomenon of "criss-crossing globalization" (Mattoo and Subramanian 2010)—which create enmeshing and interlocking private interests to a greater degree than ever before.

China itself embodies this criss-crossing globalization. It is the hub for many of the modern value-added chains resulting in a high level of imports and exports and its outward FDI is beginning to catch up with FDI inflows into China.[3] Moreover, as argued in earlier chapters, China—with its unusually high dependence on trade for completing the catching up process—will have a vested interest in an open trading system and hence act, even lead, to preserve it. And if the renminbi ascends to become an international reserve currency, China might be reluctant to lose the prestige, and any associated benefit, that comes with that status by disrupting financial and trade relations in any serious way.

So, is the current open, rules-based economic system safe? History's lesson is that one can never be sure. One cannot be certain that the enmeshing of interests will be strong enough to sustain the status quo. Nor is there a cast-iron guarantee that the current ideological embrace of markets as the predominant basis for organizing economic relations will survive the vicissitudes of intellectual fashion, the selective and self-serving interpretations of policymakers, and the financial crises that will inevitable shock the modern global economy. There is tail-side risk that interests, ideology, and institutions, both domestic and international, will be inadequate to the task of preserving the current system. And then there is always the unforeseeable and the irrational. World War I, after all, did happen.

So, there remains a small possibility of an eventual unbenign exercise of dominance by a hegemonic or near-hegemonic China. President John Quincy Adams's remarks, hysterically off the mark at the time they were made, might nevertheless carry some resonance in the future. What economic forms might such hegemony take? A dominant China could reverse some of its past liberalization (as for example it has done with its exchange rate policy); it could maintain or pursue industrial and quasi-protectionist policies domestically; it could attempt to capture essential resources (energy, food, and commodities) abroad and enter into bilateral and discriminatory arrangements with selected partners, all of which given the country's size could affect the fundamental character of the current economic system.

Historically, the United States during Pax Americana was noteworthy in refraining from exercising most if not all these forms of dominance. With ex-

---

3. In 2009, the outward and inward FDI figures were, respectively, $57 billion and $94 billion.

ceptions noted in chapter 1, its markets remained open, and until recently, it practiced nondiscriminatory trade. And as a net importer of energy and commodities, it ensured access to these resources through political and security arrangements (for example, in the Middle East and Gulf). This followed the recognition that ensuring access through ownership of these supplies across the globe was not a viable strategy in the face of a strong desire on the part of resource-owning nations not to allow majority-foreign ownership of energy resources (Yergin 2008).

China's economic dominance going forward is more likely to manifest itself in its own protectionism more than via monopolizing access to resources or by entering into discriminatory arrangements. As Aaditya Mattoo and I (forthcoming) argue, energy is becoming more diversified in terms of type and geographic location; and barriers in other countries have come down in a way that makes discriminatory trading arrangements by China less of a threat. So, it is preventing a reversal of liberalization of the Chinese market and facilitating its further opening that will be of main concern to outsiders.[4] But can these be achieved through international cooperation?

Limits to the Efficacy of Trade Reciprocity with a Dominant China

The previous chapter argued that after World War II, reasonably successful cooperation between the two dominant trading powers—the United States and Europe, the G-2 of that era—was achieved in the GATT/WTO via reciprocal exchange of market-opening commitments. Can this same mechanism help or be effective going forward with China as a dominant trader? Will it be possible to avoid the unbenign exercise of China's dominance and get greater market opening in China and reduce its policy barriers, especially in all those areas that are not covered by WTO rules such as China's government procurement, investment rules, technology indigenization, and service sector policies?

There might indeed be a structural problem, limiting the scope for reciprocity. When the United States and European Union dealt with each other in the postwar period, their markets were open, and in some areas closed, but broadly to the same extent. This symmetry facilitated reciprocity. In the future, problems could arise because the United States and European Union are in policy terms more open than China. This is a structural problem for cooperation going forward stemming from a situation in which economically dominant powers for the first time are at different stages of development.

China, although highly open in terms of trade outcomes, and although it has made great strides in removing policy barriers as part of WTO accession, is,

---

4. Charles Kindleberger argued that a benign hegemon needed to perform three functions to provide systemic stability: maintain open markets, provide countercyclical long-term lending, and supply short-term liquidity in a crisis. In the case of China, it is the first that seems most in question and hence the focus of the discussion here.

however, more closed in policy terms especially outside the traditional goods area, for example, in services, technology, and government procurement, with the closed policies taking the form of continuing state control over a large part of economic activity.[5] According to Gootiz and Mattoo (2008), China's service sector policies are about three times as restrictive as those of the United States. In any future bargain, the United States will, by virtue of previous liberalization, have less to offer China.

The paradox will be that China will have greater leverage in bargaining by virtue of its much larger trade and market size but will also have the greater policy barriers. It is as if in a duel, one party offers both the smaller target and has the pistol with greater range of shot. For example, by 2020, China's imports will be one-and-a half times that of the United States and twice as large as Germany, conferring the kind of power that comes with being able to determine access to its markets, the power that the United States has enjoyed during much of the postwar period. Future bargaining will therefore be structurally imbalanced in China's favor, and reciprocity therefore more difficult to achieve.

This structural imbalance will be a persistent source of tension between the United States and China. If the US manufacturing sector hollows out, and as the United States comes to rely to an even greater degree on services and intellectual property, it will seek to open markets overseas, including and especially in China. If China's future opening is slow, the United States, over time, might be increasingly tempted to play the unfairness card based on the disparate levels of policy openness: Why should US markets be more open than that of a rival and equal?

This imbalance in bargaining could remain at the level of sparring and skirmishing without systemic consequences. But suppose the United States has difficulty addressing its structural economic problems: high unemployment, stagnating median household income, rising inequality, and declining economic mobility, all creating a large, disaffected, and beleaguered middle class. And suppose that in this climate, the intellectual consensus in favor of openness gets increasingly frayed, as has been evident in the last few years. Recall that a stellar cast of intellectuals—from Paul Samuelson to Paul Krugman, Alan Blinder, and Larry Summers—has expressed misgivings about different aspects of globalization.[6]

---

5. It is important to stress that China is mercantilist but open in terms of trade outcomes, the latter reflecting in part that its policy barriers in agriculture and goods are reasonably low. But exceptional trade and mercantilist outcomes, which relate largely to traditional areas, are consistent with China being restrictive and maintaining high barriers in the new areas.

6. Samuelson (2004) argued that the rise of developing countries such as China and India could compromise living standards in the West by worsening the terms of trade—that is, by making imports more expensive. Krugman (2009) has focused on the impact of imports from developing countries, and China in particular, on the distribution of income in rich countries and wages of their less-skilled population. His conclusion is that, "It is likely that the rapid growth of trade since the early 1990s has had significant distributional effects," and more specifically that "it is

If the United States is frustrated by an unwillingness on China's part to open new sectors of its economy, lacks the carrots to overcome this unwillingness, faces a weak economic climate and shifting intellectual certitudes, and is goaded by perceptions that China is not making its fair contribution to keeping markets open, the United States might be tempted to threaten to close its own market to China unless China further opens its own. The implicit bargaining approach here would thus not be "first-difference reciprocity"—that is, "you open your markets for my opening mine." Rather, it would be "level reciprocity"—"you open your markets for my refraining from closing mine so that we can all be similarly open."

How can this tension be best managed—it cannot be eliminated—to prevent a major trade conflict in the years ahead? Put differently, what insurance can the world take out today against the small chance of a damagingly assertive China in the future? It seems that the only real insurance is multilateralism, or more specifically, keeping China tethered to the multilateral system. The historical analogy would be the post–World War II experience of anchoring Germany in Europe and European structures. The objective and motive then were largely political although the early instruments deployed were economic. In the case of China, the motive would be to preempt economic hegemony.

One must keep in mind a broader truth, or rather the big dirty secret, about cooperation in general. Vis-à-vis a dominant power, on the one hand, no cooperation can be effective if some critical self-interest is at stake for the dominant power, and on the other, no cooperation might even be necessary if natural forces are at work that align self-interest with the collective interest. Cooperation is only necessary, and perhaps possible, for the muddy middle, the grey zone where neither the consonance of self-interest and collective interest nor the clash between the two is particularly strong.

For that grey area, multilateralism offers the best hope for placing checks on dominant economic powers. One cannot, however, be overly confident about the efficacy of multilateralism in checking China's exercise of dominance. The experience of recent attempts to persuade China to change its exchange rate policy is instructive. The more promising prospects for inducing Chinese cooperation have arisen when a number of countries, including

---

probably true that this increase (in manufactured imports from developing countries) . . . has been a force for greater inequality in the United States and other developed countries" (Krugman 2009, 134–35). Blinder (2009) has drawn attention to the employment and wage consequences of the outsourcing that has been facilitated by technological change and trade in services. He estimates that between 22 and 29 percent of all US jobs will be offshored or offshorable within the next decade or two. And most recently, Summers (2008a, 2008b) has highlighted the problems stemming from increasing capital mobility. Hypermobile US capital creates a double whammy for American workers: First, as companies flee in search of cheaper labor abroad (the "giant sucking sound" in Ross Perot's evocative and provocative phrase), American workers become less productive (because they have less capital to work with) and hence receive lower wages; the "exit" option for capital also reduces its incentive to invest in domestic labor. Second, capital mobility also impairs the ability of domestic policy to respond to labor's problem through redistribution because of an erosion in the tax base as countries compete to attract capital by reducing their tax rates.

emerging markets such as Brazil, India, Indonesia, and Mexico, have expressed concern about China's policy, rather than when the United States has acted alone. The sobering reality—and one that should engender realism rather than optimism about multilateralism—is that even these collective efforts have had only limited success. Hence multilateralism should be viewed as a necessary rather than sufficient insurance policy.

Thus, the aim of China's trading partners—and the list must go beyond the United States to include other major ones such as the European Union, Japan, Brazil, and India, for starters—should be to make multilateralism a habit for China rather than a distraction or inconvenience. The aim would be to make multilateralism so routine and legitimized over the next several years—the period of transition to possible Chinese dominance—that there would be serious costs to China, reputationally and substantively, if it were to depart from it once its dominance becomes entrenched.

What will it take to legitimize multilateralism and make it routine? Facilitating this might require one or even two acts of self-restraint by China's major trading powers. First, they should all refrain from negotiating bilateral free trade agreements with China, at least in relation to areas covered by the WTO (goods, services, government procurement, and intellectual property). If some of these countries negotiate bilateral trade agreements, then all of them will have less multilateral dealings with China. The problem is not just that bilateral agreements with China might be imbalanced but also that enforcement of rules and agreements is likely to be more difficult bilaterally than multilaterally. In other words, China's economic dominance might get reflected in imbalanced rules and opening as well as asymmetric adherence to them. As it is, China's trading partners are concerned that China might not live up to its WTO obligations—e.g., in the area of intellectual property rights enforcement, the United States claims lost sales of about $50 billion from trademark and especially copyright infringements (USITC 2011)—or might subtly circumvent them as it has done say with its exchange rate policy. Imagine the difficulties if these obligations had to be enforced bilaterally.

The more that countries elevate the role of bilateralism in dealings with China, the less China will be anchored in the multilateral system, and the more countries will be exposed to the exercise of Chinese dominance. It is not necessary to assume that China will exert power in undesirable ways to eschew bilateralism and embrace multilateralism. Rather it should be seen as insurance against the possibility of being at the receiving end of unrestrained Chinese power.

A more difficult question is whether a second act of self-restraint by China's major trading partners might be necessary. If those countries resist deepening bilateral ties with China but then turn around and negotiate free trade or economic partnership agreements with each other, China might well see this as economic and trade encirclement from which it is excluded. A more positive and less hostile way of keeping China anchored would be for its trading partners to pronounce that they will embrace multilateralism not only in their dealings with China but also among themselves. This would signal a belief in the intrinsic worth of multilateralism rather than just as an instrument to contain China.

Alternative Approaches: Promiscuous and Hostile Bilateralism

What are the alternatives to multilateralism as the preferred way to deal with a rising China? Two such alternatives are suggested by relaxing the acts of self-restraint discussed above that would sustain the multilateralist approach. These alternatives still remain available as options because they have not as yet been overtaken by events. Although bilateral (and regional) agreements have been proliferating, the major players—the United States, European Union, China, Japan, Brazil, and India—have for the most part not entered into bilateral agreements among themselves.[7]

Promiscuous Bilateralism

The first alternative to multilateralism is the form of bilateralism advocated most forcefully by Robert Zoellick and C. Fred Bergsten, which one might call "promiscuous bilateralism." Advocates of this approach rely on the competitive dynamic it creates: If two countries negotiate preferential reductions of barriers, one or several outsiders will be hurt. These outsiders will then have an incentive to negotiate preferential agreements themselves and so on until the goal of global free trade is achieved.

In the old debate between the bilateralists and the multilateralists, the divide was not about the endpoint: All parties wanted global free trade. Rather, the divide was whether preferential (bilateral) agreements would be, in Jagdish Bhagwati's (1999) words, a "building bloc" or "stumbling bloc" toward that final goal, with the bilateralists falling in the former category and the multilateralists in the latter. To the former, the competitive dynamic argument remains unaltered in the presence of a rising China. They would disagree with both forms of restraint suggested above, that is, refraining both from making free trade agreements with China and from China's major trading partners making such agreements among themselves. In fact, they would actively pursue both (hence the "promiscuous" description).

The difficulty with this kind of promiscuous bilateralism is twofold. The success of bilateral agreements in the past in reducing barriers and generating the competitive dynamic for further liberalization simply cannot be ap-

---

7. Negotiations between Brazil and Europe toward a regional agreement have recently been revived, and those between India and Europe are close to being finalized. In the past, closer trade ties between the United States and Brazil was tried in the context of the free trade area of the Americas and closer US-Japan and EU-Japan is widely discussed in Japan. Middle tier countries such as Korea and Mexico have entered into a number of bilateral agreements.

plied to China. The most important successes of such agreements—the North American Free Trade Agreement (NAFTA) and Eastern and Central Europe—have largely involved a big economic power such as the United States or the European Union negotiating with smaller countries. As such, it is the smaller countries that have done most of the incremental liberalization. In these negotiations, it is the larger countries that have held the balance of negotiating power and influence and successfully used them.

Going forward, though, with China's growing size, the balance of negotiating power will be with China rather than its partners that are seeking bilateral agreements. The key argument for multilateralism is that there will be enough combined heft among China's trading partners such that negotiating with China on market opening can be more balanced. China might be willing to open its government procurement market in return for its major trading partners opening theirs. A multilateral negotiation among these large trading countries could conceivably lead to meaningful opening. But China's willingness to open up in a similar manner in negotiations just with the United States or European Union or with some less-weighty combination in a bilateral negotiation is far from clear. If the basic problem is the imbalance of leverage arising from China's size, bilateralism will by definition be less effective than multilateralism.

If bilateralism will be less effective in securing market opening, a similar problem carries over to enforcement and the incentives to adhere to previously agreed-upon rules. China's incentive to abide by multilateral rules will be stronger than to abide by a series of bilateral agreements because the reputational costs of being seen as errant is much greater in the former context. To picture this most starkly, consider the following alternative scenarios.

In the first, China has agreed to zero tariffs separately with Indonesia, Brazil, India, the United States, and the European Union as part of five bilateral agreements. In the second, China has agreed to reduce its multilateral tariff to zero in the WTO. In the former case, if China wanted to renege on its commitment to, say, Indonesia, it would do so under a bilateral agreement with only Indonesia as the victim. Indonesia could presumably seek recourse in some (fledgling) bilateral procedure for settling disputes between Indonesia and China. But if the commitment were a multilateral commitment, as in the second case, Indonesia could set in motion a well-established multilateral dispute settlement machinery in which all partner countries have a stake. The reputational costs and the effectiveness and legitimacy of enforcement would be a more effective deterrent in a multilateral context than regionally or bilaterally.[8] It is the opprobrium that is associated with being a deviant from the global norm—rather than a bilateral one—that is the most valuable weapon

---

8. In fact, very few regional enforcement mechanisms—not even NAFTA, which is perhaps the most well advanced—have the credibility of the WTO's dispute settlement mechanism. For example, the United States chose the WTO rather than NAFTA as the forum for its successful complaint against Mexico's telecommunications policies.

that the world can deploy in tying China today in a way that minimizes the prospects of an aggressively dominant China in the future.

Thus, in looking ahead, bilateralism's previous appeal needs to be carefully reviewed. It is not a matter of making regionalism compatible with multilateralism. With a dominant China, regionalism will be less effective in actually securing greater liberalization because of the imbalance in size. And, perhaps more importantly, regionalism will be less effective in imposing the kind of reputational costs that will be key to keeping China moored in an open, rules-based system.

Hostile Bilateralism

Instead of relaxing both strictures against bilateralism, suppose only the second one is relaxed—that is, China's major trading partners, led by the United States and Japan, enter into bilateral agreements among themselves but exclude China. The consequence if not the aim of such an approach would be to encircle China and worsen the terms of its access to the markets of its trading partners, thereby inflicting a large cost on China presumably to induce further market opening on its part. This would be, and would be viewed by China as, an act of economic aggression on the part of its trading partners. China's trading partners could justify this as waging war to secure peace, in this instance by getting China to the negotiating table and show a willingness to open its economy and address some of the major irritants of its trade policies.

The problem with this strategy is that it will probably not be effective in the short run and will certainly sour the prospects for cooperation in the medium to long run. China is already dominant and increasingly beyond the scope of influence of outsiders, especially via the threat of sanctions. China has enough market power to offer or deny to its Asian neighbors and enough cash to dangle to all those in need, from Africa to the heart (and not just the periphery) of Europe, to deter countries from pursuing this type of hostile regionalism. Long before China's trading partners can achieve encirclement, China will have negotiated free trade agreements with, invested in infrastructure in, and helped avert financial crises in some or many of these same countries.

Hence an attempt at hostile regionalism will not only be unsuccessful but also leave behind bad memories. And the system does not need a dominant China nurturing resentments and harboring grudges against a hostile outside world.

Asian-Centered Regionalism as a Medium

If desisting from bilateral deals with China and with each other is one way of keeping China anchored multilaterally, what scope might there be for regional integration efforts such as the Trans-Pacific Partnership or the Asia-Pacific Economic Cooperation (APEC) forum? The case for anchoring China in something smaller than a robustly multilateral process such as the WTO and something larger than bilateral agreements would be the following. The WTO process, especially in the wake of the failure of the Doha Round, has proven to be ineffective and in part because it is unwieldy with too many actors creating multiple veto points and stasis. Why not choose a smaller grouping that can make progress especially if an Asian-centered grouping can increase the prospect of eliciting China's cooperation?

Advocates of this view favor something like the Trans-Pacific Partnership (TPP) and the Free Trade Area of the Asia-Pacific (FTAAP), in which it is hoped that the United States and Japan would provide the kind of counterweight to China that would remedy the basic imbalance of bargaining power while the presence of China's other Asian neighbors would create a legitimately non-US dominated structure. The ardent Asian regionalists would also point to the greater strides being made on opening the more difficult behind-the-border barriers in Asia, especially in the Association of Southeast Asian Nations (ASEAN) and APEC. Why not build on that?

The key analytical point to bear in mind, and the challenge for cooperation with China, is the growing imbalance of power and influence between China and its partners, which limits the possibilities for reciprocal bargaining that has been at the heart of successful cooperation between the larger trading countries. Whether this imbalance is easier to remedy with a large group of countries (as in the WTO) or a smaller group (as within Asia) will, and should, largely be dictated by pragmatism and expediency. By definition, the larger the grouping the better the prospect of rectifying the imbalance. Equally, larger groupings can become unwieldy and ineffective. More practically, an Asia-Pacific grouping could exclude Europe, Brazil, and possibly India, whereas a WTO type collectivity would include them all. Who all should be "in" and who can be "out" are details that will have to be ironed out in the future, but it is essential to avoid the fragmentation that would arise from promiscuous bilateralism and the ineffectiveness and ill-will from hostile bilateralism.

Impediments to Revived Multilateralism

Even if multilateralism might be the preferred approach in dealing with China, the difficulties of reviving it by tethering China to it will be considerable. The proximate challenge is contending with the Doha Round, which refuses to go away. The deeper challenges relate to institutions, attitudes, and habits around the world, not just in the United States but in the larger emerging-market countries such as India and Brazil.

Proximate Impediments: The Doha Round

It is worth recalling a long-forgotten fact about the Doha Round. Even at the start, there was little appetite for launching the round, as evidenced in the string of previous, unsuccessful attempts—Seattle, Cancún, Potsdam—to do so. It was midwifed in a bout of post-9/11 solidarity that proved transient once the horrors of the terrorist attacks gave way to the routine and sordid political realities that accompany trade negotiations. Furthermore, it is not at all obvious, unlike the GATT/WTO's previous efforts, what big change, development, or opportunity the Doha Round has sought to address. The irony is that the round was planned as a development round (its official title is Doha Development Agenda) to give a boost to the economic prospects of developing countries. But the return of convergence (chapter 4) and the depressed prospects of the industrial countries in the aftermath of the global financial crisis highlight how quaint the motivating concern for the Doha Round has become. It is now developed rather than developing countries that seem to need a development boost.

Part of the current problem seems to be the view that failure to conclude the Doha Round would have devastating consequences for the WTO and the multilateral trading system. But this view needs to be questioned. Most agree that the Doha Round's substantive benefits would be minimal, largely related to providing security of future access rather than triggering new liberalization (Martin and Mattoo 2008, Hufbauer et al. 2010). This in turn explains the lack of private-sector enthusiasm for completing it because there is not a lot for that sector that rides on concluding the Doha Round. It is telling that meetings related to the round do not even rouse the wrath of the antiglobalization protesters. If an outcome has modest substantive value, how can failure to realize it have such significant costs?

More recently, it has become evident that the failure to complete the Doha Round might itself reflect China's growing dominance. In a recent paper (Mattoo, Ng, and Subramanian 2011), we argued that China looms especially large in the markets of major trading partners in sectors where protection is greatest. China's share in these sectors in Japan is over 70 percent, in Korea over 60 percent, in Brazil about 55 percent, in the United States, Canada, and the European Union about 50 percent each. Liberalization under the Doha agenda, especially in the politically charged, high-tariff sectors, is increasingly about other countries opening their markets to Chinese exports. And China's major trading partners are disinclined to do so.

This disinclination is exacerbated by the strong political perception that China's export success has been achieved, and continues to be sustained, in part by an undervalued exchange rate. It seems unlikely and politically unrealistic to expect China's trading partners to open further their markets to China when China is perceived as de facto (via the undervalued exchange rate) imposing an import tariff and export subsidy not just in selected manufacturing sectors but across the board. Unless Chinese currency policy changes significantly, and unless there can be credible checks on the use of such policies in the future, concern will remain in many countries, both industrial and emerging-market, about the increased competition from China that liberalization under Doha might unleash.

But the argument that the WTO and the multilateral trading system would be fatally undermined by the failure to complete the Doha Round rather than its unwillingness or failure to begin grappling with the real big challenge of the future—China's dominance—is somewhat like complaining about the lack of euphony in Nero's fiddling instead of attempting to put out Rome's fires.

Deeper Impediments

Collective Action and Strategic Forbearance

The more serious impediment to tethering China to the multilateral mast relates to China's trading partners and the collective action problems that must be overcome if they are to form a unified coalition for multilateralism. Consider the daunting requirements for collective action to be possible. First, all these countries—not just the United States and the advanced countries but the other emerging-market countries as well—need to take seriously the possibility of future Chinese economic dominance and the small but finite probability of this dominance being a threat.

The temptations to flout this approach—to deepen bilateral ties with China because it offers some type of market concessions (e.g., buying more French airbuses or US Boeing products) or because it is more forthcoming on cooperation on other issues such as North Korea or Iran—will be considerable. But the consequence of doing so, which could result in not being able to restrain Chinese economic and trade dominance in the future, will become evident only with time. The pursuit of multilateralism calls for a strategic patience that will be difficult to muster in the short run.

Brazil enthusiastically embarked on closer bilateral engagement a few years ago, signing a number of agreements on trade, currency, and investment with China. But Brazil has become disenchanted as it has seen its currency appreciate and its economy lose competitiveness, while China has provided no relief by way of corrective currency action of its own or the promised investments in Brazilian resources.

The sections that follow consider two examples of deeper impediments to the revival of a China-focused multilateralism, one each from the United States and India.

Anachronistic Institutional Structures: United States

In the case of the United States, there is the question of whether domestic institutions support or impede multilateralism as the preferred approach to trade. The historical experience of the United States is instructive. The constitutional right to regulate imports in the United States is vested in Congress. This imparts a strong protectionist bias to US tariff and trade policy because liberalization and increased imports affect domestic producers, to whom members of Congress are particularly sensitive. In contrast, the benefits of liberalization are spread among many consumers who have neither the same incentives nor the institutional mechanisms to express their views. Thus the concentrated interests and power of domestic producers, with political outlets for expression, tend to prevail over diffuse consumer interests.

Schattschneider (1935, 127–28) explains this asymmetry: "The political agitation concerning the tariff is profoundly influenced by the fact that, in many instances, the benefits of the legislation to an individual producer are obvious while many of the costs are obscure. . . . Benefits are concentrated while costs are distributed."

The infamous Smoot-Hawley Act of 1931 represented the perfect illustration of this dynamic whereby initial efforts to raise tariffs in agriculture led to coalitions based on vote-trading ("logrolling") in Congress, all aimed at raising particular tariffs until the exercise bequeathed a large and across-the-board increase in protectionism (Destler 1992, Irwin 2011). The act's dire consequences, however, begat a fundamental institutional change in US trade policy. In 1934, President Franklin D. Roosevelt persuaded Congress to delegate tariff-setting authority and agenda-setting power to the administration under the Reciprocal Trade Agreements Act (RTAA). Apart from Congress losing its ability to legislate specific tariffs, this change fundamentally altered the political economy of trade policy in the United States. By making the tariff an international bargaining issue, it brought exporters into the political equation. By explicitly linking domestic tariff reductions to foreign tariff reductions, it created a stake for exporters to lobby against protectionism at home, because domestic protectionism sparked protectionism abroad, which hurt exporters. Congress retained the right to periodically approve the granting of these rights to the president but had less say over specific trade and tariff issues.

Over time, this institutional structure has been broadly preserved, with Congress granting the president fast-track authority to negotiate international agreements but retaining the right to review this authority and also the right to say yes or no to agreements negotiated by the president.[9]

Under Pax Americana, this dual role of the president and Congress has worked well in that it has allowed the two branches of government to use this duality to tactical advantage in international trade relations. Congress was a credible bad cop to the administration's good cop in terms of international trade relations. Often, the refrain of successive administrations to trading partners would be: "Please accede to this deal/demand because Congress will not agree to anything else." Or, "Please accede to this demand/deal or else

---

9. Destler (1992) has argued persuasively that costs have been incurred in preserving this structure and in ensuring that the risks of a serious lapse back into protectionism in the United States are kept in check. These costs, which took the form of allowing lesser forms and magnitudes of protectionism, were embodied in an elaborate system, which included: providing "relief" in the form of safeguards, antidumping and countervailing duties to domestic producers under "unfair trade" laws; providing access to trade retaliation mechanisms to export interests such as the services and intellectual property to generate a pro free-trade momentum; and allowing special protectionist deals for special cases (steel, automobiles, and semiconductors).

Congress will authorize trade retaliation under its legislative authority, which we (the administration) will be unable to control." And often this was a successful strategy because the United State generally held the balance of negotiating power and influence relative to its trading partners.

But when the United States has to turn from being wooed by to actively wooing others, an insular, instinctively unilateral Congress is no longer a credible bad cop defining the worst case options for US trading partners but rather a potential albatross around the neck of the administration, limiting its international options. When Congress saber rattles or sets unusually high standards for international trade agreements, smaller countries have to take those threats seriously. Indeed, during the Uruguay Round of trade negotiations, the outside option of facing retaliation under laws enacted by Congress ("Special 301" in that instance) if they did not raise their intellectual property standards played a key role in countries such as Brazil and India reluctantly agreeing to higher multilateral standards in the WTO on intellectual property.

But in the case of China, congressional instincts could prove counterproductive. For example, Brazil and India could conceivably come together with the United States as part of a multilateral coalition to discuss exchange rate issues with China. But they would be loath to do so if it were to happen after Congress has authorized trade retaliation against China for manipulating its currency. They would be seen as siding with a belligerent United States rather than a cooperative one. Congressional unilateralism might thus foreclose or weaken some multilateral options for the administration.

Put starkly, under US dominance, Congress limited the options for America's relatively weak partners in negotiations with a strong US administration; under Chinese dominance, Congress will limit the negotiating options for a relatively weak administration vis-à-vis a relatively strong China. These institutional structures can come in the way of successfully mobilizing a multilateral coalition to deal with China in the future.

Perhaps what might be required—and this is radical and speculative prescription—is for the United States to make the next logical change in its domestic institutional trade arrangements inspired by the history of the first such change under the RTAA in 1934. That change would be to transfer even more authority from Congress to the administration in the design and implementation of trade policy. The aim would be to facilitate and galvanize more multilateral approaches—less constrained by a unilateral, insular Congress—that will be necessary to deal with a dominant China.

Habit and Mindset: India

If institutional mechanisms can impede forging a multilateral approach to dealing with a dominant China, so can deeply ingrained habits and mindsets. India is in the throes of formulating its own strategic economic relationship with China. The challenge for India, of course, is to some extent different and arguably greater than that of China's other partners such as the United States.

Bismarck famously said of the United States that it had managed to "surround itself on two sides with weak neighbors and on the other two sides with fish." When it comes to China, India does not enjoy this luxury of splendid isolation. Both history and geography complicate matters considerably.

On the one hand, trade and economic relations between China and India are intensifying, creating opportunities for both countries. On the other, India has to contend with what is becoming, in political terms, an imbalanced economic relationship. India runs a large and growing trade deficit with China, and the pattern of trade is reminiscent of trade during the days of empire. India exports predominantly raw materials to China and imports high-value-added and sophisticated goods. Indian industry and government officials have complained about China's trade, industrial, FDI, and exchange rate policies, which aid, often opaquely, Chinese industry and exports. China's government procurement policies have impeded Indian pharmaceutical exports and the fear is of a large China using its size to create and set standards (for example, for telecommunications equipment), which others have no choice but to follow. Not just the content but the tone of these complaints can resemble the emanations from the toughest China hawks in the United States.

India also is grappling with essentially the same question that this chapter has posed: How much should it engage with China bilaterally and how much multilaterally? India recognizes that its negotiating hands are seriously tied bilaterally because of the imbalance in size, and yet it is unable to embrace multilateralism as conviction, preferring a reluctant and opportunistic multilateralism. And the reason in part is mindset.

India, it is well known, was a habitual naysayer in the international trading system. The underlying objective of Indian economic engagement was the jealous and zealous safeguarding of India's sovereignty. India was a "sovereignty hawk." India has tried its best to minimize having to do what it would otherwise not want to do. In the trading system, for example, India lobbied hard and strong over the past three decades to preserve the right to protect its economy through tariffs and quotas. Sovereignty, in this arena, was equivalent to the freedom to protect or prevent the imposition of rules and obligations that would deprive India of this freedom. Of course, this objective in turn flowed from an economic ideology that initially viewed liberalization and market opening as unhelpful to India's interest and later started to recognize the benefits of liberalization, but still as something to be undertaken at India's pace rather than dictated by trading partners.

But if India was a naysayer, it was one with a following. India was essentially one of the intellectual leaders and the spokesperson for many developing countries (sometimes called the G-77). For example, it played a key role in getting the GATT to accord special status to developing countries, which essentially relieved them of any obligation to liberalize their trade regime in the GATT. Leading a group of like-minded developing countries became not just a position that Indian diplomats and policymakers enjoyed but it became a habit, a mindset, even an entitlement. In recent years, as India's ideological moorings have shifted, it has been able, albeit gradually and episodically, to back away from playing the recalcitrant trade partner bent on obstructing efforts to open up the international economy. But its officials have been less able to walk away from the prestigious mantle of leadership and hence less willing to join multilateral coalitions where the spotlight is necessarily diffused because leadership is shared or even sacrificed. For India and Indian policymakers, it has been easier to repudiate ideology than it has been to spurn the spotlight.

In this situation, India seems to have yielded to the temptation to become a free rider. In discussions on China's exchange rate policy, India has chosen not to align itself with the United States as part of a multilateral coalition for fear of endangering the broader relationship with China ("we live in a rough neighborhood," the Indians routinely say) and because it believes that the United States can "handle" China alone without Indian participation. The consequence, of course, is the classic free rider problem where all countries thinking similarly contribute to the breakdown of cooperation. Both these assumptions are misplaced.

Even where the need for forging coalitions is recognized, the Indian instinct is still to look to deepen relationships with developing-country partners such as South Africa, Brazil, or Indonesia rather than the United States and Europe.

For the new multilateralism to be effective, however, a country such as India must accept that it can no longer be the leader and at the same time recognize that its participation is necessary for successful coalitions that seek to tether China multilaterally. In today's world, and especially going forward, the United States cannot do it alone. Coalitions must be broad, and they require easy engagement between the old powers and emerging ones. Thus, India must not just become a visceral multilateralist but learn the new habits of multilateralism and come to terms with the demotion in status that it entails and the reaching out to all partners that it requires.

The appealing symmetry of the new multilateralism is to induce a greater humility in both the United States and India: in the former, to spurn the temptation—or rather outgrow the illusion—that it can exercise exclusive leadership and dominance in shaping outcomes, and in the latter to shed the desire to do the same by stymieing outcomes and instead participate in forging cooperation as important but humble drones rather than as the queen bee.

A "China Round" for Tethering China[10]

One way to signal that the world community recognizes the need to deal with a dominant China in the future, and to do so multilaterally, would be to put

---

10. What does it mean to "tether" China given that it is already part of the multilateral system? One answer is that there may need to be a new bargain or equilibrium such that China has an incentive to abide by it. This would be in contrast to the existing equilibrium, which has not proven

to bed the Doha Round and embark on a new round of trade negotiations (Mattoo and Subramanian, forthcoming). The aim of such a "China Round" would in fact be to anchor China, to the maximum extent possible, in the multilateral trading system.

Recall that one of the virtues of the GATT/WTO has been its ability historically to respond to five major developments in the trading system. These include (1) promoting liberalization in the immediate aftermath of World War II in the first few rounds of tariff negotiations; (2) diluting the effects of discriminatory European integration by way of most favored nation (MFN) tariff cuts in the Kennedy Round; (3) addressing the competitiveness threat against a backdrop of US decline from a then-rising Japan, which was achieved in the Tokyo Round through disciplines on subsidies and through permissiveness in the use of contingent protection against imports; (4) bringing into the multilateral fold major developing countries as they became economically important and adding new areas such as intellectual property and services that had become sources of comparative advantage for the industrial countries, as achieved at the Uruguay Round by creating a greater symmetry of obligations between all members and by developing new rules on intellectual property and services; and (5) responding to the emergence of China as a big market access opportunity by securing unprecedentedly large policy liberalization by China in agriculture, manufacturing, and services, in the context of its WTO accession.

Having responded to China as an opportunity, the next major development on the trading horizon is China as a potential threat. A China Round is thus a natural for the WTO and one consistent with its history. It would mirror the Tokyo Round, which had as one of its main objectives the accommodation of Japan in a manner that minimized the risks to the system.

What might an agenda look like for a China Round? Mattoo and I (forthcoming) spell out a possible agenda in detail, which might potentially cover a number of items in which China's role will be crucial and where China might also have an interest in other countries opening their markets (for example, in government procurement) or in other countries committing not to restrict access to energy, food, and natural resources in a way that could help China. The aim would be to create a balanced package where China would have to "give" by way of liberalizing its own policies in return for others offering commitments of interest to China. The greater the number of China's partners that participate, the better the prospects that China would have an incentive to engage in it and the more the stigma for China if it were to distance itself from the exercise. A China Round could thus revitalize the multilateral trading system. It might not succeed but it must be tried.

---

to be one, reflected in the actions of China (for example, its mercantilist policies) to de facto depart from, or renege on, it. Perhaps one should pose the question as one of trying to "re-tether" China in the multilateral system.

There is a final appeal to the multilateralism proposed here, with its forswearing of promiscuous and hostile bilateralism. The discussion has been permeated of course by a sense of China as a target or a concern. But support by China itself for stronger multilateralism today might be in its interest as well, because it would be a strong and credible signal—a kind of precommitment—that China does not intend in the future to exercise the kind of dominance that could disrupt the current open and rules-based system that has served it so well over the past three decades. Strengthening multilateralism is in China's interest and the interest of its major trading partners.

Conclusion

An ascendant China might create new challenges for cooperation. As a dominant power, China will be increasingly beyond the influence of outsiders, especially on key issues such as exchange rates, climate change, and technological protectionism. Self-interest will, largely, rule. But the pursuit of self-interest need not augur badly for the open rules-based system that the world enjoys. China's unique features—especially the fact that it is one of history's most open superpowers—will invest it with a stake in broadly maintaining the current trade and financial system. And China's stake in market openness will be of primary importance because delivering development—the basis for the regime's legitimacy—is crucially predicated on markets remaining open.

The importance of trade for China going forward, the likelihood that China will exit from its mercantilism by internationalizing the renminbi, and the relative ineffectiveness of the IMF as a forum for cooperation between systemically important countries, makes it likely that engagement—and the scope for friction—between China and the other large economies will relate more to trade than macroeconomic issues. In turn, this will make the WTO not the IMF the key forum for and locus of cooperation between China and these economies.

The odds are strong that China will act to maintain the current open rules-based trading system. But history suggests that there are no guarantees and the world requires some insurance against the possibility that China exercises its dominance by either reversing its previous policies or failing to open areas of the economy that are now highly protected. If it were to do so, and given its size, the resulting conflict could undermine the post–World War II system.

The history of post–World War II relations between trading superpowers—the United States and European Union—suggests that cooperation can be successful. That success is based on the fact that key actors in the WTO engage in reciprocal market opening and share a sense of a fair bargain to which countries feel they must adhere. The broad success of the WTO dispute settlement process owes to this perception of an equitable contract between countries, which both creates the incentive to comply and confers legitimacy in governance.

Insofar as China shares this perception after its WTO accession—and the fact that it has benefited substantially from being part of this system—it is likely that China will participate in the WTO and sustain it much as the other superpowers did in the postwar period.

The difference between the past and future is the tension that might arise as a result of the uniqueness of China as a superpower. By virtue of its income level and the historic trajectory of its development, China remains less open in terms of policy barriers, especially in the nontraditional areas, than its major trading partners. But because of its distinctive development strategy it will also be an overwhelmingly large trader—much larger over time than the major partners—rendering it less susceptible to external influence.

So the United States and European Union, by virtue of being more open, will on their own be less able to engage in reciprocal market opening with China—which has been one of the keys to the success of the WTO system. And by virtue of China's size, they will be less able to influence China's policy regime. The inability of its trading partners to influence China and the temptation to try do so anyway—especially if the US economy continues to fare poorly and if perceptions of unfairness and asymmetric contributions to keeping the trading system gain serious ground—will remain a key structural tension.

One possible insurance policy that the world can take out is to keep China tethered to the multilateral trading system, so that it would be politically difficult, and economically and reputationally costly, for China to depart from or undermine the multilateral system even once it becomes dominant.

But anchoring China in the multilateral system would require all its major trading partners—not just the United States—to become more reticent about bilateral trade deepening. This reticence should extend not just to deepening bilateral relations with China but perhaps also to trade relations with each other. China's trading partners must avoid both the temptations of a promiscuous bilateralism and a hostile regionalism. The impediments to taking out the insurance of multilateralism are going to be considerable. China's trading partners must first recognize the seriousness of the looming challenges and act now, even though those challenges may seem distant. They must resist the lure of bilateral agreements that might offer short-term gains but which might leave them exposed to China in the long run. And domestic institutions and habits may need to be adapted to successfully forge a coalition to revitalize multilateralism. China, in short, might be the raison d'être for a new multilateralism. But making that multilateralism a reality will be far from easy.

America Resurgent or America Vulnerable?

We are not now that strength which in old days
Moved earth and heaven; that which we are, we are;
One equal temper of heroic hearts,
Made weak by time and fate, but strong in will.

—Alfred Lord Tennyson, *Ulysses*

Angst about the economic future of the United States has three causes. First, in the aftermath of the recent global financial crisis, the fiscal and debt situation looks especially dire. Tax cuts, two wars, and the inexorable growth in long-term entitlements, especially related to healthcare and the response to the crisis, have combined to create serious doubts about the public-sector balance sheet. And if account is taken of the contingent liabilities that might be accumulating because of the vulnerability of the financial system, the picture looks grim.

The second and arguably more serious cause for concern is the country's structural problem arising from a combination of stagnating middle-class incomes, rising inequality (particularly pronounced at the very top of the income spectrum), declining mobility, and more recently, the apparently declining prospects for even the college-educated. A beleaguered middle class is emerging that, understandably, does not want to move down the skill spectrum but whose prospects of moving up through education and skill acquisition are increasingly affected by competition from India and China. There is the serious risk that some of the cyclical problems from the recent crisis add to, and become part of, the structural malaise. These include high levels of unemployment, the rising number of long-term unemployed, and the rising number of people who have dropped out of the labor force either directly or by becoming claimants of disability benefits.

Lawrence Katz metaphorically captured the structural malaise. In an interview with Edward Luce of the *Financial Times* he said: "Think of the American economy as a large apartment block. A century ago—even 30 years ago—it was the object of envy. But in the last generation its character has changed. The penthouses at the top keep getting larger and larger. The apartments in the middle are feeling more and more squeezed and the basement has flooded. To round it off, the elevator is no longer working. That broken elevator is what gets people down the most."[1]

The third concern relates to long-run growth. Countries at the economic frontier tend to chug along at a certain "trend" rate of growth, which I have assumed to be 2.5 percent for the United States and unaffected by the crisis. That assumption might also be unwarranted. Carmen Reinhart and Kenneth Rogoff (2010) suggest a negative correlation between the high levels of debt that the United States is approaching and growth (a correlation that is strengthened if private levels of debt also remain high). Long-term unemployment, and the attendant skill attrition and loss of human capital, combined with reductions in the labor force participation rate also exert a downward impact on growth.

The United States, in short, has a fiscal problem, possibly a growth problem, and the most intractable of all, a distributional problem, relating to the middle class. These can cumulatively lead to a downward spiral. But that is not inevitable. Indeed, after 1993, thanks to some policy reform, but especially because of finding new sources of growth, the United States was able to address its budgetary problems, turning deficits into large surpluses, and reversing, albeit for a limited time, the previous trend of stagnating median incomes.

Indeed, one of the strong beliefs in the United States is that that episode can be repeated, thereby heading off the threat to the nation's preeminence from a rising China. If the United States can fix its education problem and if it can correct its looming fiscal deficits, the argument goes, then the fundamentals are there to ensure continuing economic dominance. These fundamentals are captured in the 2009 survey by the Global Entrepreneurship Monitor, which ranked the United States ahead of other countries in opportunities for entrepreneurship "because it has a favorable business culture, the most mature venture capital industry, close relations between universities and industry, and an open immigration policy" (as quoted in Nye 2010). Supporting this is the fact that nearly all the major commercially successful companies that have embodied breakthroughs in technology continue to be US-based and founded, like Microsoft, Google, Apple, and Facebook. Moreover, the culture of innovation and entrepreneurship are conducive to America playing a crucial role in building and sustaining the global networks that are sources of power in today's fractured world (Slaughter 2009).

But confidence in America's strengths, even if warranted, conflates the absolute with the relative. Imagine a best-case scenario where the United States bounces back from the recent recession, rediscovers new sources of growth (say, in green and information technologies), reverses the trend stag-

---

1. Edward Luce, "The Crisis of Middle-Class America," *Financial Times*, July 30, 2010.

Figure P.1 Economic dominance in a scenario where America is resurgent, projection to 2030

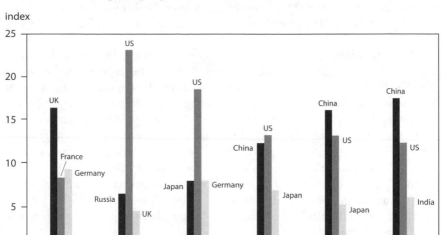

Notes: This index is a weighted average of the share of a country in world GDP, trade, and world net exports of capital. The weights are 0.35 for trade; 0.6 for GDP (split equally between GDP measured at market and purchasing power parity exchange rates, respectively); and 0.05 for net exports of capital. The United States and China are projected to grow at 3.5 percent and 5.9 percent (in purchasing power parity dollars) per year, respectively, between 2010 and 2030. All other countries are assumed to grow as in the convergence scenario described in chapter 4.

Source: Author's calculations.

nation of median household incomes, restores mobility and the prospects of attaining the American dream, and overcomes domestic political bickering to address its long-term fiscal challenges, thereby also reducing its long-run foreign indebtedness.

Let us put some numbers on these optimistic developments and see what the consequences for economic dominance might be. Suppose US growth were to average 3.5 percent over the next two decades (which would be very high by historical standards and match growth during the booming 1990s) instead of the 2.5 percent currently projected. Suppose too that the US current account deficit were to be considerably reduced as a result of bold fiscal actions.

What difference would these numbers make to the economic dominance numbers depicted in figure P.1. The answer is that while the magnitude of differential between China and the United States changes a little, the picture of Chinese dominance remains broadly unaltered.

Regardless of the disparity in dominance conveyed by the picture, could an America that grows at 3.5 percent really be dominated by a China even if it grows at 7 percent? The arithmetic difference between a growth rate of 3.5 versus 2.5 percent is not meaningful, but the practical difference might well be. A 3.5 percent growth rate, by virtue of being significantly above the long-run trend, would embody a dynamism and engender an optimism that would have a material effect on investor sentiment, confidence in the dollar as a reserve currency, and in the US model more broadly. After all, it was through strong growth that the United States saw off the threat from Japan in the early 1990s.

Indeed, the US-Japan dynamic of the early 1990s is helpful in understanding the US-China dynamic going forward. But it is the differences that stand out. The first, and most obvious, difference is that Japan, unlike China, never had the size to rival the United States. Perhaps an even more important point relates to relative dynamism. Back in the 1990s, the United States surged while Japan stagnated. Going forward, though, by virtue of being relatively poor, China will, barring a collapse, have more dynamic potential than the United States. To put it starkly, the US-Japan growth differential in the 1990s was about 2 percent in favor of the United States. Even with the United States growing at 3.5 percent, the differential will be 3.5 percent in China's favor. China might, in Alexander Gerschenkron's famous characterization, reap the advantages of "backwardness."

Quite apart from the question of whether the United States can grow at 3.5 percent and for a sufficiently long period—remembering that even in the 1990s, the high growth momentum did not last more than a decade—there are other crucial differences between the 1990s and the future. The United States headed into the 1990s with considerably less government debt than it will in the future: in 1990, the ratio of debt held by the public to GDP was about 42 percent while the latest projected figure for 2020 by the Congressional Budget Office is close to 100 percent. The external position of the United States was also less vulnerable then: for example, in 1990, foreign holdings of US government debt was 19 percent, today it is close to 50 percent.[2] Moreover, in the 1990s it was considerably farther away from the date of entitlement reckoning than it is now and will be over the next decade.

The most crucial difference might relate to America's middle class problem. Over the last 20 years, the related pathologies that have come together to create this problem may have become more entrenched, more intractable, and less easy to solve. In that case, even the 3.5 percent growth rate may not be adequate to preserve the attractions of, and confidence in, the United States and the US model, which at its core is based on the hope of a better future not for a few but for the many.

The dominance consequences can be checked under other scenarios. Under the convergence scenario discussed in chapter 4, the differential was 4.5 percent (7 percent for China and 2.5 percent for the United States). With America growing at 3.5 percent—the resurgent America scenario—the differential is narrowed to 3.5 percent. One should not rule out a growth collapse in China, where the differential with the United States is narrowed, say, to

2. David Walker, "Comeback America: The Nation's Fiscal Challenge and a Way Forward," Comeback America Initiative, available at http://tcaii.org.

Figure P.2   Economic dominance in a scenario where Chinese growth collapses, projection to 2030

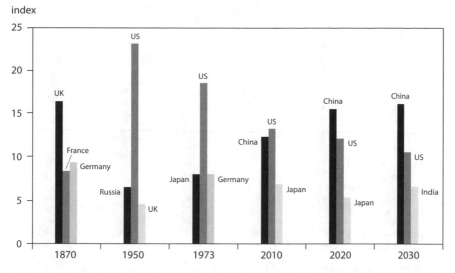

Note: This figure is identical to figure P.1 except that the United States and China are projected to grow at 2.5 and 4.9 percent (in purchasing power parity dollars) per year, respectively, between 2010 and 2030.

Source: Author's calculations.

2 percent a year; nor should one rule out, however, a China that manages to sustain reasonable momentum in its growth, in which case the differential with the United States is 5.5 percent.

These latter two scenarios are depicted in figures P.2 and P.3, respectively. Not surprisingly, even under a growth-collapse scenario, China maintains its dominance, although less so than under the convergence scenario. And in a resurgent China scenario, its dominance by 2030 starts to look similar to the United States not in 1973 but in 1950.

These scenarios cast some doubt on the central American belief that US economic preeminence is America's to lose, that is, that American preeminence can be maintained if the country undertakes the necessary policy corrections. In a world where relative performance matters for dominance, whether the differential in growth between the United States and China will be 2 percent (if China's growth collapses) or 5.5 percent (in a resurgent China scenario) will be largely—not exclusively—China's to determine, depending on its decisions and actions. In contrast, the range of possibilities for the United States is much narrower. It is unlikely to grow significantly slower than 2 to 2.5 percent, even if crises lower those numbers for shorter periods. And it is extremely unlikely to grow faster than 3.5 percent. This narrower range of possibilities is in some ways the "curse" of being at the economic frontier—both the downside and certainly the upside potential are limited. China's range of

Figure P.3   Economic dominance in a scenario where China is resurgent, projection to 2030

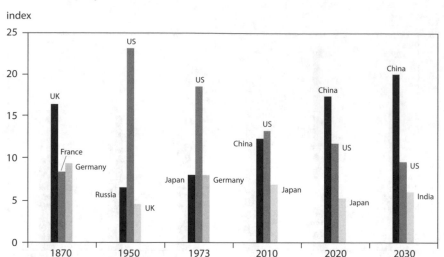

Note: This figure is identical to figure P.1 except that the United States and China are projected to grow at 2.5 and 6.9 percent (in purchasing power parity dollars) per year, respectively, between 2010 and 2030.

Source: Author's calculations.

possibilities—which are up to China to exploit or forgo—are much greater. It is this contrast that implies that China's future dominance is more China's to gain than America's to lose.

A final point relates to an inherent asymmetry in the relative possibilities and performance that strengthen the case for Chinese dominance and for attenuated American control over affecting outcomes. The asymmetry is that when the pace of technology creation by the frontier countries is slow or limited, convergence in the poorer countries is largely unaffected because the existing stock of technology is already available for all to use. But if the pace of technological progress quickens in rich countries, new technologies can become quickly usable in countries such as China and India, providing a fillip to growth in these poorer countries as well. In this case, faster growth in the rich countries need not necessarily translate into faster growth relative to countries such as China and India.

In a "flattened" world of convergence, the location of technological progress thus begins to matter less. In fact, convergence is happening precisely because the "technology" of progress is becoming more replicable worldwide. Dissemination more quickly follows discovery. And this is true in both senses of "technology." Information technologies, for example, drive innovation and production in a physical sense. But they also globalize ideas and knowledge, including how best to run an economy—the mistakes to avoid, the examples to emulate, and the learning-by-doing-and-erring to attempt.

As long as a country has the human capital skills to use, even if it cannot produce new technologies, progress is likely. According to estimates by the National Science Foundation (NSF), in 2006, the number of science and engineering undergraduates in China (about 912,000) was nearly twice that in the United States. Over time, this differential is only likely to grow. Even adjusting for what are sizable quality differentials in the education being provided, China seems well-positioned to develop and absorb technology. For example, US peer-reviewed scientific publications, which were six times Chinese publications in 2002, were merely two-and-half times in 2008 because China had posted a 175 percent growth rate compared with 20 percent by the United States.

In other words, if the United States grows at 3.5 percent, one might have to bump up the growth projections for China as well because the technological progress underlying America's acceleration is China's to emulate and adopt as well. Put starkly, the asymmetry is this: Rich countries can fall behind, but their ability to stay ahead in growth terms is inherently limited by convergence and by the nature of new technologies and the ability of countries such as China to more quickly use them.

The United States cannot escape the inherent logic of demography and convergence. A country such as China that is four times as populous as the United States will be bigger in overall economic size once its standard of living exceeds a quarter of that of the United States (which has already occurred). A converging, growing China will ensure that the gap in overall size will only get larger over time.

The baseline scenario of a dominant China can be altered materially by a resurgent America (of course, aided by a faltering China). But the preconditions are demanding. Not just will the United States have to grow substantially faster than long-run trend but it must be seen as strong fiscally and, above all, able to reverse the pall of economic and social stagnation that has enveloped its middle class. Such an America will restore the American dream domestically but will also be essential to take the lead and play a key role in shaping and strengthening the multilateralism that was described in the previous chapter as the world's best insurance against an unbenign China in the future.

Suez Canal Revisited?

A resurgent America can be a strong and vibrant nation but not necessarily one that can easily exercise power and dominance over a rising China. So the possibility of more dire scenarios under which the United States is actually dictated to must also be considered. This book began with one such scenario, in which China used its economic dominance to attain noneconomic objectives reminiscent of the experience of the United Kingdom, which "lost" the Suez Canal in part when the United States exercised its power against an economically enfeebled and indebted Britain. The fantasy scenario of the United

States going to the IMF was inspired by the Suez episode of 1956. But are the implicit comparisons appropriate and relevant? It is useful to examine how some of the specific elements of the two events, one real, one imagined, did and might play out.

First consider the incentives of the rising creditor country. In 1956, the withholding of financing for the United Kingdom by the United States—directly and indirectly via the IMF where the United States could muster a majority against the United Kingdom—had no serious consequence for the dollar and the US economy.

Today, the argument is that China's threat to not buy US treasury bonds or even to sell some of its existing stock is not credible because the consequence of China's action would be the very outcome—dollar decline and renminbi appreciation—that China has been steadfastly trying to prevent in order to sustain a mercantilist growth strategy and avoid large capital losses on the stock of foreign exchange reserves that it has acquired by running large current account surpluses for over a decade.[3] So remaining sanguine about the consequences of China wielding the creditor's weapon may be warranted by current conditions: At a time of a depressed US economy, the Federal Reserve might be only too happy to buy US treasuries dumped by China.

But the dynamic and credibility of wielding the financing weapon in the future could be very different from today's circumstances. Ten years on, it is quite easy to see China being less wedded to a weak renminbi. Indeed, if China proceeds on the path of renminbi internationalization it so clearly seems to have embarked upon, its ability and stake in maintaining a weak currency will be considerably weaker.

Moreover, in the case of the United Kingdom back in 1956, its financiers were more dispersed and included the private sector. In the case of the United States, China—and, crucially, the Chinese government—is the largest net supplier of capital to the United States, accounting for a large share of holdings of US treasury bonds, both in stock terms and as a financier of the flow deficits of the United States. Leverage over the United States is thus concentrated, not dispersed, and concentrated in the hands of those who can wield power. So when the current imperatives for a weak renminbi fade, China's ability to wield power will be considerable.

Second, consider the exchange rate policy of the indebted country. In 1956, Britain was desperately trying to maintain a fixed exchange rate peg and needed financial resources to do so, resources which the United States controlled. However, the United States today is not, and will not likely be in the years ahead, wedded to dollar fixity. Downward movements in the dollar are less of a problem, especially since the foreign liabilities of the United States are denominated in dollars and not in foreign currency.

---

3. For example, a 30 percent revaluation of the renminbi against the dollar would lead to valuation losses for China of about half a trillion dollars, or 10 percent of its GDP.

The United States in 2021 may have less to fear from a decline of the dollar, even a disorderly one but vulnerable it will be even if for slightly different reasons. Its vulnerability will arise from the combination of its fiscal fragility and the fact that it might be dependent on its potential rival to economic superpower status—the government of China—to keep supplying the foreign financing necessary to forestall that fragility.

So, the proximate vulnerabilities might be different: external in the case of the United Kingdom in 1956 and fiscal-cum-external for the United States in 2021. But the deeper parallel is this: The United Kingdom was vulnerable not just because it was a debtor but because its economy had weakened and another power had emerged. The United States is also weakening structurally, its government has become a chronically large debtor, its growth prospects have dulled, and critically, a credibly strong rival—that controls the finance spigots and that might also issue the premier reserve currency—has emerged. While not an adversary, this rival is not an ally either—unlike the United Kingdom and the United States in 1956. And it is one that has yet to sufficiently reassure the world about its internal politics and extraterritorial ambitions.

To clarify, the 2021 scenario described in the introduction is still a very low probability one. But stranger things have happened, as the recent global financial crisis showed. As John Maynard Keynes said, "the inevitable never happens, it is the unexpected always." And while the triggers may be very different than in this "handover fantasy," it is the economic fundamentals—which this book has shown are clearly moving against the United States and in favor of China—that create the vulnerability. That an economically dominant China will wield considerable economic power and that the United States will be vulnerable cannot be wished away as beyond the realm of possibility. Indeed . . .

****

. . . on that February morning in 2021, after signing the agreement with the IMF, the president of the United States makes his way through the bracing cold air toward the cavalcade of black Lincolns that will carry him and his entourage back to the White House. As he steps into his limousine, the bells of the National Cathedral erupt in somber splendor. Self-aware and history-honed—not unlike his once-removed predecessor, Barack Obama—the president is reminded of the funeral procession of King Edward VII over a century ago, as described by Barbara Tuchman in *The Guns of August*: "The muffled tongue of Big Ben tolled nine by the clock as the cortege left the palace, but on history's clock it was sunset, and the sun of the old world was setting in a dying blaze of splendor never to be seen again."

References

Acemoglu, Daron, Simon Johnson, and James Robinson. 2002. Reversal of Fortune: Geography and Institutions in the Making of the Modern World Income Distribution. *Quarterly Journal of Economics* 117, no. 4: 1231–94.

Acemoglu Daron, Simon Johnson, James A. Robinson, and Yunyong Thaicharoen. 2003. Institutional Causes, Macroeconomic Symptoms: Volatility, Crises, and Growth. *Journal of Monetary Economics* 50, no. 1: 49–123.

ADB (Asian Development Bank). 2010. *2009 ADB Annual Report*. Manila.

Ahamed, Liaquat. 2009. *Lords of Finance: The Bankers Who Broke the World*. New York: Penguin Press.

Aker, Jenny, and Issac Mbiti. 2011. Mobile Phones and Economic Development in Africa. *Journal of Economic Perspectives* (forthcoming).

Akin, Cigdem, and M. Ayhan Kose. 2007. *Changing Nature of North-South Linkages: Stylized Facts and Explanations*. IMF Working Paper 07/280. Washington: International Monetary Fund.

Aliber, Robert. 1966. *The Future of the Dollar as an International Currency*. New York: Frederick Praeger Publishers.

Alogoskoufis, George, and Richard Portes. 1992. European Monetary Union and International Currencies in a Tripolar World. In *Establishing a Central Bank: Issues in Europe and Lessons from the U.S.*, ed. Matthew Canzoneri, Vittorio Grilli, and Paul Masson. Cambridge, UK: Cambridge University Press.

Anderson, James E. 1979. A Theoretical Foundation for the Gravity Equation. *American Economic Review* 69, no. 1 (March): 106–16.

Anderson, James E., and Eric van Wincoop. 2003. Gravity with Gravitas: A Solution to the Border Puzzle. *American Economic Review* 93, no. 1: 170–92.

Andrews, David M. 2006. Monetary Coordination and Hierarchy. In *International Monetary Power*, ed. David M. Andrews. Ithaca, NY: Cornell University Press.

Åslund, Anders. 2007. *Russia's Capitalist Revolution: Why Market Reform Succeeded and Democracy Failed*. Washington: Peterson Institute for International Economics.

Balassa, Bela, and Marcus Noland. 1989. The Changing Comparative Advantage of Japan and the United States. *Journal of the Japanese and International Economies* 3, no. 2 (June): 174–88.

Bandholz, Harm, Jorg Clostermann, and Franz Seitz. 2009. Explaining the US Bond Yield Conundrum. *Taylor and Francis Journals*, 19, no. 7: 539–50.

Bayard, Thomas O., and Kimberly Ann Elliott. 1994. *Reciprocity and Retaliation in US Trade Policy*. Washington: Institute for International Economics.

Bergsten, C. Fred. 2008. A Partnership of Equals: How Washington Should Respond to China's Economic Challenge. *Foreign Affairs* 97, no. 4 (July/August): 57–69.

Bergsten, C. Fred. 2009. The Dollar and the Deficits. *Foreign Affairs* 88, no. 6 (November/December): 20–38.

Bergsten, C. Fred, and C. Randall Henning. 1996. *Global Economic Leadership and the Group of Seven*. Washington: Institute for International Economics.

Bergsten, C. Fred, and Nicholas R. Lardy. 2009. *China's Rise: Opportunities and Challenges*. Washington: Peterson Institute for International Economics.

Bhagwati, Jagdish. 1999. Free Trade in the 21st Century: Managing Viruses, Phobias and Social Agendas. Third Anita and Robert Summers Lecture, University of Pennsylvania.

Bhalla, Surjit. 2008. World Bank: Most Asians Dead in 1950. *Business Standard*, August 23.

Bhattasali, Deepak, Li Shantong, and Will Martin. 2004. *China and the WTO: Accession, Policy Reform, and Poverty Reduction Strategies*. New York: Oxford University Press for the World Bank.

Blinder, Alan S. 2009. How Many U.S. Jobs Might Be Offshorable. *World Economics* 10, no. 2 (April–June): 41–78.

Bloom, D., and D. Canning. 2001. Demographic Change and Economic Growth: The Role of Cumulative Causality. In *Population Matters: Demographic Change, Economic Growth, and Poverty in the Developing World*, ed. Nancy Birdsall, A. C. Kelley, and S.W. Sinding. New York: Oxford University Press.

Blustein, Paul. 2009. *Misadventures of the Most Favoured Nations: Clashing Egos, Inflated Ambitions and the Great Shambles of the World Trade System*. New York: Public Affairs.

Boone, Peter, and Simon Johnson. Forthcoming. *The Problem of Central Banks*. Washington: Peterson Institute for International Economics.

Bordo, Michael D., and Eugene N. White. 1991. A Tale of Two Currencies: British and French Finance During the Napoleonic Wars. *Journal of Economic History* 51, no. 2 (June): 303–16.

Boughton, James. 2001a. Northwest of Suez: The 1956 Crisis and the IMF. *IMF Staff Papers* 48, no. 3: 425–46.

Boughton, James M. 2001b. *Silent Revolution: The International Monetary Fund, 1979–1989*. Washington: International Monetary Fund.

Boughton, James. 2006. Once Upon a Quota. Business Times Guide to the 2006 Annual Meetings. *Business Times*, Singapore, September 12.

Bryant, R. C. 2010. Governance Shares for the International Monetary Fund: Principles, Guidelines, Current Status. Brookings Institution, Washington. Photocopy.

Canuto, Otaviano, and Marcelo Giugale. 2010. *The Day After Tomorrow: A Handbook on the Future of Economic Policy in the Developing World*. Washington: World Bank.

Carse, Stephen, John Williamson, and Geoffrey E. Wood. 1980. *The Financing Procedures of British Foreign Trade*. New York: Cambridge University Press.

Chang, Gordon G. 2001. *The Coming Collapse of China*. New York: Random House.

Chinn, Menzie, and Jeffrey A. Frankel. 2007. Will the Euro Eventually Surpass the Dollar as Leading International Reserve Currency? In *G7 Current Account Imbalances: Sustainability and Adjustment*. Chicago: University of Chicago Press.

Chinn, Menzie, and Jeffrey Frankel. 2008. *The Euro May Over the Next 15 Years Surpass the Dollar as Leading International Currency*. NBER Working Paper 3909. Cambridge, MA: National Bureau of Economic Research.

Citigroup Global Markets, Inc. 2011. *Global Growth Generators Moving Beyond 'Emerging Markets' and 'BRIC.'* New York.

Clark, Gregory. 2007. *A Farewell to Alms: A Brief Economic History of the World.* Princeton, NJ and Oxford, UK: Princeton University Press.

Cline, William R. 2005. *The United States as a Debtor Nation.* Washington: Institute for International Economics and Center for Global Development.

Cline, William R., and John Williamson. 2010. *Estimates of Fundamental Equilibrium Exchange Rates.* Policy Briefs in International Economics 10-15. Washington: Peterson Institute for International Economics.

Cohen, Benjamin J. 1998. The Macrofoundations of Monetary Power. In *The Geography of Money*, ed. David M. Andrews. Ithaca, NY: Cornell University Press.

Cohen, Benjamin J. 2008. *International Political Economy: An Intellectual History.* Princeton, NJ: Princeton University Press.

Cooper, Richard. 2003. Is "Economic Power" a Useful and Operational Concept? Available at www.economics.harvard.edu (accessed May 20, 2011).

Cooper, Richard. 2006. Can China Be Effectively Punished Through Global Economic Isolations? In *No More States: Globalization, National Self Determination, and Terrorism*, ed. Richard N. Rosecrance and Arthur A. Stein. Lanham, MD: Rowman & Littlefield Publishers, Inc.

Cooper, Scott. 2006. The Limits of Monetary Power: Statecraft within Currency Areas. In *International Monetary Power*, ed. David M. Andrews. Ithaca and London: Cornell University Press.

Davey, William J. 2009. Compliance Problems in WTO Dispute Settlement. *Cornell International Law Journal* 42, no. 1: 119–28.

Deardorff, Alan. V. 1998. Determinants of Bilateral Trade: Does Gravity Work in a Neoclassical World? In *The Regionalization of the World Economy*, ed. Jeffrey A. Frankel. Chicago: University of Chicago Press.

Deaton, Angus, and Alan Heston. 2010. Understanding PPPs and PPP-Based National Accounts. *American Economic Journal: Macroeconomics* 2, no. 4: 1–35.

Destler, I. M. 1992. *American Trade Politics,* 2d. ed. Washington: Institute for International Economics.

Diamond, Jared. 1997. *Guns, Germs, and Steel: The Fates of Human Societies.* New York: W. W. Norton & Co.

Eaton, Jonathan, and Samuel Kortum. 2002. Technology, Geography, and Trade. *Econometrica* 70, no. 5: 1741–779.

Edwards, Richard W., Jr. 1985. *International Monetary Cooperation.* New York: Transnational Publishers.

Eichengreen, Barry. 2009. The Dollar Dilemma: The World's Top Currency Faces Competition. *Foreign Affairs* (September/October): 53–68.

Eichengreen, Barry. 2010. *Exorbitant Privilege: The Rise and Fall of the Dollar and the Future of the International Monetary System.* New York: Oxford University Press.

Eichengreen, Barry, and Marc Flandreau. 2008. *The Rise and Fall of the Dollar, or When Did the Dollar Replace Sterling as the Leading International Currency?* NBER Working Paper 14154. Cambridge, MA: National Bureau of Economic Research.

Eichengreen, Barry, and Donald Mathieson. 2000. *The Currency Composition of Foreign Exchange Reserves: Retrospect and Prospect.* IMF Working Paper 00/131. Washington: International Monetary Fund.

Eichengreen, Barry, Donghyun Park, and Kwanho Shin. 2011. *When Fast Growing Economies Slow Down: International Development and Implications for China.* NBER Working Paper 16919. Cambridge, MA: National Bureau of Economic Research.

El-Erian, Mohamed. 2010. Navigating the New Normal in Industrial Countries. Per Jacobsson Foundation Lecture, International Monetary Fund, October 10.

Ferguson, Niall. 2000. *The House of Rothschild: The World's Banker, 1849–1998*. New York: Penguin.

Ferguson, Niall. 2008. *The Ascent of Money A Financial History of the World*. New York: Penguin Press.

Ferguson, Niall. 2009. Empire at Risk. Available at www.niallferguson.com (accessed on June 13, 2011).

Ferguson, Niall. 2010. Decline and Fall When the American Empire Goes, It Is Likely to Go Quickly. *Foreign Affairs* 89, no. 2 (March/April).

Feyrer, James Donald. 2009. *Trade and Income-Exploiting Time Series in Geography*. NBER Working Paper 14910. Cambridge, MA: National Bureau of Economic Research.

Findlay, Ronald, and Kevin H. O'Rourke. 2007. *Power and Plenty: Trade, War, and the World Economy in the Second Millennium*. Princeton, NJ: Princeton University Press.

Frankel, Jeffrey. 1992. On the Dollar. In *The New Palgrave Dictionary of Money and Finance*, ed. Peter Newman, Murray Milgate, and John Eatwell. London: Macmillan Press.

Frankel, Jeffrey. 1995. Still the Lingua Franca: The Exaggerated Death of the Dollar. *Foreign Affairs* 74, no. 4 (July/August): 9–16.

Frankel, Jeffrey A., and Andrew K. Rose. 2000. *Estimating the Effects of Currency Unions on Trade and Output*. NBER Working Paper 7857. Cambridge, MA: National Bureau of Economic Research.

Frieden, Jeffrey. 2006. *Global Capitalism: Its Fall and Rise in the Twentieth Century*. New York: W.W. Norton & Company.

Friedman, Thomas L. 2005. *The World is Flat: A Brief History of the Twenty-First Century*. New York: Farrar, Straus and Giroux.

Friedman, Thomas L., and Michael Mandelbaum. 2011. *That Used to Be Us: How America Fell Behind in the World It Invented and How We Can Come Back*. New York: Farrar, Straus and Giroux.

Fukuyama, Francis. 1992. *The End of History and the Last Man*. New York: The Free Press.

Gill, Indermit, and Homi Kharas. 2007. *An East Asian Renaissance: Ideas for Economic Growth*. Washington: World Bank.

Gilpin, Robert. 2001. *Global Political Economy: Understanding the International Economic Order*. Princeton, NJ: Princeton University Press.

Goldman Sachs. 2003. *Dreaming With BRICs: The Path to 2050*. Global Economics Paper 99. New York: Goldman Sachs.

Goldstein, Morris, and Nicholas R. Lardy. 2008. China's Exchange Rate Policy: An Overview of Some Key Issues. In *Debating China's Exchange Rate Policy*, ed. Morris Goldstein and Nicholas R. Lardy. Washington: Peterson Institute for International Economics.

Goodhart, Charles A. E. 1995. *The Central Bank and the Financial System*. Cambridge, MA: MIT Press.

Gootiz, B., and A. Mattoo. 2008. *Restrictions on Services Trade and FDI in Developing Countries*. Washington: World Bank.

Hausmann, Ricardo, Lant Pritchett, and Dani Rodrik. 2005. Growth Accelerations. *Journal of Economic Growth* 10, no. 4: 303–29.

Harrod, Roy Forbes. 1951. *The Life of John Maynard Keynes*. London: MacMillan & Co.

Helpman, Elhanan, Marc Melitz, and Yona Rubinstein. 2008. Estimating Trade Flows: Trading Partners and Trading Volumes. *Quarterly Journal of Economics* 123, no. 2 (September): 441–87.

Heston, Alan, and Bettina Aten. 1993. Real World Military Expenditures. In *Economic Issues of Disarmament: Contributions from Peace Economics and Peace Science*, ed. Jurgen Brauer and Manas Chatterji. New York: New York University Press.

Hirschman, Albert O. 1945. *National Power and the Structure of Foreign Trade*. University of California Press.

Hufbauer, Gary, and Jared C. Woollacott. 2010. *Trade Disputes Between China and the United States: Growing Pains so Far, Worse Ahead?* Working Paper 10-17. Washington: Peterson Institute for International Economics.

Hufbauer, Gary, Yee Wong, and Ketki Sheth. 2006. *US-China Trade Disputes: Rising Tide, Rising Stakes*. Policy Analyses in International Economics 78. Washington: Peterson Institute for International Economics.

Hufbauer, Gary Clyde, Jeffrey J. Schott, and Woan Foong Wong. 2010. *Figuring Out the Doha Round*. Washington: Peterson Institute for International Economics.

Hufbauer, Gary, Jeffrey J. Schott, Kimberly Ann Elliott, and Barbara Oegg. 2007. *Economic Sanctions Reconsidered*. Washington: Peterson Institute for International Economics.

IMF (International Monetary Fund). 1989. *World Economic Outlook* (World Economic and Financial Surveys, October). Washington: International Monetary Fund.

IMF (International Monetary Fund). 2009. *World Economic Outlook* (World Economic and Financial Surveys, October). Washington: International Monetary Fund.

IMF (International Monetary Fund). 2011. Currency Composition of Foreign Exchange Reserves (COFER) database. Washington: International Monetary Fund.

Irwin, Douglas A. 2011. *Peddling Protectionism Smoot-Hawley and the Great Depression*. Princeton, NJ: Princeton University Press.

Jensen, Robert T. 2007. The Digital Provide: Information (Technology), Market Performance and Welfare in the South Indian Fisheries Sector. *Quarterly Journal of Economics* 122, no. 3: 879-924.

Johnson, Simon, William Larson, Chris Papageorgiou, and Arvind Subramanian. 2009. *Is Newer Better? Penn World Table Revisions and Their Impact on Growth Estimates*. NBER Working Paper 15455. Cambridge, MA: National Bureau of Economic Research.

Kagan, Robert. 2008. *The Return of History and the End of Dreams*. New York: Alfred A. Knopf Random House.

Keay, John. 2009. *China: A History*. London: Harper Press.

Kenen, Peter. 1983. *The Role of the Dollar as an International Currency*. Group of Thirty Occasional Paper 13. New York: Group of Thirty.

Kennedy, Paul. 1989. *The Rise and Fall of the Great Powers*. New York: First Vintage Books.

Kenny, Charles. 2011. *Getting Better: Why Global Development is Succeeding—And How We Can Improve the World Even More*. New York: Basic Books.

Keynes, John Maynard. 1981. Activities 1922-1929: The Return to Gold and Industrial Policy. In *The Collected Writings of John Maynard Keynes*, ed. D. E. Moggridge. London: Macmillan, and New York: Cambridge University Press for the Royal Economic Society.

Keynes, John Maynard. 1919. *The Economic Consequences of the Peace*. London: Macmillan and Co., Limited.

Khanna, Parag. 2011. *How to Run the World: Charting a Course to the Next Renaissance*. Random House.

Kindleberger, Charles. 1973. *The World in Depression, 1929–1939*. Berkeley: University of California Press.

Kindleberger, Charles. 1981. *International Money*. London: George Allen & Unwin.

Kindleberger, Charles. 1985. The Dollar Yesterday, Today and Tomorrow. *Banca Nazionale de Lavoro Quarterly Review* 38 (December): 295–308.

Kirshner, Jonathan. 2006. Currency and Coercion in the Twenty-First Century. In *International Monetary Power*, ed. David M. Andrews. Ithaca, NY: Cornell University Press.

Kissinger, Henry. 1994. *Diplomacy*. New York: Touchstone.

Kissinger, Henry. 2011. *On China*. New York: Penguin Press.

Krugman, Paul. 1984. The International Role of the Dollar: Theory and Prospect. In *Exchange Rate Theory and Practice*, ed. John F. O. Bilson and Richard C. Marston. Chicago: University of Chicago Press.

Krugman, Paul R. 1992. The International Role of the Dollar. In *Currencies and Crises*, ed. Paul R. Krugman. Cambridge, MA: MIT Press.

Krugman, Paul. 1994. The Myth of Asia's Miracle. *Foreign Affairs* 73, no. 6 (November/December): 62–79.

Krugman, Paul. 2009. Trade and Wages, Reconsidered. In *Brookings Papers on Economic Activity* 1. Washington: Brookings Institution.

Kunz, Diane B. 1991. *The Economic Diplomacy of the Suez Crisis*. Chapel Hill, NC: University of North Carolina Press.

Lardy. Nicholas R. 2007. China: Rebalancing Economic Growth. In *The China Balance Sheet in 2007 and Beyond*, ed. C. Fred Bergsten, Nicholas R. Lardy, Bates Gill, and Derek Mitchell. Washington: Center for Strategic and International Studies and Peterson Institute for International Economics.

Lardy, Nicholas R. 2010. *The Sustainability of China's Recovery from the Global Recession*. Policy Briefs in International Economics 10-7. Washington: Peterson Institute for International Economics.

Nicholas R. Lardy. 2010. China's Growth Prospects. Unpublished manuscript, October.

Lane, Philip, and Gian Maria Milesi-Ferretti. 2007. The External Wealth of Nations Mark II: Revised and Extended Estimates of Foreign Assets and Liabilities. *Journal of International Economics* 73 (November): 223–50.

Lawrence, Robert Z. 1987. Imports in Japan: Closed Markets or Minds? *Brookings Papers on Economic Activity* 2. Washington: Brookings Institution.

Li, Cheng. 2011. *China's Midterm Jockeying: Gearing Up for 2012 (Part 4: Top Leaders of Major State-Owned Enterprises)*. Washington: Brookings Institution. Available at www.brookings.edu (accessed on May 20, 2011).

Lindert, Peter. 1969. *Key Currencies and Gold*. Princeton, NJ: Princeton University.

Lipset, Seymour M. 1959. Some Social Requisites of Democracy: Economic Development and Political Legitimacy. *American Political Science Review* 53: 69–105.

Lucas, Robert E. Jr. 2004. *The Industrial Revolution: Past and Future*. Federal Reserve Bank of Minneapolis 2003 Annual Report Essay. Federal Reserve Bank of Minneapolis.

Lucas, Robert Jr. E. 2000. Some Macroeconomics for the 21st Century. *The Journal of Economic Perspectives* 14, no. 1: 159–68.

Luce, Edward. 2010. The Crisis of Middle-Class America. *Financial Times*, July 30.

Maddison, Angus. 2001. *The World Economy: A Millennial Perspective*. Paris: Organization for Economic Cooperation and Development.

Maddison, Angus. 2010. Statistics on World Population, GDP and Per Capita GDP, 1-2008 AD. Available at www.ggdc.net/maddison/oriindex.htm.

Mandelbaum, Michael. 2010. *The Frugal Superpower: America's Global Leadership in a Cash-Strapped Era*. New York: Public Affairs.

Martin, Will, and Aaditya Mattoo. 2008. *The Doha Development Agenda: What's on the Table?* World Bank Policy Research Working Paper 4672. Washington: World Bank.

Mattoo, Aaditya, and Arvind Subramanian. 2009. *Multilateralism Beyond Doha*. Working Paper 09-8. Washington: Peterson Institute for International Economics.

Mattoo, Aaditya, and Arvind Subramanian. 2010. Crisscrossing Globalization: The Phenomenon of Uphill Skill Flows. In *Annual World Bank Conference on Development Economics 2009, Global: People, Politics, and Globalization*. Washington: World Bank.

Mattoo, Aaditya, and Arvind Subramanian. Forthcoming 2011. *A China Round of Trade Negotiations*. Washington: Peterson Institute for International Economics.

Mattoo, Aaditya, Francis Ng, and Arvind Subramanian. 2011. *The Elephant in the "Green Room": China and the Doha Round*. Policy Briefs in International Economics 11-3. Washington: Peterson Institute for International Economics.

McKinnon, Ronald. 1979. *Money in International Exchange*. New York: Oxford University Press.

Mikesell, Raymond. 1994. *The Bretton Woods Debate: A Memoir*. Princeton, NJ: Princeton University Press.

Morgenthau, Hans.1949. *Politics Among Nations*. New York: Knopf.

Morris, Ian. 2010. *Why the West Rules For Now: The Patterns of History, and What They Reveal About the Future*. New York: Farrar, Straus and Giroux.

Mussa, Michael. 2008. IMF Surveillance over China's Exchange Rate Policy. In *Debating China's Exchange Rate Policy*, ed. Morris Goldstein and Nicholas R. Lardy. Washington: Peterson Institute for International Economics.

Noland, Marcus. 1995. US-Japan Trade Friction and its Dilemmas for US Policy. *The World Economy* 18, no. 2 (March): 237-67.

Nye, Joseph S., Jr. 2010. The Future of American Power. *Foreign Affairs* 89, no. 6 (November/December): 2–13.

Nye, Joseph S., Jr. 2004. *Soft Power: The Means to Success in World Politics*. New York: Public Affairs.

Ocampo, José Antonio. 2010. Building an SDR-Based Global Reserve System. *Journal of Globalization and Development* 1, no. 2.

Parente, Stephen L., and Edward C. Prescott. 1994. Barriers to Technology Adoption and Development. *Journal of Political Economy* 102, no. 2: 298–321.

Pauly, Louis. W. 2006. Monetary Statecraft in Follower States. In *International Monetary Power*, ed. David M. Andrews. Ithaca and London: Cornell University Press.

Pei, Minxin. 2009. Will the Chinese Communist Party Survive the Crisis? How Beijing's Shrinking Economy May Threaten One-Party Rule. *Foreign Affairs* (March). Available at www.foreignaffairs.com (accessed on June 13, 2011).

Penn World Table. 2010. PWT Version 6.3 database. Philadelphia, PA: University of Pennsylvania.

Perkins, Dwight H. 2010. Rapid Growth and Changing Economic Structure: The Expenditure Side Story and Its Implications for China. *China Economic Review* (October 2). Available at www.sciencedirect.com (accessed on May 20, 2011).

Portes, Richard, and Helene Rey. 1998. *The Emergence of the Euro as an International Currency*. NBER Working Paper 6424. Cambridge, MA: National Bureau of Economic Research.

Prasad, Eswar, Raghuram Rajan, and Arvind Subramanian. 2008. Foreign Capital and Economic Growth. *Brookings Papers on Economic Activity*: 1. Washington: Brookings Institution.

Pritchett, Lant. 1996. Measuring Outward Orientation: Can It Be Done? *Journal of Development Economics* 49, no. 22: 307–35.

Pritchett, Lant H. 1997. Divergence, Big Time. *Journal of Economic Perspective* 11, no. 3: 3–17.

Rachman, Gideon. 2011. *Zero-Sum Future: American Power in an Age of Anxiety*. New York: Simon & Schuster.

Ravallion, Martin. 2010. *Price Levels and Economic Growth: Making Sense of Revisions to Data on Real Incomes*. World Bank Policy Research Working Paper 5229. Washington: World Bank.

Reinhart, Carmen M., and Kenneth S. Rogoff. 2009. *This Time is Different Eight Centuries of Financial Folly*. Princeton, NJ: Princeton University Press.

Reinhart, Carmen M., Kenneth Rogoff, and Miguel A. Savastano. 2003. Debt Intolerance. *Brookings Papers on Economic Activity*: 1. Washington: Brookings Institution.

Reinhart, Carmen M. 2010. *This Time is Different Chartbook: Country Histories on Debt, Default, and Financial Crises*. NBER Working Paper 15815. Cambridge, MA: National Bureau of Economic Research.

Rey, Helene. 2001. International Trade and Currency Exchange. *Review of Economic Studies* 68 no. 2 (April): 443–64.

Rodrik, Dani. 2009. *Growth After the Crisis*. CEPR Discussion Paper 7480. London: Centre for Economic and Policy Research.

Rodrik, Dani, and Arvind Subramanian. 2004. *From "Hindu Growth" to Productivity Surge: The Mystery of the Indian Growth Transition*. IMF Staff Papers 52, no. 2: 193–228. Washington: International Monetary Fund.

Rodrik, Dani. 2010. Making Room for China in the World Economy. *American Economic Review* 100, no. 2: 89–93.

Romer, Paul M. 1994. The Origins of Endogenous Growth. *Journal of Economic Perspectives* 8, no. 1: 3–22.

Samuelson, Paul. 2004. Where Ricardo and Mill Rebut and Confirm Arguments of Mainstream Economists Supporting Globalization. *Journal of Economic Perspectives* 18, no. 3: 135–46.

Schattschneider, Elmer Eric. 1935. *Politics, Pressures and the Tariff*. New York: Prentice-Hall.

Schenk, Catherine R. 2010a. *The Decline of Sterling: Managing the Retreat of an International Currency, 1945–1992*. New York: Cambridge University Press.

Schenk, Catherine R. 2010b. How Have Multiple Reserve Currencies Functioned in the Past? Why Were the Rules-Based Adjustment Indicator and the Stabilisation Account Abandoned in the Past? Paper prepared for seminar on the International Monetary System: Old and New Debates, sponsored by the Reinventing Bretton Woods Committee, Paris (December). Available at http://imsreform.org/reserve/pdf/schenk.pdf (accessed on May 20, 2011).

Schularick, Moritz. 2006. A Tale of Two 'Globalizations': Capital Flows from Rich to Poor in Two Eras of Global Finance. *International Journal of Finance & Economics* 11, no. 4: 339–54.

Segal, Adam. 2011. *Advantage How American Innovation Can Overcome the Asian Challenge*. New York: W.W. Norton & Company.

Shambaugh, David. 2009. *China's Communist Party: Atrophy and Adaptation*. Berkeley, CA: University of California Press.

Skidelsky, Robert. 2003. *John Maynard Keynes 1883–1946 Economist, Philosopher, Statesman*. London: Macmillan.

Slaughter, Anne-Marie. 2009. America's Edge: Power in the Networked Century. *Foreign Affairs* 88, no. 1 (January/February): 94–113.

Spence, Michael. 2011. *The Next Convergence: The Future of Economic Growth in a Multispeed World*. New York: Farrar, Straus, and Giroux.

Stiglitz, Joseph. 2009. *Emerging Thinking on Global Issues*. United Nations University Series. Office of the President of the 63rd Session of the United Nations General Assembly. Available at www.unmultimedia.org (accessed on June 9, 2011).

Stockholm International Peace Research Institute. 2010. SIPRI Military Expenditure database. http://milexdata.sipri.org (accessed on May 10, 2011).

Strange, Susan. 1987. Persistent Myth of Lost Hegemony. *International Organization* 41, no. 4 (Autumn): 551–74.

Subramanian, Arvind. 2010. *New PPP-Based Estimates of Renminbi Undervaluation and Policy Implications*. Policy Briefs in International Economics 10-8. Washington: Peterson Institute for International Economics.

Subramanian, Arvind, and Shang-Jin Wei. 2007. The WTO Promotes Trade, Strongly but Unevenly. *Journal of International Economics* 72, no. 1: 151.

Summers, Lawrence. 2008a. America Needs to Make a New Case for Trade. *Financial Times,* April 27.

Summers, Lawrence. 2008b. A Strategy to Promote Healthy Globalisation. *Financial Times*, May 4.

Summers, Lawrence H. 2010. Speech delivered at Economic Policy Institute, December 13.

Swoboda, Alexander. 1969. Vehicle Currencies in the Foreign Exchange Market: The Case of the Dollar. In *The International Market for Foreign Exchange*, ed. R. Aliber. New York: Praeger.

Tamura, Robert. 1996. From Decay to Growth: A Demographic Transition to Economic Growth. *Journal of Economic Dynamics and Control Elsevier* 20, no. 6–7: 1237–61.

Taylor, Alan M. 2002. A Century of Current Account Dynamics. *Journal of International Money and Finance* 21 (November): 725–48.

Triffin, Robert. 1961. *Gold and the Dollar Crisis The Future of Convertibility*. New Haven, CT: Yale University Press.

Truman, Edwin. 2007. Comment on Will the Euro Surpass the Dollar as International Reserve Currency? by Menzie Chinn and Jeffrey A. Frankel. In *G7 Current Account Imbalances: Sustainability and Adjustment,* ed. Richard H. Clarida. Chicago: University of Chicago Press.

Tuchman, Barbara, W. 1962. *The Guns of August*. New York: Ballantine Books.

USITC (United States International Trade Commission). 2011. *China: Effects of Intellectual Property Infringement and Indigenous Innovation Policies on the US Economy*. USITC Publication 4226 (May). Washington. www.usitc.gov (accessed on June 9, 2011).

Vogel, Ezra. 1979. *Japan as Number One: Lessons for America.* Cambridge, MA: Harvard University Press.

Virmani, Arvind. 2004. *Economic Performance, Power Potential, and Global Governance: Towards a New International Order*. Working Paper 150. Indian Council for International Economic Relations.

Warnock, Frank, and Veronica Cacdac Warnock. 2009. International Capital Flows and U.S. Interest Rates. *Journal of International Money and Finance* 28 (October): 903–19.

Weitzman, Martin L. 1970. Soviet Postwar Economic Growth and Capital-Labor Substitution. *American Economic Review* 60, no. 4: 676–92.

Williamson, John. 2009. *Understanding Special Drawing Rights (SDRs)*. Policy Briefs in International Economics 9-11. Washington: Peterson Institute for International Economics.

Williamson, John. 2011. *Getting Surplus Countries to Adjust*. Policy Briefs in International Economics 11-1. Washington: Peterson Institute for International Economics.

Wilson, Bruce 2007. Compliance by WTO Members with Adverse WTO Dispute Settlement Rulings: The Record to Date. *Journal of International Economic Law* 10, no. 2 (June): 397–403.

Wolf, Martin. 1987. Differential and More Favorable Treatment of Developing Countries and the International Trading System. *World Bank Economic Review* 1, no. 44: 647–68.

Wolf, Martin. 2010. Will China's Rise Be Peaceful? *Financial Times*, November 16.

Wolf, Martin. 2011. How China Should Rule the World? *Financial Times*, March 22.

World Bank. 2010. *World Development Indicators*. Washington.

WTO (World Trade Organization). 2007. *World Trade Report 2007*. Geneva.

Yang, Yao. 2010. The End of Beijing Consensus Can China's Model of Authoritarian Growth Survive? *Foreign Affairs* (February). www.foreignaffairs.com (accessed on June 13, 2011)

Yeager, Leland B. 1966. *International Monetary Relations*. New York: Harper and Row.

Yergin, Daniel. 2008. *The Prize: The Epic Quest for Oil, Money, and Power*. New York: Free Press.

Yu Yongding. 2010. Witness to Financial Imbalances: A Double Surplus, the Yuan Exchange Rate and the Dollar Trap. *International Economic Review* 3.

Yu Yongding. 2011. China's Best Way Forward. *Financial Times*, January 18.

Young, Alwyn. 1993. *Lessons from the East Asian NICS: A Contrarian View*. NBER Working Paper 4482. Cambridge, MA: National Bureau of Economic Research.

Zakaria, Fareed. 2008a. *The Post-American World*. London and New York: W. W. Norton and Company.

Zakaria, Fareed. 2008b. The Future of American Power Why the United States Will Survive the Rise of the Rest. *Foreign Affairs* 87, no. 3 (May/June): 18–43.

Index

intellectual property, 21, 22
interest rates, 2
International Clearing Union, 43n
International Comparison Program (ICP), 84b, 95
international currency. *See* currency dominance; reserve currency
international financial system, US influence on, 16–19, 35n
International Monetary Fund (IMF)
creation of, 16–19, 33, 35n, 43, 43n, 161
current account projections, 100
Direction of Trade Statistics, 97
emergency financing, 1–3, 15, 15n
legitimacy of, 165–66
quota formula, 17, 42–44, 43n
index of economic dominance based on, 45, 45n, 46f, 100–101, 101f
role in financial crises, 162b
special drawing rights, 52, 59, 162b–163b
US political control over, 17n, 17–18, 35n
World Economic Outlook, 84b, 137
International Stabilization Fund (ISF), 43n

Jackson-Vanik Amendment (1974), 31
Japan
dominance forecasts for, 135–36, 138
economic challenge from, 5, 20, 30, 49, 192
index of economic dominance, 49
unfair trade accusations against, 2n, 19, 23
Japan as Number One (Vogel), 136
Joyce, James, 4

Kennedy, John F., 20
Kennedy Round, 20, 185
Keynes, John Maynard, 16–17, 17n, 41, 43n, 59, 94, 135, 162b, 197
Khruschev, Nikita, 135
Kindleberger, Charles, 99, 150, 171n
Kissinger, Henry, 6, 105
Korea, 34
Krugman, Paul, 51, 53, 60–61, 107, 135, 136n, 172, 172n

Lamy, Pascal, 22
lend-lease credits, 14–15, 15n, 33
level reciprocity, 173
living standards
convergence and, 70, 140–43, 141t
economic dominance and, 9, 104–105, 119–21, 143t, 143–44

Long Term Agreement Regarding International Trade in Cotton Textiles (LTA), 21
Luce, Edward, 189

Macmillan, Harold, 1, 12
macroeconomic stability
economic cooperation and, 160–66
growth dependent upon, 75, 75n
Malaysia, 34, 56, 113n
Mao Zedong, 26
mercantilism, 30, 33
China, 9, 22, 124–33, 125t, 157–58
consumption growth and, 130, 131b–133b
demise of, 157–58
history of, 125t, 125–30
instruments used to achieve, 126b–128b
Mexico, 21
middle-income countries, economic dominance of, 9, 104–105, 119–21, 142n, 143, 195
military strength, 29–30, 36–37, 37f
Mill, John Stuart, 32n
mobile telephones, 75n
monetary cooperation, 160–66
limits to, 162b–164b
most favored nation (MFN) principle, 19n, 19–20, 32, 150n, 166, 185
Multi-Fiber Arrangement (MFA), 21
multilateralism, 169–87
alternatives to, 175–77
"China Round," 184–86
history of, 19–24, 161–66
impediments to, 178–84
as insurance, 5, 11–12, 129, 173–74, 186–87
requirements for, 174–75

Nasser, Gamal Abdel, 14
National Intelligence Council, 104
national objectives, economic dominance used for, 13, 15–16, 27, 29, 31, 34, 156
National Science Foundation (NSF), 195
newly industrialized economies (NIEs), 69
Newton, Sir Isaac, 48n
Nixon, Richard, 18n, 31
Noriega, Manuel, 35–36
North American Free Trade Agreement (NAFTA), 21, 31, 176
Nye, Joseph, 4, 25, 26, 104

Obama, Barack, 3, 24, 197
Occam razorization, 28, 28n, 36–39, 60

Other Publications from the Peterson Institute for International Economics

7   A New SDR Allocation?*
John Williamson
March 1984   ISBN 0-88132-028-5
8   An International Standard for Monetary
Stabilization*   Ronald L. McKinnon
March 1984   ISBN 0-88132-018-8
9   The Yen/Dollar Agreement: Liberalizing
Japanese Capital Markets*   Jeffrey Frankel
December 1984   ISBN 0-88132-035-8
10 Bank Lending to Developing Countries:
The Policy Alternatives*   C. Fred Bergsten,
William R. Cline, and John Williamson
April 1985   ISBN 0-88132-032-3
11 Trading for Growth: The Next Round of
Trade Negotiations*
Gary Clyde Hufbauer and Jeffrey J. Schott
September 1985   ISBN 0-88132-033-1
12 Financial Intermediation Beyond the Debt
Crisis*   Donald R. Lessard and
John Williamson
September 1985   ISBN 0-88132-021-8
13 The United States-Japan Economic
Problem*   C. Fred Bergsten and
William R. Cline
Oct. 1985, 2d ed. January 1987
                    ISBN 0-88132-060-9
14 Deficits and the Dollar: The World
Economy at Risk*   Stephen Marris
Dec. 1985, 2d ed. November 1987
                    ISBN 0-88132-067-6
15 Trade Policy for Troubled Industries*
Gary Clyde Hufbauer and Howard F. Rosen
March 1986   ISBN 0-88132-020-X
16 The United States and Canada: The Quest
for Free Trade*   Paul Wonnacott, with
an appendix by John Williamson
March 1987   ISBN 0-88132-056-0
17 Adjusting to Success: Balance of Payments
Policy in the East Asian NICs*
Bela Balassa and John Williamson
June 1987, rev. April 1990
                    ISBN 0-88132-101-X
18 Mobilizing Bank Lending to Debtor
Countries*   William R. Cline
June 1987   ISBN 0-88132-062-5
19 Auction Quotas and United States Trade
Policy*   C. Fred Bergsten,
Kimberly Ann Elliott, Jeffrey J. Schott, and
Wendy E. Takacs
September 1987   ISBN 0-88132-050-1
20 Agriculture and the GATT: Rewriting the
Rules*   Dale E. Hathaway
September 1987   ISBN 0-88132-052-8
21 Anti-Protection: Changing Forces in
United States Trade Politics*
I. M. Destler and John S. Odell
September 1987   ISBN 0-88132-043-9
22 Targets and Indicators: A Blueprint for the
International Coordination of Economic
Policy   John Williamson and
Marcus H. Miller
September 1987   ISBN 0-88132-051-X

23 Capital Flight: The Problem and Policy
Responses*   Donald R. Lessard and
John Williamson
December 1987   ISBN 0-88132-059-5
24 United States-Canada Free Trade: An
Evaluation of the Agreement*
Jeffrey J. Schott
April 1988   ISBN 0-88132-072-2
25 Voluntary Approaches to Debt Relief*
John Williamson
Sept. 1988, rev. May 1   ISBN 0-88132-098-6
26 American Trade Adjustment: The Global
Impact*   William R. Cline
March 1989   ISBN 0-88132-095-1
27 More Free Trade Areas?*   Jeffrey J. Schott
May 1989   ISBN 0-88132-085-4
28 The Progress of Policy Reform in Latin
America*   John Williamson
January 1990   ISBN 0-88132-100-1
29 The Global Trade Negotiations: What Can
Be Achieved?*   Jeffrey J. Schott
September 1990   ISBN 0-88132-137-0
30 Economic Policy Coordination: Requiem
for Prologue?*   Wendy Dobson
April 1991   ISBN 0-88132-102-8
31 The Economic Opening of Eastern Europe*
John Williamson
May 1991   ISBN 0-88132-186-9
32 Eastern Europe and the Soviet Union in the
World Economy*   Susan Collins and
Dani Rodrik
May 1991   ISBN 0-88132-157-5
33 African Economic Reform: The External
Dimension*   Carol Lancaster
June 1991   ISBN 0-88132-096-X
34 Has the Adjustment Process Worked?*
Paul R. Krugman
October 1991   ISBN 0-88132-116-8
35 From Soviet DisUnion to Eastern Economic
Community?*   Oleh Havrylyshyn and
John Williamson
October 1991   ISBN 0-88132-192-3
36 Global Warming: The Economic Stakes*
William R. Cline
May 1992   ISBN 0-88132-172-9
37 Trade and Payments after Soviet
Disintegration*   John Williamson
June 1992   ISBN 0-88132-173-7
38 Trade and Migration: NAFTA and
Agriculture*   Philip L. Martin
October 1993   ISBN 0-88132-201-6
39 The Exchange Rate System and the IMF: A
Modest Agenda   Morris Goldstein
June 1995   ISBN 0-88132-219-9
40 What Role for Currency Boards?
John Williamson
September 1995   ISBN 0-88132-222-9
41 Predicting External Imbalances for the
United States and Japan*   William R. Cline
September 1995   ISBN 0-88132-220-2
42 Standards and APEC: An Action Agenda*
John S. Wilson
October 1995   ISBN 0-88132-223-7

Completing the Uruguay Round: A Results-Oriented Approach to the GATT Trade Negotiations*   Jeffrey J. Schott, ed.
September 1990   ISBN 0-88132-130-3
Economic Sanctions Reconsidered (2 volumes)
Economic Sanctions Reconsidered:
Supplemental Case Histories
Gary Clyde Hufbauer, Jeffrey J. Schott, and Kimberly Ann Elliott
1985, 2d ed. Dec. 1990   ISBN cloth 0-88132-115-X
                              ISBN paper 0-88132-105-2
Economic Sanctions Reconsidered: History and Current Policy   Gary Clyde Hufbauer, Jeffrey J. Schott, and Kimberly Ann Elliott
December 1990   ISBN cloth 0-88132-140-0
                              ISBN paper 0-88132-136-2
Pacific Basin Developing Countries: Prospects for the Future*   Marcus Noland
January 1991   ISBN cloth 0-88132-141-9
                              ISBN paper 0-88132-081-1
Currency Convertibility in Eastern Europe*
John Williamson, ed.
October 1991   ISBN 0-88132-128-1
International Adjustment and Financing: The Lessons of 1985-1991*   C. Fred Bergsten, ed.
January 1992   ISBN 0-88132-112-5
North American Free Trade: Issues and Recommendations*   Gary Clyde Hufbauer and Jeffrey J. Schott
April 1992   ISBN 0-88132-120-6
Narrowing the U.S. Current Account Deficit*
Alan J. Lenz
June 1992   ISBN 0-88132-103-6
The Economics of Global Warming
William R. Cline
June 1992   ISBN 0-88132-132-X
US Taxation of International Income:
Blueprint for Reform   Gary Clyde Hufbauer, assisted by Joanna M. van Rooij
October 1992   ISBN 0-88132-134-6
Who's Bashing Whom? Trade Conflict in High-Technology Industries   Laura D'Andrea Tyson
November 1992   ISBN 0-88132-106-0
Korea in the World Economy*   Il SaKong
January 1993   ISBN 0-88132-183-4
Pacific Dynamism and the International Economic System*   C. Fred Bergsten and Marcus Noland, eds.
May 1993   ISBN 0-88132-196-6
Economic Consequences of Soviet Disintegration*   John Williamson, ed.
May 1993   ISBN 0-88132-190-7
Reconcilable Differences? United States-Japan Economic Conflict*   C. Fred Bergsten and Marcus Noland
June 1993   ISBN 0-88132-129-X
Does Foreign Exchange Intervention Work?
Kathryn M. Dominguez and Jeffrey A. Frankel
September 1993   ISBN 0-88132-104-4
Sizing Up U.S. Export Disincentives*
J. David Richardson
September 1993   ISBN 0-88132-107-9

NAFTA: An Assessment
Gary Clyde Hufbauer and Jeffrey J. Schott, *rev. ed.*
October 1993   ISBN 0-88132-199-0
Adjusting to Volatile Energy Prices
Philip K. Verleger, Jr.
November 1993   ISBN 0-88132-069-2
The Political Economy of Policy Reform
John Williamson, ed.
January 1994   ISBN 0-88132-195-8
Measuring the Costs of Protection in the United States   Gary Clyde Hufbauer and Kimberly Ann Elliott
January 1994   ISBN 0-88132-108-7
The Dynamics of Korean Economic Development*   Cho Soon
March 1994   ISBN 0-88132-162-1
Reviving the European Union*
C. Randall Henning, Eduard Hochreiter, and Gary Clyde Hufbauer, eds.
April 1994   ISBN 0-88132-208-3
China in the World Economy
Nicholas R. Lardy
April 1994   ISBN 0-88132-200-8
Greening the GATT: Trade, Environment, and the Future   Daniel C. Esty
July 1994   ISBN 0-88132-205-9
Western Hemisphere Economic Integration*
Gary Clyde Hufbauer and Jeffrey J. Schott
July 1994   ISBN 0-88132-159-1
Currencies and Politics in the United States, Germany, and Japan   C. Randall Henning
September 1994   ISBN 0-88132-127-3
Estimating Equilibrium Exchange Rates
John Williamson, ed.
September 1994   ISBN 0-88132-076-5
Managing the World Economy: Fifty Years after Bretton Woods   Peter B. Kenen, ed.
September 1994   ISBN 0-88132-212-1
Reciprocity and Retaliation in U.S. Trade Policy   Thomas O. Bayard and Kimberly Ann Elliott
September 1994   ISBN 0-88132-084-6
The Uruguay Round: An Assessment*
Jeffrey J. Schott, assisted by Johanna Buurman
November 1994   ISBN 0-88132-206-7
Measuring the Costs of Protection in Japan*
Yoko Sazanami, Shujiro Urata, and Hiroki Kawai
January 1995   ISBN 0-88132-211-3
Foreign Direct Investment in the United States, 3d ed.   Edward M. Graham and Paul R. Krugman
January 1995   ISBN 0-88132-204-0
The Political Economy of Korea-United States Cooperation*   C. Fred Bergsten and Il SaKong, eds.
February 1995   ISBN 0-88132-213-X
International Debt Reexamined*
William R. Cline
February 1995   ISBN 0-88132-083-8
American Trade Politics, 3d ed.   I. M. Destler
April 1995   ISBN 0-88132-215-6

Reforming the US Corporate Tax
Gary Clyde Hufbauer and Paul L. E. Grieco
September 2005   ISBN 0-88132-384-5
The United States as a Debtor Nation
William R. Cline
September 2005   ISBN 0-88132-399-3
NAFTA Revisited: Achievements and
Challenges   Gary Clyde Hufbauer and
Jeffrey J. Schott, assisted by Paul L. E. Grieco and
Yee Wong
October 2005   ISBN 0-88132-334-9
US National Security and Foreign Direct
Investment   Edward M. Graham and
David M. Marchick
May 2006   ISBN 978-0-88132-391-7
Accelerating the Globalization of America: The
Role for Information Technology
Catherine L. Mann, assisted by Jacob Funk
Kirkegaard
June 2006   ISBN 978-0-88132-390-0
Delivering on Doha: Farm Trade and the Poor
Kimberly Ann Elliott
July 2006   ISBN 978-0-88132-392-4
Case Studies in US Trade Negotiation, Vol. 1:
Making the Rules   Charan Devereaux,
Robert Z. Lawrence, and Michael Watkins
September 2006   ISBN 978-0-88132-362-7
Case Studies in US Trade Negotiation, Vol. 2:
Resolving Disputes   Charan Devereaux,
Robert Z. Lawrence, and Michael Watkins
September 2006   ISBN 978-0-88132-363-2
C. Fred Bergsten and the World Economy
Michael Mussa, ed.
December 2006   ISBN 978-0-88132-397-9
Working Papers, Volume I   Peterson Institute
December 2006   ISBN 978-0-88132-388-7
The Arab Economies in a Changing World
Marcus Noland and Howard Pack
April 2007   ISBN 978-0-88132-393-1
Working Papers, Volume II   Peterson Institute
April 2007   ISBN 978-0-88132-404-4
Global Warming and Agriculture: Impact
Estimates by Country   William R. Cline
July 2007   ISBN 978-0-88132-403-7
US Taxation of Foreign Income
Gary Clyde Hufbauer and Ariel Assa
October 2007   ISBN 978-0-88132-405-1
Russia's Capitalist Revolution: Why Market
Reform Succeeded and Democracy Failed
Anders Åslund
October 2007   ISBN 978-0-88132-409-9
Economic Sanctions Reconsidered, 3d ed.
Gary Clyde Hufbauer, Jeffrey J. Schott, Kimberly
Ann Elliott, and Barbara Oegg
November 2007
          ISBN hardcover 978-0-88132-407-5
    ISBN hardcover/CD-ROM 978-0-88132-408-2
Debating China's Exchange Rate Policy
Morris Goldstein and Nicholas R. Lardy, eds.
April 2008   ISBN 978-0-88132-415-0

Leveling the Carbon Playing Field:
International Competition and US Climate
Policy Design Trevor Houser, Rob Bradley, Britt
Childs, Jacob Werksman, and Robert Heilmayr
May 2008   ISBN 978-0-88132-420-4
Accountability and Oversight of US Exchange
Rate Policy   C. Randall Henning
June 2008   ISBN 978-0-88132-419-8
Challenges of Globalization: Imbalances and
Growth   Anders Åslund and
Marek Dabrowski, eds.
July 2008   ISBN 978-0-88132-418-1
China's Rise: Challenges and Opportunities
C. Fred Bergsten, Charles Freeman, Nicholas R.
Lardy, and Derek J. Mitchell
September 2008   ISBN 978-0-88132-417-4
Banking on Basel: The Future of International
Financial Regulation   Daniel K. Tarullo
September 2008   ISBN 978-0-88132-423-5
US Pension Reform: Lessons from Other
Countries   Martin Neil Baily and
Jacob Funk Kirkegaard
February 2009   ISBN 978-0-88132-425-9
How Ukraine Became a Market Economy and
Democracy   Anders Åslund
March 2009   ISBN 978-0-88132-427-3
Global Warming and the World Trading
System   Gary Clyde Hufbauer,
Steve Charnovitz, and Jisun Kim
March 2009   ISBN 978-0-88132-428-0
The Russia Balance Sheet   Anders Åslund and
Andrew Kuchins
March 2009   ISBN 978-0-88132-424-2
The Euro at Ten: The Next Global Currency?
Jean Pisani-Ferry and Adam S. Posen, eds.
July 2009   ISBN 978-0-88132-430-3
Financial Globalization, Economic Growth, and
the Crisis of 2007–09   William R. Cline
May 2010   ISBN 978-0-88132-4990-0
Russia after the Global Economic Crisis
Anders Åslund, Sergei Guriev, and Andrew
Kuchins, eds.
June 2010   ISBN 978-0-88132-497-6
Sovereign Wealth Funds: Threat or Salvation?
Edwin M. Truman
September 2010   ISBN 978-0-88132-498-3
The Last Shall Be the First: The East European
Financial Crisis, 2008–10   Anders Åslund
October 2010   ISBN 978-0-88132-521-8
Witness to Transformation: Refugee Insights
into North Korea   Stephan Haggard and
Marcus Noland
January 2011   ISBN 978-0-88132-438-9
Foreign Direct Investment and Development:
Launching a Second Generation of Policy
Research, Avoiding the Mistakes of the First,
Reevaluating Policies for Developed and
Developing Countries   Theodore H. Moran
April 2011   ISBN 978-0-88132-600-0
How Latvia Came through the Financial Crisis
Anders Åslund and Valdis Dombrovskis
May 2011   ISBN 978-0-88132-602-4

Global Trade in Services: Fear, Facts, and
Offshoring   J. Bradford Jensen
August 2011   ISBN 978-0-88132-601-7
NAFTA and Climate Change
Meera Fickling and Jeffrey J. Schott
September 2011   ISBN 978-0-88132-436-5
Eclipse: Living in the Shadow of China's
Economic Dominance   Arvind Subramanian
September 2011   ISBN 978-0-88132-606-2

SPECIAL REPORTS

1   Promoting World Recovery: A Statement
    on Global Economic Strategy*
    by 26 Economists from Fourteen Countries
    December 1982   ISBN 0-88132-013-7
2   Prospects for Adjustment in Argentina,
    Brazil, and Mexico: Responding to the
    Debt Crisis*   John Williamson, ed.
    June 1983   ISBN 0-88132-016-1
3   Inflation and Indexation: Argentina, Brazil,
    and Israel*   John Williamson, ed.
    March 1985   ISBN 0-88132-037-4
4   Global Economic Imbalances*
    C. Fred Bergsten, ed.
    March 1986   ISBN 0-88132-042-0
5   African Debt and Financing*
    Carol Lancaster and John Williamson, eds.
    May 1986   ISBN 0-88132-044-7
6   Resolving the Global Economic Crisis:
    After Wall Street*   by Thirty-three
    Economists from Thirteen Countries
    December 1987   ISBN 0-88132-070-6
7   World Economic Problems*
    Kimberly Ann Elliott and John Williamson,
    eds.
    April 1988   ISBN 0-88132-055-2
    Reforming World Agricultural Trade*
    by Twenty-nine Professionals from
    Seventeen Countries
    1988   ISBN 0-88132-088-9
8   Economic Relations Between the United
    States and Korea: Conflict or Cooperation?*
    Thomas O. Bayard and Soogil Young, eds.
    January 1989   ISBN 0-88132-068-4
9   Whither APEC? The Progress to Date and
    Agenda for the Future*
    C. Fred Bergsten, ed.
    October 1997   ISBN 0-88132-248-2
10 Economic Integration of the Korean
    Peninsula   Marcus Noland, ed.
    January 1998   ISBN 0-88132-255-5
11 Restarting Fast Track*   Jeffrey J. Schott, ed.
    April 1998   ISBN 0-88132-259-8
12 Launching New Global Trade Talks: An
    Action Agenda   Jeffrey J. Schott, ed.
    September 1998   ISBN 0-88132-266-0
13 Japan's Financial Crisis and Its Parallels to
    US Experience   Ryoichi Mikitani and
    Adam S. Posen, eds.
    September 2000   ISBN 0-88132-289-X

14 The Ex-Im Bank in the 21st Century: A
    New Approach   Gary Clyde Hufbauer and
    Rita M. Rodriguez, eds.
    January 2001   ISBN 0-88132-300-4
15 The Korean Diaspora in the World
    Economy   C. Fred Bergsten and
    Inbom Choi, eds.
    January 2003   ISBN 0-88132-358-6
16 Dollar Overvaluation and the World
    Economy   C. Fred Bergsten and
    John Williamson, eds.
    February 2003   ISBN 0-88132-351-9
17 Dollar Adjustment: How Far? Against
    What?   C. Fred Bergsten and
    John Williamson, eds.
    November 2004   ISBN 0-88132-378-0
18 The Euro at Five: Ready for a Global Role?
    Adam S. Posen, ed.
    April 2005   ISBN 0-88132-380-2
19 Reforming the IMF for the 21st Century
    Edwin M. Truman, ed.
    April 2006   ISBN 978-0-88132-387-0
20 The Long-Term International Economic
    Position of the United States
    C. Fred Bergsten, ed.
    May 2009   ISBN 978-0-88132-432-7

WORKS IN PROGRESS

Global Identity Theft: Economic and Policy
Implications   Catherine L. Mann
Globalized Venture Capital: Implications
for US Entrepreneurship and Innovation
Catherine L. Mann
Why Reform a Rich Country? Germany and the
Future of Capitalism   Adam S. Posen
Global Forces, American Faces: US Economic
Globalization at the Grass Roots
J. David Richardson
Banking System Fragility in Emerging
Economies   Morris Goldstein and Philip Turner
Private Rights and Public Problems: The
Global Economics of Intellectual Property in
the 21st Century   Keith Maskus
Flexible Exchange Rates for a Stable World
Economy   Joseph E. Gagnon
Inflation, Debt, and Exchange Rate Issues
Carmen M. Reinhart and Kenneth Rogoff
Launching a Comprehensive US Export
Strategy   Howard F. Rosen and
C. Fred Bergsten, editors
Sustaining China's Economic Growth after the
Global Financial Crisis   Nicholas Lardy
The Future of the World Trade Organization
Gary Clyde Hufbauer and Jeffrey J. Schott

DISTRIBUTORS OUTSIDE THE UNITED STATES

**Australia, New Zealand,
and Papua New Guinea**
D. A. Information Services
648 Whitehorse Road
Mitcham, Victoria 3132, Australia
Tel: 61-3-9210-7777
Fax: 61-3-9210-7788
Email: service@dadirect.com.au
www.dadirect.com.au

India, Bangladesh, Nepal, and Sri Lanka
Viva Books Private Limited
Mr. Vinod Vasishtha
4737/23 Ansari Road
Daryaganj, New Delhi 110002
India
Tel: 91-11-4224-2200
Fax: 91-11-4224-2240
Email: viva@vivagroupindia.net
www.vivagroupindia.com

**Mexico, Central America, South America,
and Puerto Rico**
US PubRep, Inc.
311 Dean Drive
Rockville, MD 20851
Tel: 301-838-9276
Fax: 301-838-9278
Email: c.falk@ieee.org

Asia *(Brunei, Burma, Cambodia, China,
Hong Kong, Indonesia, Korea, Laos, Malaysia,
Philippines, Singapore, Taiwan, Thailand,
and Vietnam)*
East-West Export Books (EWEB)
University of Hawaii Press
2840 Kolowalu Street
Honolulu, Hawaii 96822-1888
Tel: 808-956-8830
Fax: 808-988-6052
Email: eweb@hawaii.edu

Canada
Renouf Bookstore
5369 Canotek Road, Unit 1
Ottawa, Ontario KlJ 9J3, Canada
Tel: 613-745-2665
Fax: 613-745-7660
www.renoufbooks.com

Japan
United Publishers Services Ltd.
1-32-5, Higashi-shinagawa
Shinagawa-ku, Tokyo 140-0002
Japan
Tel: 81-3-5479-7251
Fax: 81-3-5479-7307
Email: purchasing@ups.co.jp
*For trade accounts only. Individuals will find
Institute books in leading Tokyo bookstores.*

Middle East
MERIC
2 Bahgat Ali Street, El Masry Towers
Tower D, Apt. 24
Zamalek, Cairo
Egypt
Tel. 20-2-7633824
Fax: 20-2-7369355
Email: mahmoud_fouda@mericonline.com
www.mericonline.com

United Kingdom, Europe
(including Russia and Turkey), **Africa,
and Israel**
The Eurospan Group
c/o Turpin Distribution
Pegasus Drive
Stratton Business Park
Biggleswade, Bedfordshire
SG18 8TQ
United Kingdom
Tel: 44 (0) 1767-604972
Fax: 44 (0) 1767-601640
Email: eurospan@turpin-distribution.com
www.eurospangroup.com/bookstore

**Visit our website at:
www.piie.com
E-mail orders to:
petersonmail@presswarehouse.com**